THE ORIGINS OF
PHYSIOCRACY

THE ORIGINS OF PHYSIOCRACY

Economic Revolution and Social Order in Eighteenth-Century France

ELIZABETH FOX-GENOVESE

CORNELL UNIVERSITY PRESS
ITHACA AND LONDON

Copyright © 1976 by Cornell University

First published 1976 by Cornell University Press.
Published in the United Kingdom by Cornell University Press Ltd.,
2-4 Brook Street, London W1Y 1AA.

International Standard Book Number 0-8014-1006-1
Library of Congress Catalog Card Number 75-36999
Printed in the United States of America by York Composition Co., Inc.
Librarians: Library of Congress cataloging information
appears on the last page of the book.

FOR GENE

Two are better than one; because they have a good reward for their labour.

Ecclesiastes 4:9

Contents

Preface

Physiocracy means rule of nature. The term, coined in 1767 by Pierre-Samuel du Pont de Nemours to describe the doctrine of François Quesnay (and his unacknowledged collaborator Victor Riqueti, marquis de Mirabeau), captures the complex ideological character of the first French and indeed the first modern school of economics. Quesnay transformed economics from the role it had occupied from Aristotle to Rousseau as the management of the social household—first the city, then the state—to its modern role as the science of wealth. In so doing he disengaged economic process from its anthropological role as servant of the sociopolitical order, and established its claim to be the direct manifestation of the natural order. In other words, he argued that economic process itself embodied natural law and should thus dictate the sociopolitical order.

Quesnay had arrived at his theories of a free market and economic individualism by studying the emergence of a national market in England. But he always understood that in eighteenth-century France the unfettered pursuit of individual interest might not result in the natural order he sought to establish: men could fail to behave "economically." Quesnay believed that his introduction of arithmetic precision into economics provided a scientific rule that should dictate appropriate political arrangements—and even the obedience of sovereigns. He was never willing, however, to trust the spontaneous development of the proper sociopolitical order. Nature required the assistance of an absolute authority capable of forcing natural order upon recalcitrant humans.

Quesnay's economic achievement has never lacked the deep, if puzzled, respect of subsequent economists, and he would have been gratified by the admiration it now commands among scientific economists. He would, however, have been surprised to see it shorn of his larger social and political concerns and reduced to "the science of wealth." For him, as for all the physiocrats, political economy was "the science of natural law applied, as it should be, to civilized societies," and of "enlightened justice in all social relations—internal and external."[1] Quesnay's success in grounding his economic analysis in the social and political dilemmas of his own society and tying it to a specific ideological perspective, however paradoxically, largely accounts for the failure of subsequent generations to appreciate his accomplishment fully. For if the "nature" of physiocracy corresponds to those fundamental economic relationships described by Adam Smith and sanctified by Anglo-Saxon social science, the "rule" reflects a particularly French problem of social control—of directing that natural order which cannot be trusted to realize itself.

Physiocracy has not survived as an economics, much less as a political economy or social philosophy; the word and the concepts it embodies have passed from the mainstream of our intellectual tradition. It has succumbed to the increasingly homogenized modern vision of social and economic process—to the triumph of neomarginal economics and liberal social science. Quesnay's frank concern with the immediate problems of French society under the ancien régime and his determination to avoid anarchy help account for the bypassing of his thought. But as Marx and Schumpeter so well understood, Quesnay's contribution to economic analysis transcends his specific concerns and can legitimately be divorced from them, even from his always central

1. "Pierre-Samuel du Pont de Nemours to Jean-Baptiste Say, Letter of 22 April 1815," in Eugene Daire, ed., *Physiocrates*, 2 vols. (Paris, 1846), I, 397.

dictum that agriculture constitutes the source of all wealth. For Quesnay simultaneously described the essential dynamics of capitalist production, including a market in labor-power, and repudiated the artisanal and industrial forms through which the capitalist mode of production would rise to world dominance.

Physiocracy never proclaimed itself as a doctrine directed solely to the modernization of France. To the contrary, the physiocrats rapidly appraised the mortal dangers inherent in addressing French political and social problems head on. In economic matters they talked openly about France; in political and social matters they talked in abstract terms about the natural order appropriate to all times and places, or pretended to talk about Switzerland or China or elsewhere. Their method encouraged others who confronted similar problems to espouse physiocracy, for it promised to modernize traditional society without the sacrifice of traditional notions of order and without the price of social conflict. But the success of Adam Smith in formulating an alternative science of the "wealth of nations," and the failure of Turgot in implementing physiocratic policy in France in the mid-1770s, simultaneously discredited the physiocrats' claims to having a practical and theoretical blueprint for a new socio-economic order. And the gradual triumph of industrial capitalism, whether through the workings of the market as in England, or through the subsequent dictates of the state as in Prussia, increasingly deprived physiocracy of its raison d'être and reduced it to an antiquarian curiosity.

During the latter part of the eighteenth century, when the process of modernization presented an immediate political, economic, and social challenge, physiocracy claimed such devoted adherents as Thomas Jefferson, Leopold I of Tuscany, Holy Roman Emperor Joseph II, Karl Friedrich, Margrave of Baden, members of several French Parlements, and numerous intellectuals and enlightened administrators throughout Europe, the United States, and Latin America. Even Catherine II of Russia, while scoffing at anything so naive as "legal" despotism, called upon the physiocrat Le Mercier de la Rivière to help her reorganize her government. None of these contemporary fellow travelers, however, felt bound to accept the doctrine as a whole; they simply discarded those features not suited to their immediate purposes. Throughout the nineteenth century, particularly in countries still caught in the struggles between the traditional hierarchical and modern individualistic values, physiocracy continued to command the respectful attention of many students of political economy. In France, where the events of the 1840s apparently fostered a rediscovery of the virtues of the science of natural order, those who presided over the resurrection could, with the advantage of historical distance, pick and choose among the facets of a doctrine originally devised as a total science of society.

Modern commentators have never found it necessary to restore the original complexity of physiocracy, especially since economists long ago abstracted economic analysis from its social and political moorings. Recently, critics have even liberated Quesnay from his belief in the exclusive productivity of agriculture, thus establishing him as the first analyst of capitalism. This process entails staring down or apologetically passing over many of the physiocrats' own most cherished pronouncements, but modern Whigs rise to the occasion and happily assimilate Quesnay and Mirabeau to the forward march of humanity from Adam Smith to Alfred Marshall. With similar *largesse d'esprit*, some political economists, particularly during the early years of the twentieth century, claimed to find in physiocracy the origins of the French Revolution's Declaration of the Rights of Man and the Citizen, including the sanctity of private property. Finally, some historians, generously overlooking physiocracy's theoretical and ideological pretensions, have come to honor it as a penetrating description of the ancien régime. All these interpretations capture important aspects of physiocratic thought, but taken separately they distort the parts as well as the whole. A full understanding of the doctrine and of its place in the history of France and of the Enlightenment depends upon at least the provisional acceptance of the physiocrats' own assessment of their accomplishment.

None of the many commentators on physiocratic thought has satisfactorily considered legal despotism, the primacy of agriculture, capitalist production, and free trade in grain as parts of a coherent whole. The most important books on the subject discuss either Quesnay or Mirabeau, either the economics of physiocracy or the history of the physiocratic school. Paradoxically, the most enthusiastic of the physiocratic disciples, du Pont, bears considerable responsibility for this fragmentary treatment. Du Pont's histories of physiocracy, written in the 1760s at the height of physiocratic influence, set the tone for all subsequent histories of the doctrine. Despite his notorious predilection for embellishment and minor distortion, he provided an accurate transcription of the public history of physiocracy, but he did not know the whole story. Du Pont claimed, as have all subsequent scholars, that the history of physiocracy began in 1756 with the publication of the article "Fermiers" in volume VI of the *Encyclopédie*. He then dramatically recounted how in 1757 its author François Quesnay, personal physician to Madame de Pompadour, acquired as a collaborator Victor de Riqueti, marquis de Mirabeau, the flamboyant author of the year's best seller, *L'ami des hommes*.

Du Pont's account assumed that Quesnay created physiocracy more or less whole at the time he was writing the economic articles and that he subsequently converted Mirabeau, who became the willing vessel for and exponent of a fully formed truth. Subsequent scholars, to their cost and ours, have accepted the essentials of du Pont's interpretation. Yet when Quesnay wrote the economic articles he was in no meaningful sense a physiocrat. And despite his command of sophisticated economic analysis, he never succeeded unilaterally in imposing his views on Mirabeau. Du Pont, who knew Mirabeau, should have known better. Apparently, however, du Pont did not learn the full history of

Quesnay's diagram of the monetary circuit, the "Tableau écono-mique," and was not aware of Quesnay's and Mirabeau's un-published joint work, "Le traité de la monarchie."

The manuscript of the "Traité" helps piece together the tale that du Pont never fully understood, and it reveals the extent to which Quesnay and Mirabeau both contributed to the formula-tion of physiocracy. It also reveals the way in which they elabo-rated a broadly ideological assessment of history and social process. In the "Traité," Quesnay and Mirabeau directly discussed the nature and the problems of the French monarchy. Quesnay brought to the work a revolutionary economic analysis and a firm statist bias. Mirabeau brought an unshakable commitment to the restoration of an organic social order under the aegis of a divine monarch free of intendants and other bureaucratic trap-pings. Their joint investigation of the monarchy they revered and regarded as the necessary mainspring of France exposed to them the major obstacles to rational reform. The experience taught them that they could not address the political dimension of social and economic reform directly. Worse, it suggested at least implicitly that, although their apparently conflicting commit-ments could be welded together and mutually reinforced in a new system, that very system would require a complete repudia-tion of the principles upon which their revered monarchy rested.

Not only did Quesnay and Mirabeau not publish their "Traité," they never discussed contemporaneous French politics in print again. Instead, they abstracted from their analysis a number of general principles, which they gradually framed into a purportedly harmless "rural philosophy." The book that they published under that title in 1763—formally inaugurating the physiocratic doctrine—nevertheless bore as its subtitle *Economie générale et politique de l'agriculture, réduite à l'ordre immuable des loix physiques et morales, qui assurent la prospérité des empires*. Criticism of the monarchy had surfaced in the guise of a consideration of im-personal laws.

Neither Quesnay nor Mirabeau ever explained the method by

which they had arrived at their conclusions. Their disciples simply accepted their general principles and specific projects for reform —such as the supposedly apolitical freeing of the grain trade, abolition of the corvée, and free use of land including enclosure —and handed physiocracy down to posterity in an abstract formulation designed to convert the very authority that it implicitly repudiated. The physiocrats always claimed that their program had been designed to strengthen the monarchy. They always remained committed to the notion of a single or absolute embodiment of sovereignty and would never entertain any breath of political pluralism. Certainly they never broadcast that the implementation of their economic policies would have entailed recasting the monarchy according to revolutionary principles. They did come to recognize that the practices of the monarchy departed from their conception of natural order, but in political terms they may have assumed that since both the monarchy and their legal despotism represented absolute authority, the one could be substituted for the other by administrative fiat. Like so many other philosophes, the physiocrats abhorred the prospect of social chaos and desperately assumed that men of good will could rationalize their world without paying that ultimate price. It never seems to have occurred to them that the mere implementation of their economic program could lead inexorably to the very social and political disruption they dreaded. Ironically, that fateful silence, which has never been recognized much less understood, accounts for the passion with which so many either accepted or rejected physiocracy, and explains how value-free social science passes into ideology.

The physiocratic doctrine that grew from the confrontation between Quesnay's and Mirabeau's independent perspectives disguised all the tensions of its origins. Mature physiocracy thus appears as something of an anomaly in the context of the eighteenth century. The formalistic rhetoric of physiocratic tracts cannot entirely mask the underlying contradictions, but its rigidity has deceived commentators into overly stressing either the medieval or the precociously modern aspects of physiocratic thought. In fact, Quesnay and Mirabeau addressed themselves to the same political, economic, social, and intellectual problems as did the other philosophes. If anything, their early work suggests an unseemly amount of direct, unacknowledged borrowing from French and English theorists. Their commitment to rigorous economic individualism, grounded in absolute property and embedded in an organic social system, proved, however, more alarming in its political implications than did other more personal quests for liberation of thought. In covering their political tracks with an abstract model, Quesnay and Mirabeau obscured the profound ties between physiocracy and the broader currents of French thought.

In mature form physiocracy foreshadowed the development of French social theory and of modern economic thought, as a number of scholars have skillfully demonstrated. The importance of the physiocratic legacy, however, lies not in this or that specific chain of ideas, but rather in the deeper problems of adapting free market economics and possessive individualism to the specifically French experience. From this perspective, the origins of physiocracy acquire greater importance than the official pronouncements of its mature formulation. Physiocracy derived from Quesnay's and Mirabeau's prephysiocratic work—which itself derived from venerable European intellectual traditions—and from their early collaboration. It cannot be understood if removed from the historical context in which its founders worked—the intellectual ferment, economic maladjustment, and politization of pre-Revolutionary France.

The story told in the following pages contains neither much direct action, nor a large cast of characters, nor a backdrop of dramatic change or sanguinary uprising. But this absence of supporting personnel and historical event does not represent some willful abstraction from a complex reality. In intellectual history, this kind of supporting texture does in fact vary in quality from figure to figure. Felix Gilbert has provided a masterly demonstration of how political events influenced the shaping of Machiavelli's political theory.[2] Peter Gay has recreated the Genevan backdrop of Voltaire's political reflections.[3] Gordon Wood and Bernard Bailyn have immeasurably advanced our understanding of the political theory of the American Revolution by careful reading of pamphlets and tracts in context.[4] In another vein, scholars such as John Clive and Arthur Mitzman, in their respective works on Macaulay and Max Weber, have subtly combined a more or less theoretical psychological sensitivity with scrupulous attention to immediate events.[5] Finally, for one last example among the many available, Steven Marcus has afforded us a fresh view of Engels by carefully situating him in family drama, in the city of Manchester, and in the cauldron of industrial revolution.[6]

A history of physiocracy for the years following 1763 would lend itself to comparable treatment. Georges Weulersse's classic study of the physiocratic movement already affords the outlines, although his picture now needs significant revision.[7] The public career of physiocracy unfolded against a dramatic backdrop of administrative reform, grain shortage, urban uprising, debates in the Parlements, and public controversy. Almost all the physiocratic works written between 1763 and the French Revolution could be understood in part as *pièces d'occasion*. As Edgar Faure has shown in his elegant study of Turgot, even court intrigue con-

2. *Machiavelli and Guicciardini: Politics and History in Sixteenth-Century Florence* (Princeton, 1965).

3. *Voltaire's Politics: The Poet as Realist* (New York, 1959).

4. *The Creation of the American Republic, 1776–1787* (Chapel Hill, N.C., 1969); and *The Ideological Origins of the American Revolution* (Cambridge, Mass., 1967).

5. *Macaulay: The Shaping of the Historian* (New York, 1974); and *The Iron Cage: An Historical Interpretation of Max Weber* (New York, 1969).

6. *Engels, Manchester, and the Working Class* (New York, 1974).

7. *Mouvement*. Weulersse exaggerates the interest group approach at the expense of larger intellectual and ideological interpretations, in a manner reminiscent of Charles Beard's work on the American Constitution.

stitutes an important dimension of the physiocratic saga.[8] Some
of the physiocrats, most notably du Pont, have left private papers
that merit careful consideration and could lead to an increased
awareness of the psychological mainsprings of pre-Revolutionary
reform, aggressive individualism (not necessarily directly political), passive-aggressive discipleship, and generational conflict.

The present account, however, does not easily lend itself to
such treatment. Quesnay and Mirabeau, individually and as col-
laborators, offer tantalizing subjects for psychological speculation.
But as the indispensable materials do not exist, the speculation
must remain precisely that. I shall suggest, albeit indirectly, that
Quesnay, for whom we have no personal papers at all, arrived at a
successful sublimation of early conflicts characterized by a
definite (if essentially loving) identification with the aggressor.
Or to put it differently, he came to identify with authority,
rather than openly rebelling against it. When prompted to
criticism, he invariably couched resistance to the powers that be
in terms of service to a higher truth. Mirabeau, for whom there
is more but still inadequate documentation, remained far more
tempestuous and openly belligerent. He, however, redirected his
violence against his family—the very concept that he so cogently
defended in the political realm—even as he accepted Quesnay's
intellectual seniority with that highly suspect deference which
has duped most commentators into casting the full partner as
"the oldest son."

In a general way, Quesnay's and Mirabeau's attitudes toward
authority constitute an important psychological dimension of
physiocratic thought. Nevertheless, the actual elaboration of the
physiocratic doctrine can be followed and understood independent of these psychological considerations, and assuredly—lack
of adequate materials notwithstanding—does not result directly
from any specific psychodrama. It is enough to understand that
Quesnay sought through his economic work a new necessity, or
higher authority, that would command obedience—unquestioning

8. *La disgrâce de Turgot* (Paris, 1961).

and conflict-free obedience, even on the part of sovereigns; and that Quesnay's disciples, beginning with Mirabeau, found in Quesnay's forceful personality and new economic language a cause to which they ought to subordinate their own rebellious instincts. Any comprehensive study of the physiocratic sect will have to take account of these psychological tensions in evaluating the unusual strength of the ties binding the members of the *Secte* to the master, and the related evidence of sibling rivalry that surfaces in the disciples' correspondence with and about each other.[9] But in the period I am analyzing there were no disciples other than Mirabeau. And unlike du Pont, who came to physiocracy as a late adolescent in search of a vocation, Mirabeau participated in the forging of the doctrine as an independent and already formed forty-year-old.

The formulation of physiocratic thought, from the publication of the article "Fermiers" in 1756 to that of *La philosophie rurale* in 1763, exactly spanned the Seven Years' War; the process of most intense intellectual collaboration transpired before 1760. The immediate background of war and accelerating fiscal pressures made its impact upon physiocracy, which originated, at least in part, in a desire to rationalize and increase royal revenues.

As early as the 1740s the financial problems that would plague the monarchy until its demise had begun to take on deadly clarity. The peasant tax base on which king and privileged estates had been able to compromise no longer sufficed for royal purposes. The two new *capitations* (head taxes) of 1747, which affected nobles as well as commoners, and the second *vingtième* (tax on income) of 1749, followed by a third in 1756, which in principle taxed noble and clerical incomes, raised virulent op-

9. EMHL, Winterthur MSS, group 2, series A, esp. du Pont's letters to Baudeau and Le Mercier de la Rivière, and those to Quesnay and Mirabeau about Baudeau and Le Mercier de la Rivière. See also group 2, series E, esp. letters from Baudeau, and Le Mercier de la Rivière's letters from Russia.

position from the privileged orders. By 1751 the clergy had managed to reaffirm their traditional immunity. The Parlements, for their part, carried forward the cause of noble exemption. The complex history of their resistance to royal despotism has been recounted elsewhere.[10] The prolonged struggle, however, included a sustained attempt in the Parlements to create a constitutional theory that placed the locus of sovereignty in themselves rather than in the crown. The crown, which had little tolerance for notions of representation, noble or other, scored a decisive if temporary victory when, in January 1771, the Maupeou government abolished the Parlements. The coup provoked mixed reactions, but before it had time to prove its merits Louis XV died. And Louis XVI upon his accession in 1774 restored the Parlements.

The resistance to fiscal reform, specifically to the taxing of the privileged orders, forced the crown to rely increasingly upon its bankers. Its perilous financial condition, however, exposed it to exorbitant interest rates. This situation not only aggravated the problems of servicing the rapidly mounting royal debt, but also distracted capital from other, and in Quesnay's words more economic, forms of investment. Contemporaries understood the problem well. From the end of the reign of Louis XIV, when Vauban and Boisguilbert sketched their criticisms of taxation and grain policies, the debate on reform had been opened. The relatively prosperous years of the early part of the personal reign of Louis XV somewhat muted public controversy, but during the 1740s war resumed, fiscal needs mounted, and the opposition surfaced.

10. Jean Egret, *Le Parlement de Dauphiné et les affaires publiques au XVIIIe siècle* (Paris, 1942), and his *Louis XV et l'opposition parlementaire* (Paris, 1970). See also James D. Hardy, Jr., *Judicial Politics in the Old Regime: The Parlement of Paris during the Regency* (Baton Rouge, 1967); A. Molinier's "Introduction" to his *Inventaire sommaire de la Collection Joly de Fleury* (Paris, 1881); J. H. Shennan, *The Parlement of Paris* (Ithaca, 1968), 285-325; and Roger Bickart, *Les Parlements et la notion de souveraineté nationale au XVIIIe siècle* (Paris, 1933).

The political debates of the 1750s and afterward defy easy classification. In particular, the issues of religion and privilege cut across the Parlementary and the royal camps. Enlightened thought merely complicated the issue: the Parlementary side produced Montesquieu; the crown found one of its ablest defenders in Voltaire. Both Parlement and king depended upon and vigorously defended many privileges. In one sense their struggle turned on the question of who should have the deciding voice in governing France. Neither Parlement nor king, royal taxation to the contrary notwithstanding, proposed abolishing traditional hierarchy or feudal privilege. Royal government was frequently accused of tending toward a leveling despotism, but no serious modern student of France during the ancien régime believes that the king's attempt to govern efficiently and remuneratively included plans for abolishing his nobility or religion. In their internecine warfare, however, both the Parlements and the administrative agents of the crown developed theoretical and constitutional principles to justify their position.[11] Their mistake, as Voltaire so well understood, lay in discussing such things before the servants, who might sooner or later draw their own conclusions.

The fiscal crisis and the conflicts it engendered constitute the immediate political background for Quesnay's and Mirabeau's early work. Mirabeau perceived royal taxation, particularly taxation of the privileged second estate, as a direct personal threat, but his opposition ran much deeper than concern over

11. See, among many, *Dissertation sur l'origine et les fonctions essentielles du parlement, sur la pairie et le droit des pairs, et sur les lois fondamentales de la monarchie française* . . . 2 vols. in 1 vol. (Amsterdam, 1764). For a general collection, see Jules Flammermont, ed., *Remontrances du Parlement de Paris au XVIIIe siècle*, 3 vols. (Paris, 1888–1898). See also Bernard Plongeron, *Théologie et politique au siècle des lumières (1770–1820)* (Geneva, 1973); Furio Diaz, *Filosofia e politica nel Settecento francese* (Turin, 1962), 428–70; Keith Baker, *Condorcet: From Natural Philosophy to Social Mathematics* (Chicago, 1975); and Eberhard Schmitt, *Repräsentation und Revolution* (Munich, 1969).

his pocketbook. Quesnay and Mirabeau both addressed themselves not to specific abuses but to the entire chronicle of
abuses that had accompanied monarchical rule since the beginning
of the personal reign of Louis XV. Their attempt to deal with
these abuses rapidly led them to a consideration of the monarchy's
fundamental nature and of its structural relationship to French
society.

Their concerns in this respect belong to a larger preoccupation
with social and economic theory that characterized much French
thought in the years following the publication of Montesquieu's
De l'esprit des lois in 1748, and that must be intimately tied to
the publication of the *Encyclopédie* in the 1750s. Quesnay's and
Mirabeau's work also drew significantly upon older intellectual
traditions, in particular upon the long-standing theoretical debates
about the nature of the monarchy. In the course of this work, I
have indicated the most important direct affiliations between
their thought and that of their predecessors and contemporaries.
But it must be emphasized that the vocabulary and arguments
upon which they drew to discuss the monarchy, and eventually
the nature of natural law and political authority, were derived
almost entirely from the most generally known intellectual traditions of their time. They, like Rousseau, use, misuse, and reinterpret
Pufendorf, Grotius, Hobbes, Locke, Barbeyrac, Burlamaqui, Fénelon, and many others without direct references. In other words, to
draw upon J. G. A. Pocock's illuminating discussion of Burke,
they work within a clearly defined paradigm and draw freely
upon the theoretical traditions that contribute to the paradigm,
even traditions that had long lain dormant.[12] In this respect, only
Quesnay's economic analysis radically differentiated their thought
from that of their contemporaries and predecessors.

Quesnay's and Mirabeau's attempt to resolve the conflicts between their respectively "statist" and "feudal" views of monarchical authority and to ground their synthesis in the new

12. J. G. A. Pocock, *Politics, Language, and Time: Essays on Political
Thought and History* [1960] (New York, 1973), 202–32.

language of economics thus remains a properly intellectual drama. The story would have been enlivened by anecdotes of their life during these critical years, but precious few have survived. Du Pont, in his autobiography, recounts how Quesnay introduced Louis XV to the Tableau by presenting it as an exercise in type-setting for the royal amusement. Louis XV, however, tired of playing printer before he had completed setting the type.[13] There exist other stray accounts embedded in memoirs and correspon-dence of those who frequented the court or Paris intellectual circles, but nothing more substantial than the fragmentary *Mémoires de Madame du Hausset . . .* , lady-in-waiting to Madame de Pompadour. The picture that emerges from the fragments shows little more than Quesnay pursuing his daily life at Versailles, and Mirabeau his in Paris and on his estate at Bignon. The two met fairly regularly and at least occasionally corresponded. Most likely, they wrote separately and passed manuscripts back and forth for editorial comment. They un-doubtedly discussed their ideas with others, but only acquired their first convert, du Pont, in 1763.

France in the early 1750s remained an essentially landed society. Wealth derived, as Quesnay insisted, from land. The agricultural base had undergone no revolution; as Michel Morineau so cogently argues, we can point to no transformation of the key productive sector.[14] Agricultural practice remained bound by routine. Enclosure had made no significant inroads upon com-mon lands. Few landed proprietors had substituted large-scale systematic exploitation for the collection of seigneurial dues or rents. The gains in economic rationalization and the transfers of

13. EMHL, Winterthur MSS, group 2, series B, P. S. du Pont de Nemours, "L'enfance et la jeunesse de du Pont de Nemours, racontées par lui-même," ch. 13, 6.

14. *Les faux-semblants d'un démarrage économique: Agriculture et démographie en France au XVIIIe siècle* (Paris, 1971); and William H. Newell, "The Agricultural Revolution in Nineteenth-Century France," *Journal of Economic History*, XXXIII (1973), 697–731.

titles (particularly in favor of robe nobles at the expense of sword nobles) that had characterized the last quarter of the seventeenth century in some areas had yielded little further advance. No major improvements in transportation had bound disparate regions into a national market. An antiquated residue of internal tolls and tariff barriers further divided the various regions, as did differences in weights, measures, and means of payment. In the area of administrative action, as in that of title to and use of land, little substantial progress had been accomplished since the building of the canal du Midi and the administrative reforms of Colbert during the late seventeenth century.[15]

Contemporaries in the 1750s knew France to be a prosperous kingdom, and in retrospect historians can point to a marked increase in population and rise in prices dating from the 1730s. Growth, however, occurred within the traditional framework without promoting structural change. Grain production and distribution thus became an increasingly sensitive and pivotal issue. The problem of grain supply, particularly the provisioning of cities, had plagued the monarchy for centuries, but by the mid-eighteenth century two pivotal and paradoxical changes had occurred. First, famine had disappeared. Although in any given bad year dearth might bring hunger, increased susceptibility to disease, and even urban disturbance, no longer did large numbers of people die of starvation. Second, with surplus population moving from the saturated land to the cities, urban areas outgrew

15. See Gaston Roupnel, *La ville et la campagne au XVIIe siècle* (Paris, 1955); Marc Vénard, *Bourgeois et paysans au XVIIe siècle* (Paris, 1957); Georges Frêche, *Toulouse et la région Midi-Pyrénées au siècle des lumières vers 1670–1789* ([Toulouse], 1974); and Henri Enjalbert, "Le commerce de Bordeaux et la vie économique dans le bassin Aquitain au XVIIe siècle," *Annales du Midi*, LXII (1950), 21–37. See also my review of Jacob Price, *France and the Chesapeake*, in *Journal of Modern History*, XLVI (1974), 691–701. And see André Rémond, *Etudes sur la circulation marchande en France aux XVIIIe et XIXe siècles* (Paris, 1956); and Georges Livet, "La route royale et la civilisation française, de la fin du XVe au milieu du XVIIIe siècle," in Georges Livet, ed., *Les routes de France depuis les origines jusqu'à nos jours* (Paris, 1958).

their traditional lines of supply. A. P. Usher, in his classic study, locates the breakdown of the medieval market system about 1710. Certainly by 1750 cities such as Paris and Rouen could no longer count on feeding their populations from their traditional hinterlands.[16]

The crown and the urban magistrates dealt with the problem of provisioning by fixing prices for the honest loaf that constituted the staple of the popular diet. In addition, they enforced all the traditional regulations in their arsenal: they coerced peasants to bring their grain to market; forced peasants to sell regardless of price after three days' display; prohibited wholesale buying of and speculation on the preharvest crop in the immediate urban hinterland; and generally discouraged forestalling, engrossing, and all those other antisocial, proto-capitalist practices to which the enterprising might be tempted. Under no conditions, they argued, should urban peace be gambled on the problematical operations of a patently nonexistent market. The authorities and the people concurred in damning free market capitalism in matters of grain supply.[17]

16. *The History of the Grain Trade in France, 1400-1710* (Cambridge, Mass., 1913); Georges Afanassiev, *Le commerce des céréales en France au dix-huitième siècle* (Paris, 1894); Jean Meuvret, "Les crises de subsistance et la démographie de la France d'ancien régime" [1946], in his *Etudes d'histoire économique* (Paris, 1971), 271-78; Charles Desmarest, *Le commerce des grains dans la généralité de Rouen à la fin de l'ancien régime* (Paris, 1926); Jean Letaconnoux, "La question des subsistances et du commerce des grains en France au XVIIIe siècle: Travaux, sources, et questions à traiter," *Revue d'histoire moderne et contemporaine*, VIII (1906-1907), 409-45.

17. Charles Musart, *La réglementation du commerce des grains en France au XVIIIe siècle: La théorie de Delamare* (Paris and Mende, 1921); Nicolas de Lamare, *Traité de la police*, 4 vols. (Paris, 1705-1738); Jean Martineau, *Les Halles de Paris des origines à 1789* (Paris, 1960); T. J. A. Le Goff, "An Eighteenth-Century Grain Merchant: Ignace Advisse Desruisseaux," in John Bosher, ed., *French Government and Society 1500-1850* (London, 1973), 92-122; Leon Biollay, *Le pacte de famine et les opérations sur les grains* (Paris, 1885); Léon Cahen, "La question du pain à Paris à la fin du XVIIIe siècle," *Cahiers de la Révolution française*, I (1934), 51-76; Guy Lemarchand, "Les troubles de subsistance dans la généralité de

Grain producers did not see the problem from the same angle. The physiocratic defense of free trade in grain found both precedent and echo in the words and practices of nobles who were anxious to market their surplus at the highest possible price or who were determined to export, as well as in those of prosperous peasants who, according to trustworthy report, preferred to let their fields lie fallow than to plant them with a crop the sale of which would not cover the costs of production. Adopting the producer's perspective, the physiocrats maintained that free internal circulation of grain, free export of grain, and destruction of all traditional marketing regulations would encourage maximum production and assure an adequate urban supply. When the partial implementation of their system in 1763 and 1764 had failed by 1770 to produce the announced results, the physiocrats argued that the failure derived from insufficient cooperation and from the temporary phenomenon of unusually bad harvests. They failed to recognize that France might confront a particular deadlock between population increase and structural and technological rigidity (particularly in transportation) that irreconcilably pitted producers and consumers against each other.[18] The

Rouen (seconde moitié XVIIIe siècle)," *Annales historiques de la Révolution française*, XXXV (1963); and R. B. Rose, "Eighteenth Century Price Riots, the French Revolution, and the Jacobin Maximum," *International Review of Social History*, IV (1959).

18. See, among many, Louis-Paul Abeille, *Faits qui ont influé sur la cherté des grains en France et en Angleterre* (Paris, 1768); Nicolas Baudeau, *Avis au peuple sur son premier besoin* . . . (Amsterdam and Paris, 1768); J. A. N. de Caritat, marquis de Condorcet, *Du commerce des bleds* . . . (Paris, 1775), and his *Lettres sur le commerce des grains* (Paris, 1774); Guillaume-François Le Trosne, *La liberté du commerce des grains, toujours utile et jamais nuisible* (Paris, 1765); P. F. de Quelen de Sterer de Caursade, duc de La Vauguyon, duc de St. Mégrin, *Lettre de M. D. à un magistrat du Parlement de Bourgogne sur la liberté du commerce des grains* (Dijon, 1768); Joseph-André Roubaud, *Récréations économiques* . . . (Amsterdam and Paris, 1770), and his *Représentations aux magistrats* . . . (Paris, 1769); Jean-François Vauvilliers, *Lettres d'un gentilhomme des états de Languedoc à un magistrat du Parlement de Rouen sur le commerce des bleds, des farines, et du pain* (n.p., 1768). On the problems of producers, see AN, H 1511, "Correspondance du ministre avec les sociétés d'agriculture."

last major grain shortage occurred in 1848, and not until the advent of the departmental railroad system in the 1870s did a national market really exist.

In the course of their discussion of the production and distribution of grain, however, the physiocrats encountered a host of other features of eighteenth-century France that contributed to the resistance to rational reform. The France of the ancien régime remained a society of estates rather than one of classes. Or to put it differently, the juridical and political structure of the country remained essentially feudal. Privilege more than income divided social groups and distorted access to social or economic advancement. The feudalism of the eighteenth century, as Mirabeau woefully complained, had moved far from its medieval origins. Trade and commerce had wreaked their damage upon ordered, land-based social relations. The crown, with its absolutist pretensions and administrative agents, had significantly distorted organic patterns. Port cities, as Quesnay shrewdly and disapprovingly noted, had mushroomed into quasi-independent societies or republics with radically different interests than those of the true landed kingdom. Financiers, those greedy leeches, had wrapped their tentacles around the throne itself and were busily milking French society of its vital forces. Quesnay's and Mirabeau's catalogue of villains accurately mirrors the conditions of the France of Louis XV. Their catalogue, however, significantly excludes the social group the defense of whose privileges permitted and indeed forced the triumph of finance capital. Both Quesnay and Mirabeau refrained from any direct attack upon the legally constituted nobility.

Only when they formulated a coherent theory of absolute property and then established that property as the necessary cornerstone of a truly economic society did they confront the nobility, or the feudal base of the monarchy, and then they did so indirectly. Neither man had any desire to substitute a capitalist bourgeoisie for noble landholders. Rather, they intended to reconstitute the nobility as a landed aristocracy on a capitalist basis.

To Quesnay and Mirabeau, "bourgeois" meant what it means to any modern historian of ancien régime France. It meant merchants, financiers, shopkeepers, urban dwellers, *rentiers*, notaries, lawyers, and so forth. The bourgeoisie did not constitute a homogeneous social group, much less a clearly defined class owning the means of production. Régine Robin has suggested that we refer to this group as the *bourgeoisie d'ancien régime*. The problems of classification worsen with the recognition that almost anyone who could be rightfully termed bourgeois could be a candidate for nobility, through purchase of office or royal patent. In fact, the group of individuals who could discretely be termed bourgeois performed a wide variety of social functions and came from a range of income levels. Quesnay and Mirabeau, even as they called for an economic—in effect a capitalist—revolution, rejected all of these individuals as uneconomic, parasitic, or antisocial and narrowly self-interested.[19]

In modern terms, however, Quesnay's and Mirabeau's economic program explicitly required a capitalist class that would own the means of production. Without such absolute ownership, as they repeatedly insisted, there could be no hope of economic transformation and therefore no hope of a financially secure government or of national prosperity. In this specific sense, they favored a bourgeois revolution. They did not favor industrialism and they loathed industrial capitalists. They only wanted absolute ownership, legal uniformity, and an unassailable national market complete with the buying and selling of human labor-power. They even divorced bourgeois ownership (landlords) from bourgeois

19. *La société française en 1789: Semur-en-Auxois* (Paris, 1970). See also Michel Vovelle and D. Roche, "Bourgeois, rentiers, propriétaires: Eléments pour la définition d'une catégorie sociale à la fin du XVIIIe siècle," *Actes du 80e Congrès national des sociétés savantes (Section d'histoire moderne et contemporaine)* (Dijon, 1959), 419–52; and Michel Vovelle, "L'élite ou le mensonge des mots," *Annales ESC*, XXIX (1974), 49–72.

entrepreneurship (farmers). In my judgment their program can best be described as bourgeois in the objective sense of the word. Yet the western world of the mid-eighteenth century offered no clear examples of such a bourgeoisie. The closest approximation could be found in the economically rational English landed aristocracy that Quesnay so admired for its capitalist (or in the objective sense, bourgeois) ethic. Lacking models, the physiocrats nonetheless established criteria for a legitimate ruling class that can be retrospectively identified as bourgeois. They insisted that a ruling class must owe its hegemony to its defense of individualistic and economic values. Its economic position must rest upon absolute property and free competition. It should need no privilege or legal protection other than that of its right to property, which must be shared by all individuals.

Such a description would serve perfectly for the nineteenth-century European bourgeoisie, which should not be described as simply middle class in the American sense. I shall, accordingly, use the word bourgeois in the sense that it was used by Karl Marx and Max Weber, among many nineteenth-century theorists. I can only hope that this usage will not create extraneous confusion about capitalism in pre-Revolutionary France or social classification in advanced industrial society. I mean no more than a class that owns the means of production, employs labor under conditions in which labor-power has itself become a commodity, and defends the vision of equality before a rational and uniform legal system. In relation to the French Revolution, the halting development of French industrial capitalism remains irrelevant. The Revolution did institute a uniform legal code based on individual rights and absolute property. In that sense it created the framework for a bourgeois society even if small peasant property, inadequate transportation, and a host of other ideological and economic problems delayed the emergence of a fully industrialized economy. Again, in this sense, the post-Revolutionary ruling class, however traditional its values and however land-based its fortunes, was bourgeois.

Historians of physiocracy have agreed almost unanimously on the bourgeois or capitalist character of the doctrine.[20] But the importance of physiocracy, much less of its origins, should not be reduced to that of a proto-capitalist harbinger of a preordained nineteenth-century capitalist society and bourgeois world view. The excitement of close textual and theoretical analysis, at least for those engaged in it, lies in following the creation of a thought in the minds of men who had no notion that they were realizing subsequent historians' divine or historicist plans. Such work becomes particularly illuminating when directed toward the thought of a generation that did ultimately, and sometimes against its own conscious intentions, contribute to a shift in intellectual paradigms.

No single Enlightenment theorist stands as indisputably and unambiguously modern. Excellent recent work has called attention to enlightened doubts, pessimism, and even "preromantic" individualism.[21] Eighteenth-century conservatism should not be submerged in the vision of a rising tide of triumphant individualism. Arthur Wilson's and Jacques Proust's works on Diderot have admirably demonstrated the complexity of the *encyclopédiste*'s thought.[22] They have taught us to accept Diderot's traditionalism as well as to respect more than ever his revolutionary attention to the psychological and productive details of human life. They have shown how self-conscious observation of the external world becomes, in Diderot's hands, a radical affirmation of human consciousness. This one strand of Enlightenment

20. The starkest exception to this general consensus is Max Beer, *An Inquiry into Physiocracy* (London, 1939).

21. See, among many, Henry Vyverberg, *Historical Pessimism in the French Enlightenment* (Cambridge, Mass., 1958); Jean A. Perkins, *The Concept of the Self in the French Enlightenment* (Geneva, 1969); Jean Starobinski, *J. J. Rousseau: La transparence et l'obstacle* (Paris, 1971); Gita May, *De Jean-Jacques Rousseau à Madame Roland* (Geneva, 1964); Aram Vartanian, "Diderot and the Phenomenology of the Dream," *Diderot Studies*, III (1966), 217–53; Eric Voeglin, *From Enlightenment to Revolution* (Durham, N. C., 1975).

22. *Diderot* (New York, 1973); *Diderot et l'Encyclopédie* (Paris, 1962). See also Anthony Strugnell, *Diderot's Politics* (The Hague, 1973).

thought constitutes an essential ingredient of the emerging individualistic paradigm.

Like Diderot, the physiocrats also contributed to the new paradigm. No more than he did they singlehandedly shape a new world view. No more than his vision did theirs triumph in the form in which they had cast it. For the physiocrats, as for Diderot, much of the experience they analyzed remained embedded in traditional forms. Similarly, much of their debates derived from an older language. Yet their discrete contributions merged to revolutionize the basic theoretical prism through which the human mind perceived and legitimized the human condition. The shift from early modern thought to theoretical individualism stands as one of the major revolutions in human consciousness. In this context, physiocracy can be seen not only as the first sustained attempt to integrate economics into social and political theory, but as a major constitutive element in the new paradigm. The very failures of physiocracy to triumph as political program or as social science elucidate the transition in thought. In this perspective, Quesnay's and Mirabeau's attachment to their myth of an ordered past matches in significance their vision of an individualistic future. Their particular intellectual hegira helps to elucidate the complexities of the formulation of modern thought and the creation of a new intellectual paradigm, as well as a new ideology.

ELIZABETH FOX-GENOVESE

Rochester, New York

Acknowledgments

For some of us, books present an irresistible opportunity to acknowledge: one wants to thank not only those who contributed in one way or another to the manuscript, but also those who helped keep the author alive long enough to complete it. I am not immune to the temptation but shall try to resist its excesses. Thus my friends and mentors (including Felix Gilbert, David Herlihy, Caroline Robbins, Alain Silvera, and those two rare and remarkable deans, Dorothy Marshall and Mabel Lang) at Bryn Mawr College shall have to forgive my not doing full justice to their important if indirect contributions. Franklin Ford, generously spelled by David Landes, presided over the wayward progress of an earlier version of this book, and provided much need encouragement.

A series of grants-in-aid from the Eleutherian Mills Historical Library supported the final stages of my research. I should especially like to thank Mrs. B. Bright Low, whose wisdom and scholarship contributed in a multitude of ways to my work. I am further indebted to the staff of the Center for Advanced Study in Behavioral Sciences at Stanford, especially Preston Cutler and Jane Kielsmeyer, for their generosity to the wife of a fellow; to Ann Schwertz of the Interlibrary Loan Department of the University of Rochester Library; to the staff of the Kress Library at Harvard University; and to the staff of the Bibliothèque de l'Arsenal in Paris.

Over the past couple of years a number of friends and colleagues have read this book in various stages. For such invaluable assistance I should like to thank Sanford Elwitt, Donald Kelley, Alan Kors, Robert Kreiser, John Laffey, Christopher Lasch, Brenda Meehan-Waters, Traian Stoianovich, Mary Young, and Perez Zagorin. Stanley Engerman, with his customary generosity, read the manuscript not once but twice and helped me cover my economic flank. Claude Jessua shared freely his vast knowledge of early modern economic thought and discussed at length the fine points of economic analysis with a warmth that transcends national and ideological differences. Sheila Kamerick provided that particular blend of appreciation and sharp criticism that only one's students can give.

Jean DeGroat and Lorraine Murray uncomplainingly typed the manuscript, duplicated it, and sent it out, and Anne Kallenberg took time from her own work to check the footnotes. The staff of Cornell University Press has been helpful throughout the stages of publication.

On the venerable principle, known to all four-year-olds and Greek dramatists, of saving the best for the last, I should like finally to acknowledge the contributions of those who have most consistently supported my work. My sister Rebecca Fox Leach and my friend Nancy Arnstein Wilson both opened their homes to me when I was on research trips, read the entire manuscript in a field far removed from their own, offered criticism and freely shared insights, and most important, provided a steady acceptance and support that eased my way to participating actively, as a woman, in what is still a man's world.

My parents, Elizabeth Simon Fox and Edward Whiting Fox, alone can appreciate the debt owed them by a frequently intractable daughter. My mother has always given freely of her knowledge and love of literature. Her influence accounts in no small measure for my taste for intellectual history. My father, having introduced me to the joys of history somewhere around my second year, has continued to share his own phenomenal wisdom, learning, and sheer delight in the subject over the intervening years. In this specific instance he gave generously of his time, his knowledge, and his editorial skill to closely criticize the manuscript and to force me to say what I meant. This book is better for his rare talent as a teacher—and teaching a daughter is the toughest test that talent can face.

My debt to my husband, Eugene Dominick Genovese, to whom this book is dedicated and without whose commitment it might never have been written, defies expression. In the interests of promoting my intellectual development and happiness, he has sacrificed time, money, domestic peace, and his own most cherished principles about the proper role of women. In sheer material terms his generosity has rivaled the largesse of his southern planters: he financed my trips to Paris, my microfilming, and my book-buying; he took time from the preparation of his own manuscript to read mine; he painstakingly taught me to write according to Fowler; he proofread the final draft. Intellectually, he combined the role of critic extraordinaire with that of comrade and companion. Most important, however, he has shared the living of this work with me, he has contributed to a community that permits my individualism to flourish, and in so generously valuing my efforts has helped me to enjoy them myself.

E. F.-G.

Selected Works of
Quesnay and Mirabeau

1743

Quesnay, "Préface" to the first volume of the *Mémoires de l'Académie royal de chirurgie.*

1747

Quesnay, *L'essai physique sur l'oeconomie animale* . . ., 2d ed.

1750

Mirabeau, *Mémoire concernant l'utilité des états provinciaux.*

1756

Quesnay, "Evidence" and "Fermiers," in the *Encyclopédie,* vol. VI.

1757

Mirabeau, *L'ami des hommes, ou traité de la population.*
Quesnay, "Grains," "Hommes," and "Impôts," in the *Encyclopédie,* vol. VI.

1758

Mirabeau and Quesnay, "Le traité de la monarchie" (unpublished).
Mirabeau, *L'ami des hommes,* part IV (includes "Introduction" and Quesnay's "Questions intéressantes."
Quesnay, first edition of the "Tableau oeconomique" (unpublished).

1759

Mirabeau, *L'ami des hommes,* part V (includes "Mémoire sur l'agriculture envoyé à la très-louable société d'agriculture de Berne").

Quesnay, second edition of the "Tableau oeconomique" (unpublished).

Quesnay, third edition of the "Tableau oeconomique" (privately printed at Versailles).

Mirabeau, *L'ami des hommes,* part VI (includes "Le Tableau oeconomique avec ses explications").

1760

Mirabeau, *Théorie de l'impôt.*

1763

Mirabeau, with the collaboration of Quesnay, *La philosophie rurale.*

Abbreviations

ADY, "Inventaire": Archives départementales des Yvelines, Etude Huber de Versailles, Minutes Thibault, 1774, "Inventaire après le décès de M. François Quesnay (29 décembre 1774)."

AN: Archives nationales.

EMHL: Eleutherian Mills Historical Library.

INED: Institut national d'études démographiques, *François Quesnay et la physiocratie*, 2 vols. (Paris, 1958).

Labrousse *et al.*: Ernest Labrousse, Pierre Léon, Pierre Goubert, Jean Bouvier, Charles Carrière, and Paul Harsin, *Histoire économique et sociale de la France*, vol. II, *Des derniers temps de l'âge seigneurial aux préludes de l'âge industriel (1660–1789)* (Paris, 1970).

Meek, *Economics:* Ronald Meek, *The Economics of Physiocracy: Essays and Translations* (Cambridge, Mass., 1963).

Onken, *Oeuvres:* Auguste Onken, ed., *Oeuvres économiques et philosophiques de F. Quesnay, fondateur du système physiocratique*, with other biographical works on Quesnay (Frankfort and Paris, 1888).

Quesnay's Tableau: Marguerite Kuczynski and Ronald Meek, eds., *Quesnay's Tableau Economique*, with new materials, translations, and notes (London and New York, 1972).

RHDES: Revue d'histoire des doctrines économiques et sociales.

RHES: Revue d'histoire économique et sociale.

Weulersse, *Manuscrits:* Georges Weulersse, *Les manuscrits économiques de François Quesnay et du Marquis de Mirabeau aux Archives nationales (M 778 à 785)*, with inventory, extracts, and notes (Paris, 1910).

Weulersse, *Mouvement:* Georges Weulersse, *Le mouvement physiocratique en France de 1756 à 1770*, 2 vols. (Paris, 1910).

THE ORIGINS OF
PHYSIOCRACY

ᵛᵉᵍ I

Introduction

> Instead of calling Governments sometimes *Monarchy*, some-
> times *aristocracy*, sometimes *Democracy*, we should have called
> them all *Theocracy* since God is the true master and lord
> of men.
>
> Plato, *The Laws*, Book 4, as quoted by du Pont

The Enlightenment proudly proclaimed the values of rational
individualism, and philosophes of all lands joined in constructing
the new "science of freedom." Even those who, like Hume,
enjoyed the benefits of relative political freedom and representative government enlisted as combatants in the great battle to free
men's minds from the ignorance and superstition of religion.
They assiduously cultivated the scientific method as their most
formidable weapon. Science could demonstrate the true origins
of the human species and its myths, explain the establishment of
societies, catalogue the phenomena of the natural world, establish
the true principles of human perception, chronicle the progress
of civilization and the arts, and lay down the rational guidelines
for the creation of a more humane society. Science, in a word,
would permit men to tailor society to fit their own needs; it
would release them from the contorted postures imposed by
priests and kings in the name of an irrational higher truth.

In this sense, the Enlightenment, despite its diversity, represented an emerging ideology. Man, it claimed, was made for
freedom. Established authority had perpetrated inhuman subser-
vience long enough. The ideological chains of the traditional

world view within which human society existed to serve the greater glory of God's inscrutable purpose had to be broken. If the concept of God was not banished entirely from the workings of the universe, it was commonly confined to the sphere of general providence; thus the particular regulation of human affairs was left to man. Considered as a whole, the Enlightenment proposed to change the consciousness of man.

In its largest claims, the Enlightenment sought to liberate all men in all countries. Its most generous aspect embodied a view of universal human equality which rested upon the concept a uniform human nature. Philosophes in different countries, however, emphasized different aspects of the struggle for freedom. In France, the home of enlightenment par excellence, the pursuit of human freedom carried an implicit political thrust, however much discretion its exponents had to exercise. The contributors to Diderot's *Encyclopédie* played a well-chronicled game of political hide-and-seek. Their numerous articles on religious and political subjects probed the limits of censorship and risked imprisonment at every turn. And their discrete works on psychology, biology, and literary criticism also and inevitably proclaimed, as Peter Gay has shown, their "bourgeois ideology."[1] In France, the philosophes sought, like their English counterparts, to replace an outmoded and authoritarian world view with a more liberal and humane one. In France unlike in England, however, the old world view still enjoyed the protection of all officially sanctioned social, political, and religious institutions. The French philosophes not only challenged the convictions of their contemporaries but also the entrenched institutions of the society in which they lived. However problematical the specific ties between the Enlightenment and the Revolution, the aspirations of the one could not easily have been realized without the actions of the other.

The philosophes by and large were not themselves revolu-

1. Peter Gay, *The Enlightenment: An Interpretation*, vol. II, *The Science of Freedom* (New York, 1969), 261.

tionaries. Like Diderot at the end of his life, they valued social order and had no wish to tear their world apart.[2] On the contrary, they sought to disseminate a larger truth that would unite all men of good will and peacefully command their allegiance. Their experience might have taught them that they labored under an illusion, but they shrank from the logical conclusions of that experience. They nevertheless could not escape informing their rational social science with a passionate commitment to change. By presenting it as science, they claimed that it did no more than record the eternal, nonpartisan laws of the universe. The philosophes, with their insistence upon the pre-eminence of rational, economic man, contributed to the emergence of the bourgeois paradigm, but they did so indirectly by helping to create an appropriate ideological vision. Their proclamation of the inalienable natural rights of man translated the specific goals of a particular group into a program worthy of the loyalty of all mankind.

The physiocrats, more commonly known then as the *Economistes* or the *Secte*, shared the values, characteristics, and general socioeconomic background of the other French philosophes. They differed from the other philosophes primarily in their unilateral acceptance of the new truth forged by François Quesnay and Victor de Riqueti, marquis de Mirabeau, and in their insistence upon the determining role of economics in human life. Their campaign to free trade—particularly in grain—and human labor from feudal and absolutist restrictions, however, led them into a range of proto-political activities and earned them considerable openly-political support and opposition. Despite the objective political content of many of their activities, the physiocrats did not constitute a political group by modern standards. Most of them directly served the state in one capacity or another. Most of those who held no particular royal appointments were associated with the traditional social elite either as clerics or

2. Denis Diderot, *Oeuvres politiques,* ed. Paul Vernière (Paris, 1963), esp. xxxii–xlii.

nobles. None would have considered himself an enemy of the traditional order or a threat to royal authority. The group that formed around Quesnay and Mirabeau were drawn by an apparently apolitical (value-free) economic analysis and the promise of a new truth that would command the willing compliance of established authority. By 1763 the group included Pierre Le Mercier de la Rivière, a member of the Parlement of Paris and sometime intendant of Martinique, and Pierre-Samuel du Pont de Nemours, the young secretary to the intendant of Soissons. By 1767 their tight ranks also included Louis-Paul Abeille, Pierre Roubaud, Guillaume-François Le Trosne, and the abbé Nicolas Baudeau with his essential dowry, the journal *Les éphémérides du citoyen*.[3] Physiocracy, in its method and aspirations, belongs to the history of the French Enlightenment. It participated fully in the tensions characterizing that movement for the liberation of the human mind and person. It shared with other currents of enlightened thought a commitment to what has been called the "geometric spirit," a repudiation of feudal privilege in all its forms, and a deep faith in education. The physiocrats, however, departed from the more eclectic liberalism of their contemporaries in their insistence upon the need for a new absolute truth that would legitimize individualism. Their intellectual absolutism ultimately earned them the implacable hostility of so bourgeois a philosophe as Diderot. More important, the political authoritarianism they welded onto their market economics hid the deep affinities between their doctrine and the larger Enlightenment ideology.

Physiocratic economics, however, cannot be understood apart from physiocratic political theory. The authoritarian system of politics was derived directly from a determination to protect—if not to institute—the market. The physiocrats saw both political and economic theory as integral parts of a single science grounded in private property. Like so many other theorists, the physiocrats

3. The best history of the physiocrats as a school remains Weulersse, *Mouvement*.

sought to forge an individualistic world view to replace traditional notions of hierarchy. Protection of private property, the necessary prerequisite to economic progress, furnished the law for political life. Physiocracy constituted a total social theory, the science of "L'ordre naturel et essentiel des sociétés politiques."[4]

The members of the sect, following Quesnay's lead, sought to explain the nature of men's relations in society and to describe the political form those relations should take. They assumed that a natural law determines the proper rules of life and that an essential political order follows logically. The physiocratic doctrine held that the roots of human social existence lie in the material conditions of life which provide for survival and physical well-being.

The physiocrats usually insisted upon the dictates of nature, or material conditions, as the prime determinant of human behavior, but their rhetoric cannot obscure a fundamental commitment to the ultimate role of divine intelligence. Nature realizes the plan that first existed in the eye of God. Like their contemporaries in the Scottish historical school, the physiocrats never abandoned the notion of divine purpose behind man's most mundane actions. The physiocrats insisted that the human animal, like all others, must eat, but that unlike the others, it stands unique in creation by its possession of an intelligence directly linking it to the deity whose purpose informs the universe. In other words, although they shared the physiological materialism of a Diderot, they supplemented it with an idealist conception of human intelligence (as distinct from animal intelligence) as an emanation from God —literally a divine light that informs the human mind.

When they turned to political theory, the physiocrats insisted upon the necessary interconnectedness of the most basic human activities and all derivative social institutions. Everything, they maintained, "is linked here below," or in the words of Mirabeau, "In politics everything hangs together and all politics starts with

4. P. P. F. J. H. Le Mercier de la Rivière, *L'ordre naturel et essentiel des sociétés politiques* [1767], ed. Edgar Depître (Paris, 1910).

a grain of wheat."[5] Nevertheless, they explicitly rejected all notions of struggle, whether between classes or between ruler and subjects, as either the motive force of continuous social development or as the initial rationale for the institution of society. The physiocrats described society as a totally natural institution, which does no more than confirm and guarantee the rights with which nature endows man.

In physiocratic thought private property constitutes man's first natural social right. Man arrives in the world with the fundamental physical obligation of keeping himself alive, and his survival depends upon his right to property in himself. The original obligation to live can only be fulfilled by eating. The physiocrats reasoned that to eat with moral sanction, man must have a natural right to the fruits of the earth. They defended that right with particular vehemence in order to refute Hobbes' contention that society rests on struggle. The first man simply collected the fruits freely offered by nature.

In time the species multiplied and nature's bounty no longer sufficed to meet human needs. Men then turned to active cultivation of the soil. But as everyone can recognize from his own experience, or in Quesnay's chosen phrase, as is evident, no one in his right mind willingly undertakes hard labor without being assured of the absolute right to the fruits of that labor. And here the physiocrats meant more than a right based on superior force. Society must approve human action, efforts, and tools, and must positively sanction property as a social good. It must recognize individual self-interest as the most respectable motive for social action. In this defense of the individual's right to property, in contrast to the traditional notion of the community's right to preserve social harmony, lies the heart of the physiocratic ideology, which they summed up in the words: Property, Liberty, Security.[6]

5. *Lettres sur la législation, ou l'ordre légal, dépravé, rétabli et perpétué,* 3 vols. (Berne, 1775), I, 123.
6. For example, du Pont's "Avis de l'éditeur," *Physiocratie, ou constitu-*

All social institutions derive from the right of property. Personal property implies the freedom of labor. Movable property represents no more than personal property in use. Freedom to trade cannot be separated from personal and movable property because every individual must enjoy the right to dispose of his own. Cultivation of the soil also requires the free use of personal and movable property; landed property forms its necessary extension, and like all other properties must be completely unrestricted. Without security, property would be a theoretical right constantly violated in practice.

The need for security of private property justifies government, the principle duty of which is to guarantee that security. Physiocratic political theory thus echoes Lockean liberal political theory in its contention that "the less government the better." In all other respects, physiocratic notions of government reverse the liberal model. The physiocrats invented the name "legal despotism" (for which they occasionally substituted "tutelary authority") to describe the government they favored. It included a sovereign, assisted by administrators, and a group of magistrates to serve as the custodians of the fundamental laws of the realm. No restrictions except the sovereign's own sense of responsibility to observe the laws hampered the free exercise of authority. The true rulers, argued the physiocrats, were the laws, which derived inexorably from nature.

Formally, the physiocrats followed the Lockean tradition in their insistence that the natural pursuit of self-interest by the discrete members of society would result in the maximum social good. Nature, or the market, best knows its own requirements. Any artificial interference with the natural process, however well-intentioned, can only distort the natural order. But individual pursuit of self-interest has no place in political life and must be confined to the economic sphere.

Few of the philosophes would have gainsaid the physiocrats'

tion naturelle du gouvernement le plus avantageux au genre humain (Leyden and Paris, 1768), I, xx–lxxv.

mistrust of political individualism. The physiocrats' major departure from French enlightened thought lay in their total confidence in economic individualism. Nevertheless, their choice of the term despotism provoked outrage. Repeatedly, they felt obliged to explain that their despotism sanctioned only the power of those laws clearly derived from nature, and hence from God. Legal despotism, they explained, only expressed the general belief that it was better to accept the hegemony of the natural order than to risk the arbitrary interference of men.

The political concerns of the physiocrats did not differ as much from those of their contemporaries as their rhetoric would suggest. Quesnay's economic analysis, however, grounded their discussions of natural law, origin of society, authority, and other commonly discussed matters in a specific form of materialism. The economic analysis rests upon a few clear propositions. It begins with the central contention that land, the source of all wealth, furnishes the only disposable national economic surplus, which should, in modern economic terms, be thought of as "that portion of the total value of goods and services generated in an optimal circular-flow equilibrium not exhausted by factor costs."[7] It follows that all commerce and industry must be recognized as "sterile"—that is, non-surplus producing. It also follows that the only source of a real surplus is the rent of land, and that therefore it alone can be taxed without crippling the productive process that regularly reproduces the surplus that supports society and the state. Royal finances and general social prosperity alike depend upon the extent of the surplus, called by the physiocrats the "net product." The greater the net product, argued Quesnay, the more men can be freed from the direct cultivation of the soil and the more men can engage in transformative manufacturing, in commerce, in the arts, in government service. To render the analytic insights of his economic writings more graphic, Quesnay prepared his famous "Tableau économique"—the first presenta-

7. James L. Cochrane, *Macro-Economics before Keynes* (New York, 1970), 12.

tion of a circular-flow equilibrium in the history of economic thought. He believed that the Tableau proved, as scientifically as Newton had proved the existence of gravity, the rule for the expenditure of the net product.

In the micro-economic sphere, Quesnay analyzed capitalist production, which he restricted to the agricultural sector, and established the distinction between profit and factor costs, including the entrepreneurial. In the macro-economic sphere, he analyzed the circular-flow equilibrium and located, in a manner some recent writers drolly attribute to Keynes, the key to development on the side of demand. Both his micro- and his macro-analyses depend upon a number of institutional arrangements, especially private property, which permit men to dispose freely of their goods and their labor in an unfettered market. Both systems also contradicted all the reigning mercantilist notions by their confident insistence upon the essential harmony of different economic interests. This contradiction pushed Quesnay to develop his narrow analysis into a political economy which he regarded as its necessary derivative.

In Anglo-Saxon countries, liberal political economy has usually been attended by a firm commitment to a weak state and representative political institutions dependent upon the proprietors of the nation. Political rights may be compared to voting shares in a joint stock company, which the defenders of parliamentary liberalism have taken to embody the maximum amount of political justice: Men should participate in the direction of society's affairs in rough proportion to their proprietary stake. And taxation has taken pride of place among the issues to be settled by proprietary consent.

In physiocracy, nature, not man, determines the extent of taxation. Only the surplus afforded by the bounty of nature is available for taxation, and a share of that surplus must remain in the hands of the landed proprietors so that their spending lubricates the circular flow of goods and services that sustains the economy. At the same time the physiocrats held the monarch, or legal despot, to be coproprietor of all lands in the kingdom. They believed that the collection of funds by the state does not threaten the inviolability of property. Rather it is the natural attribution of a portion of the surplus to the upkeep of the market (roads, police, education), just as the proprietors' spending guarantees the market's proper functioning, or as their demand elicits a corresponding supply and thus stimulates the productive sector. The margin for debate about specific allocation remains very slim and that about principles nonexistent. The proprietors might retain a little more, the state collect a little less, or vice versa, but basically nature itself, as interpreted by positive economic science, determines the just and necessary proportions. Thus legal despotism would serve much better than representative institutions to allow the maximum free play to the natural law. Political negotiation, the physiocrats argued, would slow down progress and might even prevent it. For as Quesnay's metaphysics demonstrated, if nature offers man the indisputable laws for his greatest happiness, man retains the freedom to disregard those laws.

A capsule description of physiocratic doctrine can neither do justice to its originality nor explain the bitter and fearful criticism it evoked among contemporaries. Physiocratic political thought remained an intellectual exercise. Legal, as opposed to enlightened, despotism offered a logical model of the essence of government rather than a realistic policy for an existing government; it represented the physiocrats' attempt to break the deadlock between their liberal economic premises and the reality of a legally defined traditional society. As an obvious abstraction their political theory could have been dismissed with faint scorn, but the substantive questions it raised struck sensitive nerves, as did the specific proposals for reform it engendered.

When Quesnay formulated his analysis from his study of English economic performance, particularly the agricultural progress accomplished prior to 1750, he selected as his model the most highly developed economy in the world. For a scientist who wished to analyze the process of economic development his choice made sense. For a Frenchman who wished to succor an almost bankrupt monarchy, it augured confusion and trouble. Quesnay's attempt to develop a scientific theory of economic activity, particularly of economic development, led him to emphasize the necessity for a geometric acceleration of agricultural production as the base for a comparable acceleration of the nonagricultural population that any given territory could support. Observing the startling increase of English wealth during the preceding century, he naturally sought its cause and believed that he found it in a rational, capital-intensive agriculture under the direction of modern entrepreneurial farmers. His analysis concentrated upon a close investigation of a single estate and emphasized the transformation of a number of small autarchic plots into homogeneous economies of scale, the product of which was marketed at a price sufficiently high to cover costs and yield a rent. He then arbitrarily extended his model to an entire kingdom and argued that the proliferation of such capitalist enterprises would amply provide for the needs of government.

Quesnay's economic analysis rested upon the understanding that mere subsistence farming does not produce wealth. In answer to the populationists, who argued that greater population promoted greater national wealth, he argued that powerful, monarchical states require not men, but money. For such monarchies to obtain cash, the product of the land, to which men owe their continued physical existence, must be endowed with a monetary value. Progress beyond autarchy demands that the agricultural product exceed the needs of those engaged in its production and that the excess be converted into monetary wealth. Continued prosperity also requires the continuous return to the land of some portion of the surplus. Quesnay thus isolates the separation of men from the land—the creation of a market in labor-power—as the decisive factor in escaping what has since become known as the Malthusian population-subsistence scissors.[8] Ever increasing social division of

8. See Bernard Semmel, "Malthus: 'Physiocracy' and the Commercial System," *Economic History Review*, XVII (1965), 522–35.

labor affords not only the varied delights of advanced civilization, but also the necessary market for the advantageous sale of raw materials. Agriculture may be the source of all wealth, but society, organized as the market, imparts value to agriculture.

Quesnay's program thus aimed to promote social as well as economic development. He implicitly presents the two as inseparable: as production changes, so do its social relations. His understanding of the English experience, confirmed as it is by the most modern scholarship, reveals him as a great economic historian. But in extrapolating a rule of development valid for all times and places, he failed to take sufficient account of the social and economic transformations that initially fostered the English agricultural revolution or of those social and economic institutions which might impede the generation of such a revolution in France. His sound historical analysis that societies must move beyond subsistence farming if they are to support an increasing nonagricultural population, which can then produce the conveniences and refinements of civilized life, obscures the role of seigneurial property relations. The most recent work in economic history supports his emphasis upon the decisive role of agriculture in promoting accelerated economic growth. But modern economists are only beginning to address themselves to the role of property relations in economic development. Quesnay, certainly, did not wish to acknowledge that the simple creation of economies of scale might, above all, pose a political problem.[9]

9. See Paul Bairoch, "Commerce international et genèse de la révolution industrielle anglaise," *Annales* ESC, XVIII (1973), 541–71, and his *Révolution industrielle et sous-développement*, 4th ed. (Paris and The Hague, 1974); E. L. Jones and S. J. Woolf, eds., *Agrarian Change and Economic Development* (London, 1969); E. L. Jones, "Le origini agricole dell'industria," *Studi storici*, IX (1968), 564–93; Witold Kula, "Secteurs et régions arriérés dans l'économie du capitalisme naissant," *Studi storici*, IX (1968), 594–622. For a new but debatable synthesis, see Immanuel Wallerstein, *The Modern World-System: Capitalist Agriculture and the Origins of the European World-Economy in the Sixteenth Century* (New York, 1974). On property and economic development, see Armen Alchian and Harold Demsetz, "The Property Rights Paradigm," *Journal of Economic History*,

Quesnay did not adequately assess France's international position in his discussion of economic development. The state, the interests of which he desired to promote, regarded the economy as a treasure chest, not as a book of natural law. Quesnay would not see what his gifted neomercantilist opponent, François Véron de Forbonnais, and Diderot understood quite as well as the ministers of the crown, namely that international commercial activity, colonial plunder, and luxury production might have contributed to France's ability to compete internationally even without an agricultural revolution.[10] Quesnay did see what others did not, that the problem was to assure qualitative economic development, not merely quantitative growth. But his unwillingness to consider explicitly the political implications of his model led him to obscure this very issue. His economic model failed to confront the probable social dislocation attendant upon the shift from a seigneurial agriculture to a capitalist agriculture with a market in labor-power.

Having to his own satisfaction isolated the crucial factor in English development, Quesnay applied his insight to France, where the initial transformation had not occurred. Quesnay understood the French economic system. Under the ancien régime the basis of economic life lay, as he claimed, in the agricultural sector. His insistence upon the exclusive productivity of agricul-

---

XXXIII (1973), 16–27; Jan De Vries, "On the Modernity of the Dutch Republic," *ibid.*, 191–202; Stanley Engerman, "Property Rights in Man," *ibid.*, 43–65; for a historically naive attempt to integrate a discussion of property into the economic development of Europe, see Douglass C. North and Robert Paul Thomas, *The Rise of the Western World: A New Economic History* (Cambridge, 1973). For a fine treatment of the relationship of property to eighteenth-century economic theory and development, see Giorgio Rebuffa, *Origine della ricchezza e diritto di proprietà: Quesnay e Turgot* (Milan, 1974). See also Rudolf Vierhaus, ed., *Eigentum und Verfassung: Zur Eigentums-Diskussion im angehenden 18. Jahrhundert* (Göttingen, 1972).

10. François Véron de Forbonnais, *Principes et observations oeconomiques: Sur divers points du système de l'auteur du Tableau oeconomique*, 2 vols. (Amsterdam, 1767), I, esp. 146–50; Diderot, "Apologie de l'Abbé Galiani," *Oeuvres politiques*, 87.

ture expressed a historical reality. Furthermore, all informed Frenchman of his day, like subsequent analysts, shared his belief that French agricultural production remained depressingly sluggish in relation to the apparent potential natural wealth of the country, and that the monarchy, having in desperation taxed agriculture beyond endurance, increasingly had to rely upon exorbitantly priced loans and indirect taxes.

Quesnay also knew that French agriculture suffered under the political weight of feudal property rights and under the material weight of an essentially local and fragmentary market system hampered by a severe lack of transportation facilities. He understood less well, however, that although these counterweights to economic development common to all the predominantly landed empires of Europe had discouraged the modernization of agriculture, the French monarchy, by its substantial contributions to the progress in overseas trade and industrial production, had enabled France to maintain a competitive international position relative to the predominantly commercial states. Quesnay scorned such efforts and argued that enduring economic progress, as opposed to hot-house enterprises that fed like leeches off the creative strength of the nation, had to come from the rationalization of agriculture. He could not, or did not wish to, understand that such rationalization might be physically impossible in the existing state of technological development, or might be politically unacceptable under the existing alignment of privileged orders. He seems to have assumed that the state could create an agricultural revolution as easily as it had created a few trading companies and tax-farmers.

If Quesnay's economics owed much to English development, his political theory owed equally much to English theorists. C. B. MacPherson has demonstrated how much Locke's political thought was grounded in the historical reality of seventeenth-century England, and it is clear that Locke's thought helped Quesnay understand the implications of his independent economic analysis of English conditions.[11] When Locke spoke of property as the foundation of society, he had in mind the absolute (bourgeois) property that had triumphed with the Glorious Revolution of 1688, but when Quesnay read the same word, he confronted a gap between his own acceptance of absolute property and the contingent seigneurial property of French historical experience.

The difference between the English experience and the French did not escape the physiocrats, but they limited their admiration for England to its economic miracle. Quesnay admired the English market and understood that it required buyers and sellers who enjoyed complete freedom to pursue their economic interest and unrestricted possession of their goods. He would have asked nothing better than to introduce the structure and techniques of the English market into France. But he never suspected that liberal political institutions, however high their social price, constitute the obvious political link between the economic system he desired and his own marketplace ideology, and that without such institutions the requisite form of property would never be secure. Theoretically, Quesnay understood absolute property as the indispensable material guarantee of individual liberty. Practically, he appreciated its necessary relationship to a functioning market. He nevertheless always passed in silence over the political chasm between the need for absolute property and the seigneurial reality of France. In his effort to avoid all hint of social struggle, he preferred to announce, as a dictate of natural law, that the maximization of the economic product could only occur as the result of spontaneous self-realization of the natural economic order, and to leave his readers with the problems of matching that order with existing property arrangements.

If England seemed to prove that individual freedom to pursue gain resulted in a maximum social product and to demonstrate

11. C. B. MacPherson, *The Political Theory of Possessive Individualism from Hobbes to Locke* (London, New York, Toronto, 1962).

that pursuit of selfish interests contributed to the realization of the general interest, France, towards which he directed all his prescriptions, offered no such assurances. However realistic his analysis of the French economy, his reliance upon the market to assure development partially supports those who charge him with a doctrinaire utopianism. His reliance upon that imaginary market explains his need to translate his political economy into a total world view. His support of free trade in grain—in opposition to traditional notions of provisioning—unveiled to others, if not to him, the gulf that separated the world of physiocracy and that of the old regime.

Bread occupied the central position in the French popular diet and a place of overwhelming importance in the popular consciousness. All except a few Frenchmen depended upon grain for their physical existence. With the price of grain, rather than the price of labor-power, still determining the level of popular well-being, an inexpensive, honest loaf acquired immeasurable social and psychological significance. As in England, popular standards of moral economy demanded regular supplies at possible prices. Since distribution in France encountered serious technical difficulties, it remains problematical whether the removal of all restraints upon the production and marketing of grain would have resulted in as adequate a social distribution as did the old system of provisioning. The removal of all traditional constraints upon the grain trade, nevertheless, constituted the irreducible core of the physiocratic program. From the first move of Bertin (controller-general 1759–1763) toward liberalization of the internal trade in 1763 until the fall of Turgot in 1776, the physiocrats waged an unremitting propaganda war in favor of total free trade, which they expected to result in a high, or as they chose to call it, "good," price.

Derived from those requirements of an adequate return to economies of scale which they postulated for a healthy agricultural sector, the physiocratic good price remained primarily the producer's price. It had to cover costs, including those of entrepreneurship, depreciation of fixed capital, and replacement of working capital, and it had to assure a net product large enough to sustain the social division of labor. In fact, argued the physiocrats, it would also foster the maximum popular prosperity. To demonstrate their point the physiocrats relied upon Quesnay's arithmetical calculations, introduced in his first economic articles, which claimed that a good, high price—in contradistinction to a famine price—would support an increase in the wages of labor, and ultimately cost consumers no more as a proportion of their total budget.

Quesnay's arithmetic failed to convince the magistrates responsible for urban tranquillity, let alone the urban populace, which periodically saw the price of grain consume its entire budget. Nor did it convince the rural poor who saw their own wheat crop disappearing into seigneurial and clerical granges while they made do on rye in good years and chestnuts in bad. And if the calculations pleased the few commercial estate owners with easy access to transportation or the seigneurial lords who lived off the proceeds from the sale of rents in kind, they constituted no more than an intellectual grace note to the most time-honored patterns of exploitation.

Le Mercier could entitle his paradigmatic, if little read, treatise on the grain trade *L'intérêt général*, but he impressed none but the converted.[12] And by and large, the faith of the converted rested upon their ability to use the existing property and market relations to their own advantage, rather than upon their desire to usher in the new world of a free market economy. The mushrooming literature answering the physiocrats took various tacks. Some authors, like Galiani, demonstrated—in his case with devastating wit—that the requisite market did not exist: free circulation

12. P. P. F. J. H. Le Mercier de la Rivière, *L'intérêt général de l'état; ou la liberté du commerce des blés, démontrée conforme au droit naturel; au droit public de la France; aux loix fondamentales du royaume; à l'intérêt commun du souverain et de ses sujets dans tous les temps* . . . (Amsterdam and Paris, 1770).

might be every bit as desirable as the physiocrats proclaimed, but it remained a material impossibility. Others, like Necker, evoked traditional notions of provisioning and waxed eloquent about that social interest which, in any responsible society, must override the producer's interest. Necker's fortune, after all, derived from banking—not from anything so antisocial as starving the poor. Finally, some, like Linguet and Mably, addressed themselves from widely divergent perspectives—Mably favored communism and Linguet the reinstitution of serfdom, if not slavery—to the justifications for social organization and to problems of social morality.[13]

The grain trade debate, more than any other issue, illustrates the tensions which beset physiocracy. An uncompromising defense of the legitimacy of free trade in grain implies a repudiation of traditional notions of social justice. It implies that laborpower is a commodity, and that the lives of laboring men depend upon the vagaries of the market. This commitment to capitalism, as opposed to a general commitment to the increase of wealth, entails acceptance of such corollaries as the idea that all men must be free; that the rich must be allowed to buy and sell as they choose; and that the poor must be suffered to starve if they must. The physiocrats' defense of capitalism in this sense, much more than their political thought or obscure language, has been responsible for the praise or criticism accorded their doctrine.

Interpreters who emphasize the modernity of physiocracy have frequently obscured the complexity of the doctrine by suggesting

13. Abbé Ferdinand Galiani, *Dialogues sur le commerce des bleds* (London, 1770); Jacques Necker, *Sur la législation et le commerce des grains* (Paris, 1775); Simon-Nicolas-Henri Linguet, *Du pain et du bled* (London, 1774), *Réponse aux docteurs modernes, ou apologie pour l'auteur de la théorie des loix et des lettres sur cette théorie. Avec la réfutation du système des philosophes économistes* . . . 3 pts. in 2 vols., (n.p., 1771), and *Théorie des loix civiles, ou principes fondamentaux de la société*, 2 vols. (London, 1767); and Gabriel Bonnot de Mably, *Doutes proposés aux philosophes économistes sur l'ordre naturel et essentiel des sociétés politiques* (The Hague and Paris, 1768). See also Henri Grange, *Les idées de Necker* (Paris, 1974).

that the physiocrats intended their program to serve the interests of a nascent bourgeois class or class-conscious third estate—a reading that cannot be sustained by the evidence.[14] The physiocrats made no intentional contribution to the development either of the subjective consciousness or the objective interests of the bourgeoisie as it existed under the ancien régime. They explicitly avoided formulating a class interpretation of historical development. In retrospect, the physiocratic paean to capitalist production and to a market in labor-power can be seen to have foreshadowed a classical liberal and even a Marxian social analysis, to the extent that it presented social relations as a direct emanation of the relations of production. Their model could be enlivened by adding a rising capitalist class composed of specific individuals, but unfortunately, no such class existed. Yet the physiocrats, eschewing a call to class struggle, did formulate an ostensibly struggle-free ideology that, in its largest implications, contradicted the most cherished premises of the traditional order, favored those conditions most essential to the eventual emergence of a bourgeois class, and outlined a justification for bourgeois hegemony. The physiocrats never advertised and probably never considered their world view as an irreconcilable alternative to the existing order. But their position in the grain trade debate—their claims and the opposition they aroused—revealed how far their idea of social justice departed from that espoused by the majority of the king's magistrates. Their judgment that the maximization of the net product alone could determine the social distribution of bread directly challenged the monarchy's most solemn view of itself as responsible for the just provisioning of the French people.

Quesnay never intended to sap the foundations of the mon-

14. For example, Albert Mathiez, "Les doctrines politiques des physiocrates," *Annales historiques de la Révolution française*, XIII (1936), 193–203; Lucien Goldmann, *Sciences humaines et philosophie* (Paris, 1952), 122–27. Cf. Michel Bernard, *Introduction à une sociologie des doctrines économiques des Physiocrates à Stuart Mill* (Paris and The Hague, 1963), 27–29; and Norman J. Ware, "The Physiocrats: A Study in Economic Rationalization," *American Economic Review*, XXI (1931), 607–19.

archy. On the contrary, he began by trying to strengthen the power of the state through a program for augmentation of its resources. His early economic articles suggest no ideological innovation. In fact, they display a sturdy realism about the course the pursuit of individual interest would be likely to follow in a society in which individual interest clearly meant legal privileges. Writing his early economic articles, however, led him to an understanding of the market and to the conviction that value resides in the freely determined market price of commodities. So by 1757 he had concluded that the monarchy, to ease its financial plight, had to raise the productivity, and specifically the net product, of society as a whole, and that to do so it must transform agricultural produce into marketable commodities.

The political dilemmas confronted by the physiocrats troubled other philosophes as well. Diderot, for example, long remained committed to the monarchy. He, like Quesnay, deeply mistrusted the free play of individual interests. D'Holbach (1723–1789), one of the leading philosophes, had taught Diderot that the vaunted English political system constituted only the thinnest veil for corruption and the domination of the powerful. Diderot broke with the physiocrats over the question of grain. The same Diderot who wrote that "it is property that makes the citizen," that "the land is the physical and political basis of a state," and that "the right of property is sacred from individual to individual, and if it is not sacred, then society must dissolve itself," also doubted that there could be "any sacred right when it is a question of public affairs, of general utility, real or simulated."[15] Diderot, in other words, accepted the verdicts of Galiani, Linguet, Necker, and Mably that the social interest must override individual interests when provisioning the country was at stake. When confronted by such questions, all these theorists fell back on the most traditional monarchical claims.

Provisioning had been a major royal responsibility since time

15. Oeuvres politiques, 48, 49, 85.

immemorial. As "the father of his people," the king had a sacred obligation to see to it that his people survived. He could not always live up to that responsibility, as the history of famines shows, but he continued to try. For sound political reasons, the city of Paris received his special attention, but by extension, all urban areas benefitted from protective regulations. The progress of royal centralization and the rationalization of administration never altered this traditional mentality. The king adopted these modern techniques to buttress his position, never to transform the ideological bases on which the monarchy rested. With the passage of time, French kings could no longer dole out bread as Saint Louis had doled out justice, but their ever more numerous and efficient agents perpetuated a time-honored spirit of royal concern through close control of the trade in grain.

From the late middle ages until the end of the reign of Louis XIV, most cities had ensured an adequate grain supply through close control of their immediate hinterland and close supervision of marketing practices within the city itself. With the increase in urban population, the strain upon neighboring resources increased. Inadequate transportation facilities made indefinite extension of the lines of urban supply uneconomical. The increase in urban demand exacerbated the age-old war between town and country. The magistrates responsible for urban peace felt justified in using the most rigorous controls to provide an adequate supply of cheap loaves. The producers, forced to sell below the market price or unable to export, preferred to let their fields lie fallow rather than to cultivate them at a loss.[16]

Had town-country relations remained in equilibrium, the monarchy and its agents would undoubtedly have continued to support the policy of provisioning. But the patent inadequacies of the old system compelled their reluctant consideration of free trade. The eloquent pleas of Boisguilbert and Herbert, expressing the interest of producers and arguing for national development,

16. Louis-Paul Abeille, ed., *Corps d'observations de la Société d'agriculture, de commerce et des arts de Bretagne*, 2 vols. (Paris, 1758–1759), I, 180.

initially commanded scant attention.[17] By the 1760s, however, reforming ministers were ready to try another approach to provisioning. Like the physiocrats, the controller-general Bertin and his successor L'Averdy (1723–1793) maintained that free trade would better assure a plentiful supply than could any amount of regulations. Support for their policy came from many unlikely quarters, including the notoriously reactionary Breton nobility. But the bad harvests of the late sixties aborted these schemes by triggering a wave of rioting and pillaging, especially in Rouen. L'Averdy was dismissed from office in 1768 and in 1770 Terray restored the old controls.

L'abbé Terray (1715–1778) was controller-general in the Maupeou ministry which in 1771 abolished the Parlements. The collaboration of the two men neatly illustrates the complexity of political life in the last decades of the old regime. As chancellor, Maupeou pursued a polity of ruthless reform and austerity. While Terray desperately tried to balance the budget (or at least service the debt), he took on the Parlements whose opposition had stymied so many previous efforts. Enlightened opinion divided on all their policies. Was the restoration of control over the grain trade progressive or reactionary? Was abolition of the Parlements enlightened or despotic? Many of the Parlements had supported free trade in grain—those of Languedoc, Dauphiné, and Brittany eloquently defended private property and the interest of the citizen. Yet the physiocrats, as well as men like Voltaire, applauded the abolition. Diderot, who followed Galiani in supporting Terray's grain policy, condemned the attack on the Parlements as the triumph of despotism. The crown had simultaneously reaffirmed its duty as the custodian of social justice and demolished the last vestiges of consultative restraint.

Traditional polity broke down in eighteenth-century France.

17. INED, *Pierre de Boisguilbert, ou la naissance de l'économie politique*, 2 vols., (Paris, 1966); C. J. Herbert, *Essai sur la police générale des grains, sur leurs prix et sur les effets de l'agriculture* [1755], ed. Edgar Depître (Paris, 1910).

The absolutism perfected under Louis XIV still enjoyed official sanction, but its plausibility was steadily decreasing. The long-established channels by which the various segments of the population represented their special interests to the crown still followed the old hierarchical patterns. Everyone's political identity turned upon his relationship to the crown. Society had no place for autonomous political activity. Despite pervasive dissent, no cohesive party of opposition emerged. If many Frenchmen addressed themselves to a piecemeal discussion of the abuses of the state, none formulated a comprehensive alternative to the traditional reliance on altar and throne. Indeed, most still looked to the state to remove its own abuses, for underlying even the most hostile critiques lay a common assumption that the state created society—or to put it differently, that human rights derive from social function. Those who most strongly defended natural law, like the philosophes, looked to the state to enforce it; those who broke most sharply with the statist consensus, like the *parlementaires,* did so to defend their own special legal privileges. Their attempt to rechristen those feudal claims as inalienable, contractual rights, and to present them as the cornerstone of the common social interest never fooled Voltaire or the physiocrats, but it educated many more credulous Frenchmen in the language of liberalism.

The grain trade debate cut across the already confused political lines. The physiocratic defense of free trade implicitly attacked the traditional notion of the monarchy by openly attacking the monarch's responsibility for the direct implementation of social justice. The physiocrats looked to the monarch to force free trade upon a recalcitrant nation, but they left the distribution of justice to nature. Furthermore, the free trade position rested upon an uncompromising defense of private property that implicitly challenged the social system upon which the monarchy itself rested. The physiocrats' commitment to absolute property dismissed all claims of society to a direct role in the allocation of resources. Galiani, with his customary insight, understood the implications perfectly: "He who will dare to overhaul completely the administration of grain in France, if he succeeds, will have at the same time changed the form of the government."[18]

The physiocrats lobbied vigorously to change the administration of grain in France, but always by asking the existing state to alter its practices, never by attacking it directly. They never quite shook the attitude of "if only the tsar knew." And on occasion, especially while Turgot was controller-general, the state tried to implement physiocratic policies. As Turgot's experience made clear, however, systematic defense of free trade would require shooting down some rioters in the streets. Furthermore, beyond the immediate unpleasantness, free trade would require the abolition of corvées, guilds, and private tolls, all of which belonged to powerful interests. Turgot, more the enlightened administrator than a physiocrat, accepted the less palatable aspects of enforcing his policy, but as the opposition increased, he had to rely more and more upon the personal support of Louis XVI, who was not made of such stern stuff. The triumph of Necker assured the maintenance of provisioning.

Turgot always refused to associate himself with the more doctrinaire aspects of physiocracy. He never admitted the exclusive productivity of agriculture, and he doubted the miraculous powers of the Tableau. Above all, he rejected the ideological pretensions of physiocracy. Time has served Turgot well. His enlightened eclecticism has earned him the admiration of most subsequent generations and a secure niche in the gallery of the true, liberalizing reformers of the ancien régime. He has continued to speak to civilized men whom the physiocrats repel. Yet his failure to understand the ideological dimension of physiocracy goes far toward explaining his rather naive confidence in the triumph of reason in general and his own program in particular.

Quesnay also had begun his economic career as a loyal reformer, not an opponent, of the ancien régime. No more than Turgot

18. Galiani to the comte de Schonberg, 19 May 1770, cited by Camille Bloch, *Etudes sur l'histoire économique de la France* (Paris, 1900), 71.

did he make an ideological connection between the human dimension of existing institutions and his own program for change. His economic articles did not investigate the human dimension of society in an intellectually rigorous way. The early work of his friend and collaborator Mirabeau did. Mirabeau, faced with the abuses and overweening power of the monarchy, or at least of its administrative agents, directed his efforts to restoring the traditional social order in all its purity and to reformulating traditional values as a coherent modern ideology. Mirabeau's traditionalism, superficially so opposed to all that Quesnay and Turgot stood for, provided the decisive impetus for the physiocratic ideology. Physiocracy, as distinct from more eclectic reformist critiques, retained Mirabeau's aspiration to restore some sense of coherence to the social relations of the nation without challenging the established order directly. By the time Mirabeau began his work, French experience had moved so far from its own legitimizing principles that the ordered exposition of those principles took on an ideological and proto-political character. Mirabeau's vision, however, would have been relegated to the status of an antiquarian curiosity had not Quesnay's economics provided a new mode of discourse that not only introduced scientific precision into the discussion of social relations, but also afforded a new criterion—the net product—by which economic performance could be measured. Furthermore, Quesnay's metaphysics raised his economics from the level of technical manipulation to the level of cultural symbol, and pointed the way to preserving Mirabeau's image of social order by transforming it into a new world view.

2

Quesnay—Physician
and Metaphysician

When François Quesnay turned his attention to the economics
that was to establish his reputation, he had already reached the
peak of an eminently successful medical career. In 1756, when
Quesnay contributed his first economic article, "Fermiers," to the
Encyclopédie, he was sixty-two years of age, personal physician
to the royal mistress, first *médecin ordinaire* of the king, and a
highly respected figure in the scientific community of Paris. His
wife was dead, his children grown, and his future as secure as
any that hung on a court appointment. His years of struggle and
achievement apparently lay behind him.[1]

This disjuncture colors most accounts of Quesnay's life. His
first sixty years, which bear no obvious relationship to his most
important work, are passed over lightly by those interested primarily in the economics. But to begin the story with the publication of "Fermiers," no matter how convenient for the narrow
history of economic analysis, proves inadequate in relation to
Quesnay's broader political and social thought. Economics does

1. This biographical sketch is distilled from Jacqueline Hecht, "La vie de
François Quesnay," in INED, I, 211–93. The only other recent treatment
of Quesnay's life can be found in Marguerite Kuczynski's excellent and
lengthy introduction to François Quesnay, *Oekonomische Schriften*, 2
vols. (Berlin, 1972). *Mémoires de Madame du Hausset, femme de chambre
de Madame de Pompadour* . . . (Paris, 1824) contains scattered personal
reminiscences, and the sections pertaining to Quesnay have been reprinted
in Onken, *Oeuvres*, as have the other important contemporary eulogies. For
other useful treatments, see my bibliographical note.

not provide the connecting thread of Quesnay's intellectual life. His overriding concern remained the study of man—man as a thinking, acting being, as a member of society, and as a part of the universe or divine plan. In particular, Quesnay sought to understand the nature of external reality and human perception. Only an adequate metaphysics and epistemology could afford a guide to enlightened human action or freedom of choice in medicine, economics, or administration.

Medicine provided Quesnay's introduction to humans as material beings. Metaphysics and epistemology provided his method of understanding the dialectical relationship between material and spiritual existence. Economics alone, however, provided a discourse adequate to understand social reality and simultaneously to prescribe human action. For Quesnay, humans did not exist independent of their physical constitution, and society did not exist independent of its economic base—or more accurately, society derived from human economic cooperation. Neither society nor economic life, however, could be reduced to its material anchor, for the men who composed society and who suffered under the constraints of finite—that is, human, not divine —reason, made decisions that determined the extent to which they would benefit from the natural socioeconomic order.

The legend perpetrated at Quesnay's death by his immediate circle depicts the master as a youth teaching himself to read by poring, in isolation and as if by divine intent, over a classic sixteenth-century agricultural treatise, *Maison rustique et agriculture* (1586), written by two doctors, Charles Estienne and Jean Liébault. Unfortunately, beyond vague references to traditional medical recipes, the legend does not explain how the predestined economist pursued his mission via a career in surgery. Quesnay's economic analysis and political economy can neither be understood apart from his earlier career and his intellectual formation nor treated as a necessary result of that formation. Nor can either be fully explained in biographical terms. Few of Quesnay's personal papers remain and none directly reflect his state of mind.

By the time he had addressed himself to economic questions, Quesnay had resolved, or successfully sublimated, any turbulent personal feelings and had made his peace with his past. Despite lack of direct evidence, the condensed passion of Quesnay's intellectual work suggests an intense, if tightly reined, personality. His thought, in contrast with that of Diderot, Rousseau, or even Voltaire, bears a rigorously impersonal stamp. His attempt to establish a new absolute truth undoubtedly contains its own measure of rebellion, but it betrays no immediate traces of anger or of personal revolt.

Quesnay was born in 1694, the eighth child (only four of thirteen survived) and second son of a middling peasant family. During his early years his father acted as *receveur des tailles* (petty rent and tithe collector) for the neighboring Abbaye Saint Magloire, which left Quesnay's mother responsible for the farm as well as the children. Quesnay cannot have received a great deal of attention during his childhood, although he seems always to have been close to his mother. By the age of eleven, he still could not read. Whether he began with the *Maison rustique* or not, he did suddenly start reading, and he systematically devoted himself to acquiring an education which dramatically exceeded that of his milieu. Taught Greek and Latin, perhaps by the village curé or a benevolent neighbor, he acquired a grounding in the classics by reading Plato, Aristole, and Cicero.

Intellectual ambition notwithstanding, Quesnay had to earn a living, especially after his father's death in 1707. By 1711 he had abandoned earlier plans for a theological career and had decided, in accord with his mother's views, to pursue that of surgery. In the meantime, he began a five-year apprenticeship to a Parisian engraver.

This position served not only to train him in a lucrative trade but also to associate him closely with the world of medicine (heavily reliant upon accurate diagrams of human physiology), and to permit him sufficient free time to attend courses at the Faculté de Médecine and the surgeon's college, St. Côme. By

1717 he had finished the engraving apprenticeship, taken all the necessary courses in surgery, and married the daughter of a small Parisian shopkeeper. He and his wife moved to Mantes, where Quesnay gradually emerged as a respected surgeon and local notable. The rising social status of the godparents of each subsequent child testifies to his social and professional progress. But the death of his mother, followed by the premature death of his wife at the birth of their fourth and last child and the subsequent death of two of the children, severed most of Quesnay's ties to his past by the time he was thirty. He generously provided for the two remaining children, both of whom went on to lead independent lives.

During the next quarter century Quesnay moved increasingly from the practice of surgery to that of medicine. He began to write extensively on medical questions and even engaged in a public debate with Silva, one of the leading physicians of the day. He entered the personal service of the duc de Villeroy, who procured him, in addition to access to noble circles, a *commission des guerres* of Lyon and membership in the Académie of that city. In 1744 Villeroy led Quesnay to the Flanders theater of the War of the Austrian Succession and thence back to Paris, and to a chance encounter with the Marquise d'Entrades, whom he eased through an epileptic attack with such discretion that she recommended him to her friend the Marquise de Pompadour. During the 1740s, Quesnay also became acquainted with La Peyronie, a leading surgeon who sponsored his entry into the Parisian Académie des Chrirugiens and his appointment as its perpetual secretary. That gentleman in addition lent him money to purchase the *survivance* as first ordinary physician to the king and subsequently remembered him generously in his will.

Quesnay's medical career unfolded between two poles. He frequently benefited from the generous support and patronage of his professional superiors, but he also suffered from the contempt and hostility of the community of physicians. His personal experience reflected the struggle shaking the Paris medical community. Since 1656 French surgeons, as a corporation, had been joined to that of the barbers. Their medical brethren enjoyed the monopoly of prescription, treatment of disease, and the use of Latin. In a word, surgeons performed a carefully delineated craft, and physicians cured disease and passed as intellectuals. The increasingly sophisticated and well-trained surgeons naturally chafed under these restrictions, and the arcane pretensions of the physicians alienated the public. As Barbier, among others, indicates, the literate populace, sated with a medical art immortalized by Molière, turned with growing enthusiasm to the skills of men like Quesnay.[2] Finally in 1743 a royal declaration divorced the corporation of surgeons from that of barbers. By then, Quesnay had already acquired his doctorate of medicine, but he had had to do so at Pont-à-Mousson, rather than Paris. He had therefore experienced the constraints of the ancien régime's corporate structure, but his participation in the battle to have the surgeons properly sanctioned by the regime testifies to his larger acceptance of the monarchy as the appropriate vehicle for change.

Quesnay's experience with the ancien régime did not make him a political or cultural radical, despite his earthy skepticism about the presumptive claims of birth as against those of talent and wealth. His services to the royal family earned him a patent of nobility, and his numerous activities secured him a comfortable fortune.[3] The same taste for reality that led him to materialism

2. E. J. F. Barbier, *Journal historique et anecdotique du règne de Louis XV*, ed. A. de la Villegille (Paris, 1849), II, 365–66; Denis Diderot, *Correspondance*, vol. I (*1713–1757*), ed. Georges Roth (Paris, 1955), 59–71.

3. ADY, "Inventaire," confirms the judgment of Felix Lorin, "Mémoire sur la fortune de François Quesnay," in *Extrait du Bulletin des sciences économiques et sociales du Comité des Travaux historiques et scientifiques* (Paris, 1897), esp. 229–35, that Quesnay did not leave a large fortune at his death. Most scholars, however, have insisted upon Quesnay's comfortable situation during his years at Versailles, and have pointed to the large landholdings he had already given his children. Cf. Hecht, "Vie de Quesnay";

accounts for his healthy regard for the established power. As he told Madame du Hausset, the lady-in-waiting to Madame de Pompadour and his loyal friend, at the time of Mirabeau's imprisonment, "When I am in a room with the king, I say to myself: There is a man who can have my head cut off; and this idea troubles me." Madame du Hausset's memoirs frequently testify that he nonetheless shared with his visitors Turgot and Duclos respect for the French monarchy as the legitimate focus of its subjects' love, and for the Bourbon dynasty as a family of talented men.[4] A scrupulous respect for royal censorship as well as for royal sensibilities distinguishes him from those more rebellious Encyclopédistes who periodically tested the patience of the crown. Yet his critical engagement with the major issues of the day earned him an honorable place in the great Enlightenment adventure.

The bourgeois implications of Quesnay's political economy cannot be ascribed to some personal dissatisfaction. The many testimonies to his personal stability concur in portraying a charming, contented, and fully mature man. A successful professional courtier, he made the reigning system of patronage work to his advantage. Always he kept his own counsel and extended his discretion to the affairs of others. The man who treated Madame de Pompadour for frigidity, and her royal lord for an acute indigestion that had caught him in her bed, retained the trust and friendship of both his compromised patients.[5] The reverence that Quesnay inspired in his disciples derived from the intellectual virtuosity and intransigence that accompanied his personal magnetism. Like most commanding personalities, Quesnay, a well-documented modesty notwithstanding, undoubtedly en-

Kuczynski's introduction to Quesnay, *Oekonomische Schriften*, I, lx; and Auguste Onken, "Entstehen und Werden der physiokratischen Theorie," *Vierteljahrschrift für Staats- und Volkswirtschaft Literatur und Geschichte der Staatswissenschaft* (1896), V, 123–50, 272–309.

4. Madame du Hausset, "Mémoires," in Onken, *Oeuvres*, 119–20.

5. *Ibid.*, 121–22.

couraged others to accept him as mentor. His manuscript for *Le despotisme de la Chine* contains a few pages on the life of Confucius which were deleted from the published version, but which provide a disarmingly close approximation to an autobiographical assessment and statement of personal purpose. Indeed, the title given him by his disciples—"The Confucius of Europe"—originated, however unconsciously, in his own self-image.[6]

Confucius, writes Quesnay, invoking by analogy the intellectual constellation of his own day, belonged to the generation succeeding that of Thales and including Pythagorus, Solon, and by slight extension, Socrates. In comparison with the Greeks, his doctrine did not spread widely during his lifetime. But his "glory only increased with the passage of the years, and it subsists in its entirety in the greatest Empire of the world which attributes to it its duration and splendor." Unlike the Greeks, Confucius did not indulge in sterile speculation. Confucius concentrated on humans as they exist, and recognized in them one main principle. He limited his work to inspiring mortals with "the respect, the fear, the recognition" which they owed that guiding force, to persuading them "that it knows all, that it knows even the most secret recesses of the heart, that it never leaves virtue without reward or crime without punishment." Such, Quesnay insists, was the basic precept through which Confucius attempted "to reform the morals of the human race."[7]

Having established the religious and human focus of Confucius' thought, Quesnay adds some biographical facts and psychological insights. From the tenderest years Confucius displayed "the wisdom that ordinarily is only the fruit of maturity." The games and amusements of childhood never distracted him. Indeed, his "grave, modest and serious air" earned him the veneration of all who came in contact with him and paralled Quesnay's own sobriety. And like Quesnay, in later years Confucius made great

6. EMHL, Winterthur MSS, group 2, series E, "Histoire sommaire de Confucius," in "Le despotisme de la Chine," 60–72.
7. *Ibid.*, 60, 61.

strides in the study of the past. Having, through his studies, "acquired the most profound knowledge, he proposed to reestablish the form of government on wise principles, and to reform, by this path, the morals and the customs of the various little kingdoms which then composed the Chinese Empire." Through exhortation and example, Confucius sought to lead men to the path of morality. Indeed, the resplendence of his own virtues, the profundity of his "lumières," and his integrity all contributed to the recognition of his worth. He accepted several official positions, "but with the only intent of spreading his doctrine and working for the reformation of men."[8]

Throughout a long career, the actions of Confucius never contravened his maxims. "By his gravity, his modesty, his sweetness and his frugality, by his scorn of terrestrial pleasures, and by a continual vigilance on his own conduct, he was himself an example of the precepts he advanced in his writings and his discourses. . . ." And again: "Never did one hear him speak advantageously of himself, and the praises that he received from others he listened to only with repugnance." Just as Confucius attributed his own wisdom "to the great legislators Yao and Xun," so would Quesnay place his maxims in the mouth of the great Sully.

The great Chinese philosopher always worked to reestablish human nature in its original purity, to counteract and eradicate the errors introduced by a history of superstition and false reasoning. "Human nature, he frequently said to his disciples, came to us from heaven very pure, very perfect: subsequently, ignorance, the passions, the bad examples corrupted it; and to be perfect, it is necessary to reascend to the point from which we are descended."[9]

In thus describing Confucius, Quesnay described his own character, at least as he wished it to be, and provided his most direct statement of purpose. The restoration of the integrity of

8. *Ibid.*, 62, 63.
9. *Ibid.*, 66, 67.

human nature ran like a thread through both his medical and economic work. The vision of divine presence as the origin of human perfection remains inseparable from even his most materialist analyses. Quesnay, for all his innovations, always saw his work as a restoration. New forms might be needed, but their purpose would always be to realize the potential in God's design as manifested in nature.

Quesnay's move to Versailles in 1749 constitutes a watershed in his career, but no break in his intellectual development. The Versailles appointment brought Quesnay increased honors and public attention. In 1751 he was elected to the Académie des Sciences and to the Royal Society of London; a year later he received his letters of nobility. His new position, as well as his publications, particularly the new edition of *L'essai physique sur l'oeconomie animale* (1747) and *Traité des fièvres continues* (1751), earned him considerable recognition, not always favorable, among Paris intellectuals. In the *Année littéraire* of 1756, Fréron denigrates another physician by saying that his work adds nothing to that of Boerhaave or Quesnay.[10] As early as 1748, Diderot had written to a friend, speaking of the physician-surgeon conflict, "What! an adroit man, a Quesnay, because he is only a surgeon, should keep silent in front of a P. . . . [Procope]?" And by 1753 Diderot, who had obviously met Quesnay in the interim, was enlisting his support in a matter of patronage. During these same years Quesnay made the acquaintance of the naturalist Buffon, probably through the offices of Madame de Pompadour, Buffon's patron.[11] Quesnay's new friends also included a group of *agronomes*, particularly Le Roy, Butré, and Patullo, and members of the group of reformist administrators around the influential, liberal intendant of commerce, Vincent de Gournay. Quesnay undoubtedly knew d'Alembert either

10. Elie Fréron, *L'année littéraire*, VI [1756] (Geneva, 1966), 468. All references to *L'essai physique sur l'oeconomie animale*, 3 vols. (Paris, 1747), will be to Onken, *Oeuvres*, 758–63.

11. Diderot, *Correspondance*, 60, 149ff.

through the Académie des Sciences or through Diderot, although the critic Marmontel's account of the two at dinner cannot be taken at face value. Quesnay, who also knew the philosopher-critics Helvétius and Condillac, was regarded as sympathetic enough to the philosophes' cause to be a natural contributor to the *Encyclopédie*.[12]

In addition to other advantages, the royal position afforded Quesnay his first opportunity to indulge fully the intellectual restlessness that had spurred him from his native village of Méré. Madame du Hausset portrays him in his *entresol*, immersed in a dozen books at once, tirelessly questioning everyone he met, and continually trying to work all his new information into a coherent whole. After the *Traité des fièvres* in 1751 he abandoned his medical studies, and until his article "Evidence" appeared in the *Encyclopédie* in 1756, he published nothing. Only the sketchiest hints of his preoccupations during these years remain—for example his correspondence with the Abbé Le Blanc, a translator of Hume, and his visits from Turgot and Duclos.[13] This silence might suggest some profound reorientation of his thought, but his portrait of Confucius suggests, and a close investigation of his metaphysics confirms, a shift in subject matter, not a break in method or point of view.

Nearly two centuries of scholarly interest have failed to produce a satisfactory view of the chain of Quesnay's thought. He has been variously identified as a rationalist and an empiricist, as a Cartesian and a Lockean. His thought has been linked to that of Plato, the Schoolmen, Shaftesbury, Cumberland, Descartes, Leibniz, and Wolff. Even his general and self-proclaimed debt to Malebranche has found its skeptics. No single attribution can account for Quesnay's intellectual complexity. His thought must

12. Hecht, "Vie de Quesnay," 252, 254; Cf. Jacques Proust, *Diderot et l'Encyclopédie*, rev. ed. (Paris, 1962), 15–27; and [Jean-François] Marmontel, *Mémoires* [1804], ed. John Renwick (Clermont-Ferrand, 1972), I, 137–39.

13. Madame du Hausset, "Mémoires," esp. 134–35, 137; Hecht, "Vie de Quesnay," 252.

be situated within the unfolding epistemological and metaphysical debates of the early Enlightenment, for as Wesley Mitchell said of Adam Smith, he "was primarily a philosopher. He lived at a time when economics was just beginning to disassociate itself rather clearly from the general body of philosophical interests."[14] Where Smith had specialized professionally in moral philosophy, Quesnay had specialized in medicine. Quesnay's highly individual philosophical method and commitment derived in nearly equal parts from his experience in medicine and his readings in philosophy, theology, history, and science. Furthermore, both sets of interests progressed in tandem; speculative philosophy and social theory only took the lead over medicine when he was approaching his sixtieth year. Because Quesnay's economic work appeared in the late 1750s and the 1760s, many scholars automatically place his thought in the intellectual context of mid-century. Alternatively, because the record of his middle years is buried in medical tracts, other scholars reach back indiscriminately into a general liberal, Lockean, or Cartesian tradition.

Quesnay did not belong to the intellectual generation of Diderot, Rousseau, Grimm, or d'Holbach; he was the exact contemporary of Voltaire, and only five years younger than Montesquieu. In his youthful reading he concentrated on the classics, with Cicero a particular favorite, and also included some Malebranche and Thomas' *Eloge de Descartes*. In the following years, his apprenticeship in Paris must have forced concentration on medical courses, but he probably followed the currents of Cartesian and neo-Cartesian science as well. Given his early predilection for theology, he may well have pursued the theoretical works generated by the Jansenist controversy, including those of Duguet, who also wrote about agriculture.[15] Probably, however, Quesnay had little opportunity for nonprofessional reading during this period of marriage, the birth of children, and the establishment of a surgical practice in Mantes.

14. *Types of Economic Theory*, 2 vols. (New York, 1967), I, 14.
15. Réne Taveneaux, *Jansénisme et politique* (Paris, 1965), 100–121.

Scholars, beginning with Quesnay's earliest biographers, have attempted to find the logical relationship between his interest in medicine and political economy. Most directly, they point to a natural relationship between the act of healing a human and that of healing a society and note that Locke and William Petty, the English political economist, also began their careers as doctors. In a particularly sophisticated version of physiocracy-as-medicine, Ronald Meek argues that for Quesnay the curing of a society required "knowledge of the physiology of the social order. Since for Quesnay the basis of the social order lay in the economic order, an understanding of the laws and regularities governing economic life appeared to be of primary necessity if the sickness of society was to be cured."[16] However attractive it may be, this interpretation misguidingly suggests that Quesnay began his economic studies with a particular interest in the social order. In fact, he began with an interest in the mechanics of the production of wealth and in the means of increasing the revenues of the state independent of the social order upon which it rested. The general sickness of society, in contrast to specific problems of production and of the treasury, long remained the question Quesnay wished to avoid.

Quesnay's study of medicine influenced his economics primarily through his attempt to construct a method of scientific investigation capable of reconciling empirical research and theoretical speculation. No ordinary concept of physiology in particular, or the biological sciences in general, affords an adequate model for his conception of economic science. Peter Gay, without mentioning Quesnay, has offered a very fruitful and new way of looking at eighteenth-century medicine as both a prototype for, and an influence on, the emerging social sciences. Noting the Dutch physician and teacher Boerhaave's tremendous sway over early eighteenth-century medical thought, Gay reminds us

16. Meek, *Economics*, 18. See also V. Foley, "An Origin of the *Tableau économique*," *History of Political Economy*, V (1973), 121-50.

that Boerhaave "taught medical Newtonianism, lectured on Newton, and tried to embody Newton's empirical methods in his theoretical writings and clinical practice." But if this particular medical tradition placed a refreshing emphasis upon empirical methods, it still retained a deep commitment to a unicausal explanation of material phenomena. "Down to about 1750, a whole tribe of would-be medical Newtonians obstructed progress with their search for a single cause of disease, of principle, of cure, and it was not until mid-century, when the philosophes were at the height of their influence, and partly as a result of their propaganda, that pluralistic empiricism changed the course of medical research."[17]

Quesnay had not himself studied with Boerhaave, but he owned copies of his works. Although Quesnay's reputation as a skilled and sensitive practitioner weathered the many conflicts of his career, his works published in the late 1740s and early 1750s already seemed dated to many of his enlightened contemporaries. In addition to Haller's important and thoughtful criticism, he received harsher and less balanced evaluations in the French press, including one that wondered whether he had not earned his recognition as the "French translator of Boerhaave."[18]

In his last medical works, Quesnay used medicine as a vehicle for epistemology. He implicitly addressed himself to the conflict between Newtonianism and Cartesianism. The Newtonianism and the Cartesianism of the 1730s and 1740s, however, owed as much to the work of commentators as they did to Newton and Descartes. Cartesian thought, as Aram Vartanian has argued, had, under the aegis of biologists, broken through the dualistic

17. "The Enlightenment as Medicine and as Cure," in *The Age of the Enlightenment: Studies Presented to Theodore Besterman* (Edinburgh and London, 1967), 384–85. ADY, "Inventaire," shows that Quesnay's library included the works of Boerhaave as well as a number of other treatises on physics, optics, and chemistry.

18. Hecht, "Vie de Quesnay," 228, 237; Albrecht von Haller, "Analyse critique," in *Gottinger Gelehrte Anzeigen* (1748) repr. in Onken, *Oeuvres*, 239–47.

prison of its inception and was well on the way to the most intransigent materialism, while Newtonian thought, under the patronage of Voltaire, had been shorn of much of its original religious fervor. Nevertheless, even the French Newtonians retained a commitment to a method, a mechanics, and a deism that distinguished them from the avant-garde of neo-Cartesians.[19] Quesnay owned copies of Voltaire's works and knew them well. He had undoubtedly read those of Fontenelle, of Maupertuis, and of La Mettrie, and kept abreast of new work by Buffon and Diderot. Nevertheless, he had first encountered Descartes through Thomas, and Newton through Boerhaave. Whatever his subsequent reading of the originals or the glosses, he formed his basic intellectual perspective in the context of the thinking of 1715–1720 rather than of 1750.

As early as the "Préface" for the *Mémoires de l'Académie royale de chirurgie,* published in 1743, Quesnay laid out the general principles which he would develop into a full-blown metaphysics in "Evidence." To modern readers the "Préface" appears unoriginal, but Quesnay's contemporaries greeted it with enthusiasm. In it he maintains that in scientific research, experience and theory should move hand in hand, serving rather than combating each other. Physical observation and experience, he explains, are as lights "which must unite to dissipate obscurity." He then develops this theme into a number of concepts that stamp his later work. Thus he proposes that in observation "the mind is only a simple spectator." False impressions, those not sufficiently grounded in material reality, infect theory "with false opinions," which, passed from generation to generation, promote more false views. Only a constant return to individual experiments can provide an adequate check against the emergence of an entirely misleading science. But experiments alone cannot

19. Aram Vartanian, *Diderot and Descartes* (Princeton, 1953), esp. 8–21, 85–86, 96–97; Proust, *Diderot,* 286–87; and Jean Ehrard, *L'idée de la nature en France dans la première moitié du XVIIIe siècle,* 2 vols. (Paris, 1963), I, 125–78.

produce a brilliant surgeon. Knowledge progresses through theoretical insight and innovation, as well as through practice.[20]

The most original if least successful aspect of Quesnay's "Préface" is his attempt to distinguish between constructive theory and idle speculation. He has no trouble defining speculation, which he calls "those fictions of the imagination, those ideas which are not drawn from the depth of things, those principles founded on possibilities and on appearances." The delirium of speculation has led to the modern habit of constructing "systems," a word Quesnay mistrusts as much as do his enlightened colleagues. "On foundations built by imagination alone . . . philosophers have complacently erected the entire machine of the universe." The antidote to such false procedures seems simple: construct a theory based on experience alone. Quesnay, however, rejects that unilateral solution on the grounds that nature does not yield all her secrets in rational form. Her various manifestations permit an infinite number of possible solutions. Sooner or later scientists must resort to the deceptive but indispensable guides of conjecture and analogy, and accept the consequences of that uncertainty which plagues all operations of the human mind.[21]

Quesnay makes a valiant attempt to establish the proper balance between the operations of the mind and the practice of experimentation, but his resolution of the problem hardly qualifies as epistemology: he simply denies that "limited or unenlightened minds" can ever translate theory into practice and even doubts whether "superior geniuses who possess the most extensive knowledge" can manage to do so.[22] In subsequent works Quesnay would devote greater attention to the problem of the human mind. The impasse reached in the "Préface" led him to reflect seriously upon epistemological questions, and shortly, to relate the problem of knowledge to that of human freedom.

20. "Préface," in Onken, *Oeuvres,* 724, 725–27.
21. *Ibid.,* 733, 734, 735.
22. *Ibid.,* 735. A. D. Yvelines, "Inventaire."

By the time Quesnay wrote his sketch of Confucius in 1766 or 1767, it had become clear to him that the central thread of his own life's work lay in the study of man. His early leaning toward theology prefigured a lifelong preoccupation with human nature, from which his medical practice had only temporarily distracted him. Presumably, at about this time he read or reread Malebranche, Leibniz, Wolff, Locke, and Bayle. The evidence of his library would also suggest that he pursued his interest in theology through the *Dictionnaire de Trévoux* and other religious works, including histories of the papacy and the Council of Trent.[23]

No particular philosopher decisively influenced his thought at this juncture. The intellectual debates of the 1730s and 1740s had pushed Quesnay back toward Descartes and Newton and Locke. Quesnay does not explain his own thought processes and intellectual goals for the benefit of posterity. Only his subsequent work with Mirabeau on the monarchy, to be discussed later, suggests a method for understanding his development. The origins of legal despotism, for example, would remain obscure were it not for the unpublished manuscript "Le traité de la monarchie," which shows that Quesnay directly attacked a range of problems he never mentioned in print. In legal despotism he fashioned a model sufficiently abstracted from reality to avoid dangerous repercussions.

In his metaphysical and epistemological work he apparently followed a comparable procedure in addressing problems he does not identify explicitly. His section on liberty in *L'essai physique*, and the essay "Evidence" suggest that he sought to reconcile and transcend the Cartesian and Newtonian systems, although he does not state this purpose. Quesnay avoided the worst pitfalls of the Cartesian-Newtonian controversy by rejecting all attempts to understand the nature of the universe. He did, however, try to adapt these points of view to an understanding of man's

23. Ehrard, *L'idée de la nature,* 176–77; Vartanian, *Diderot and Descartes,* 237; Proust, *Diderot,* 260.

nature and ability to know reality. As early as the "Préface" he wished to preserve the empirical rigor of Newtonian practice but doubted its ability to solve, unassisted, scientific problems. He thus took his stand in favor of a deductive method, but did not, like so many of his most able peers, banish the spiritual side of Cartesian dualism. Where the great biologists came increasingly to insist upon the effect of the body upon the mind, Quesnay, in his medical practice as well as in his writing, looked for the effect of the mind upon the body. He followed neo-Cartesian materialism in his emphasis upon material reality, but he did not trust material being to understand that reality. His epistemology carries unmistakeable Newtonian overtones.

French Newtonians, following Voltaire, had gradually mitigated the force of Newton's theism. Furthermore, they increasingly assumed that gravity, that force of attraction which Newton had placed outside matter, actually constituted a property of matter itself.[24] Over time this position permitted a kind of uneasy synthesis of Cartesian and Newtonian thought in the works of men like Buffon and Diderot. Quesnay, while working toward a similar synthesis, proceeded differently. Rather than assimilate attraction to matter, he apparently converted the general notion of attraction into the quality of human intelligence. Like the Cartesian materialists, he recognized a general notion of physical evolution which linked man and animals. Unlike them, he held out for a radical break between animal and human intelligence. Human intelligence—and here the influence of Malebranche is clear—partakes of the divine. That self-consciousness or intellectual clarity which permits at least the occasional genius to bridge the gap between theory and practice derives from a different realm than simple material being. It is a gift of God. Quesnay's great originality lies in substituting his own version of the Newtonian conception of attraction for the old Cartesian mind-body dualism. The brain is a natural or material phenomenon common to animals and men. Quesnay does not

24. Vartanian, *Diderot and Descartes*, 241–42.

waste time on pituitary glands or other problematical material seats of intelligence. Intelligence, like Newton's original gravity, is a force from outside. Quesnay describes intelligence as a light from God that illuminates the mind.

Like so many other philosophes, Quesnay had learned from Locke to mistrust the notion of innate ideas, but he also came to reject doctrinaire sensualism. His epistemology viewed external experience as the source of knowledge, but argued that knowledge without judgment or intelligence led to abstract speculations or to a mere catalogue of meaningless facts. A coherent or true picture of reality depended upon the exercise of an active intelligence that derived from God.

When Quesnay prepared the second edition of *L'essai physique* in 1747, he included a section on liberty in which he developed his ideas on human freedom. Freedom, according to Quesnay, cannot be identified with arbitrary action. Even when men believe that they will their actions, they may be operating under the influence of passion, illness, or physical idiosyncrasy (a clear but unidentified reference to Diderot's discussion of Saunderson's blindness in *Lettre sur les aveugles*). Freedom resides not in action, but in the deliberation or choices that precede action. But the decision that dictates action may be less than fully conscious, and even conscious decision does not guarantee the value of an action. Since men can choose to do evil they therefore need a standard to guide the exercise of their freedom. Deeply imprisoned in their own material being, with its attendant weaknesses of soul and body, they cannot always evaluate the merit or fault of their choices: "Only God can be our judge."[25]

Men can, however, derive strengths and standards from their society. Habit, custom, and education inculcate norms of be-

25. "Préface," in Onken, *Oeuvres*, 749, 751-52; the superficially puzzling "lack of limbs" undoubtedly is a reference to Diderot's *Lettre sur les aveugles*, in *Oeuvres philosophiques*, ed. Paul Vernière (Paris, 1964), 81-146.

havior: "Man lives in society with other men who like him have rights that he must respect, and that he can hardly violate with impunity; those rights are *natural* or *legitimate*." Quesnay then explains that natural rights such as our right to self-preservation derive from the natural order. Legitimate rights derive from the arrangements of men, which also recognize the right to self-preservation. Men can either live like animals who each day appropriate what is necessary to their continued survival, or they can arrive at an arrangement "that assures each individual of the part that he should have, and then the portion allotted to each man will belong to him by natural law and legitimate law."[26]

Quesnay abandons his first attempt to discuss natural law at this vague and inconclusive stage. He had at least begun his extensive reading in natural law doctrine. His passing mention of the right of each to everything suggests Hobbes' warlike conception of the state of nature which he would later explicitly repudiate. His reference to *partage* or division further suggests that he also accepted the idea of social contract, which he might have acquired from Hobbes or Locke and which he would also subsequently repudiate. Clearly, he was deeply immersed in the current natural law debates, from which his contemporaries like Rousseau and the chevalier de Jaucourt, who wrote so many legal and political articles for the *Encyclopédie*, also drew. He owned Richard Cumberland's *Traité philosophique des lois naturelles*, as well as the works of the German political theorist Pufendorf, and those of Pufendorf's French translator Barbeyrac (1674–1744). He also undoubtedly knew the works of the Genevan jurist Jacques Burlamaqui (1794–1748), whose many treatises on natural law lacked originality but served to popularize the thought of Grotius, Pufendorf, and Locke. He had not yet read Hume, whose rejection of the idea of contract subsequently may have influenced his own. His blending of theological and political arguments suggests knowledge of the debates between Jesuits

26. "Préface," 754, 755.

and Jansenists. The precise influences upon his thought, however, cannot be determined. Quesnay's early forays into natural law theory platitudinously reflect the common discussions of his day. Assuredly, he had not yet addressed himself to economics, let alone discovered the "net product" that would provide the necessary rule for his subsequent treatment of natural law; but he would never completely shake Barbeyrac's argument that religion constitutes the only cement of society.[27] "Without Divinity," Barbeyrac had written, "one sees nothing that imposes the indispensible necessity to act or not to act in a certain manner." Certainly, Quesnay's section in *L'essai physique* entitled "De l'immortalité de l'âme" demonstrates the depth of his commitment in 1747 to Christianity as the necessary anchor for human obligation. Men are different from animals in having immortal souls. God alone ultimately can judge their conduct. But since God is reasonable, conformity with the natural order should ensure salvation.

Quesnay has finally assembled all the elements, save the economics, of his analysis of the human condition. Man, a frail creature, can approximate divinity by the exercise of reason. He cannot, however, attain divinity and pretend to centrality in the universe, for his reason does not suffice either to apprehend all reality or to judge himself accurately. Collectively men can arrive at a series of rules to guarantee social harmony and individual existence, but divine sanction, understood as absolute standard, alone can secure the justice of a human community.

For Quesnay, men have not yet succeeded in agreeing upon the nature of divine justice. Quesnay bravely dismisses theological and conceptual arguments as "the fruit of our ignorance and our fictions." The intellectual disputes in philosophy, metaphysics,

27. Quoted in Pierre Rétat, *Le dictionnaire de Bayle et la lutte philosophique au XVIIIe siècle* (Paris, 1971), 40. On Barbeyrac and his influence, see also Roger Derathé, *Jean-Jacques Rousseau et la science politique de son temps*, 2d ed. (Paris, 1974), esp. 28–33, 89–92. See also Philippe Meylan, *Jean Barbeyrac (1674–1744) et les débuts de l'enseignement de droit dans l'ancienne Académie de Lausanne* (Lausanne, 1937).

and natural theology can never be resolved on their own terms. The question of divine purpose matters deeply, but the discussions about divine purpose, particularly in relation to the affairs of men, have moved so far from the real issues they claim to address that they can no longer offer anything. The important questions, he concludes, "can only be decided by evidence."[28]

Quesnay's introduction of the word "evidence," which would constitute the title of his first article, and his only metaphysical one, for the *Encyclopédie,* underscores the continuity in his methodological sensibility and hints at the new direction of his interests between 1747 and 1756. By the time he wrote "Evidence," he had turned from medicine to economics and appears to have been reading largely in political theory and political economy. His large new circle of authors most prominently included a host of political economists. Predictably, the reformers and early free-trade advocates Vauban, Boisguilbert, and Claude Herbert received close attention. In addition, however, he read extensively in the neomercantilist literature associated with the Law and post-Law periods. In particular, he studied the work of Jean François Melon (1675–1738), a financial official and close associate of John Law, whose *Essai politique sur le commerce* foreshadows Quesnay's early work in its combination of mercantilist presuppositions with an insistence upon the importance of agriculture, but remains far more conservative in its economic analysis and its support of regulation. He also read the *Réflexions politiques sur le commerce et les finances* (1738) of Charles Dutot (exact dates unknown), another close associate of Law and one of the principal officers of Law's Compagnie des Indes. In different ways, both Melon and Dutot demonstrated considerable sophistication in problems of money and credit, although Melon emphasized the importance of money as a sign of value whereas Dutot insisted upon its intrinsic value as a commodity. Quesnay also drew upon English political economy, notably the work of

28. "De l'immortalité de l'âme," in Onken, *Oeuvres,* 761–63.

Petty and Charles Davenant, and followed the arguments of his contemporaries, Forbonnais, Hume, and Rousseau, as they appeared.[29] This new reading, however, did not alter his basic epistemology and metaphysics. In "Evidence," he hones and polishes, but he develops rather than repudiates his original dualism.

Quesnay defines evidence as "a certainty so clear and manifest in itself that the mind cannot refuse it."[30] The certainty of evidence, however, he distinguishes from that of faith. Quesnay then re-evaluates the psychological and epistemological problems he had raised in "Immortalité de l'âme," and reaffirms his commitment to sensual psychology and to the pivotal role of memory in organizing sensations into rational judgments and interpretations. Despite his acceptance of the certitude afforded by the immediate registering of material reality, he rejects neo-Cartesian materialism and insists that the property of sensation does not derive from the organization of the body. Quesnay further insists that we can never directly know another being or any other external reality: we can only know the sensations that other objects cause in us.[31] Sensations thus afford men their only path to certain knowledge. But they cannot themselves assure the validity of knowledge, since memory, the only mechanism for organizing and comparing impressions, can fail. The memories of the insane, idiots, even normal men in dreams convey distortions, not reality, although even these memories derive from sensations.

Sensations cause us "to perceive two kinds of truth; real truths and purely speculative or ideal truths."[32] Both artificial truths and

---

29. See note 37 below. Also see Dutot, *Réflexions politiques sur les finances et le commerce,* ed. Paul Harsin (Paris, 1935); Auguste Dubois, *Précis de l'histoire des doctrines économiques dans leurs rapports avec les faits et avec les institutions: L'époque antérieure aux physiocrates* [1903] (Geneva, 1970), esp. 248–70. For a recent general treatment with a good comparative perspective, see Fritz Blaich, *Die Epoche des Merkantilismus* (Wiesbaden, 1973).

30. INED, II, 397–426. All citations to "Evidence" will be to this edition.

31. *Ibid.,* 397, 400–5.

32. *Ibid.,* 410.

abstract general ideas lead us to misconstrue evidence, which can lead to the impression that our knowledge affords no certainty. Quesnay has returned to the problem, raised in the "Préface" to the *Mémoires de l'Académie*, of establishing certainty, or a body of objective, scientific knowledge. He argues in "Evidence" against absolute relativism or skepticism: all men who deduce their truths direct from their immediate sensations will insist on the certainty of such immediate truths whether deduced by themselves or others. And science has afforded men a language that can reduce the element of uncertainty in even the soundest personal judgment. "A rule of arithmetic decisively subjects men in the disputes they entertain over their interests; because in that case their calculation has an exact and evident relation with the truths which interest them." Ideas can only be anchored to evidence by being rigorously subjected to established truths.[33]

Quesnay believed that his epistemology could explain man's knowledge of the external world. The rule of arithmetic would minimize extraneous debate and obscure philosophical systems. He seems not to have realized how subjective a criterion his evidence remained. Certainly, many of his contemporaries doubted that there was anything evident about it. As Quesnay's discussion of memory shows, he did remain alert to the tricks played by sensations and defective thought processes and did attempt to complete his epistemology with a metaphysics that situated man in relation to himself and to God.

Developing an argument enunciated in the section "Liberté" from *L'essai physique*, Quesnay returns to a discussion of human motives and action, and repeats his dictum that free will resides in the moment of choice. Faith assists the choice by elevating man to the knowledge of moral good and evil "by which he can direct himself with reason and equity in the exercise of his lib-

33. *Ibid.*, 411. See Keith Baker, *Condorcet: From Natural Philosophy to Social Mathematics* (Chicago, 1975), 65, for Condorcet's similar concern with a precise standard.

erty."[34] Quesnay defines both faith and God as "intelligence in essence." To reason intelligently, therefore, is to emulate God to whatever extent possible. Action based on reasonable motives thus merges with action based on faith; it has as its intent sound order and enlightened self-interest. In other words, man's enlightened self-interest merges with the divine order. To act thus is to choose freedom.

Quesnay was neither a systematic materialist nor a relaxed deist. His quest for absolute certainty in the knowledge of physical and social reality led him to reject both materialist and idealist determinism. Quesnay placed humanity at the center of his thought and attempted to establish the nature of and limitations on man's ability to know reality. His answer, the emphasis on mathematical calculation notwithstanding, retains man's will at its center. Man, by observing the proper rules of investigation, can know reality. Man, with the assistance of divine faith, can know himself and shape his own existence within given material possibilities. In teleological terms, however, Quesnay does not place man at the center of the universe. For Quesnay, perfect knowledge would consist in total apprehension of all physical reality at a single moment, something of which only God is capable. He suggests that if man could so apprehend material reality, knowledge would become one with existence, and our senses would register all experience directly and simultaneously. Man could then dispense with the agency of memory and reasoning and thus eliminate human fallibility.[35]

Quesnay's epistemology addresses a crucial problem that has plagued modern thought since his time. He willingly accords a major role to the individual human intelligence. Like Diderot, he reveres genius, but he rejects the subjectivism inherent in a systematic individualism that casts man as the pivot of the universe. It is easy to misread Quesnay's self-proclaimed commit-

34. *Ibid.,* 423.
35. *Ibid.,* 409.

ment to religious orthodoxy as backward-looking, or conversely to dismiss it as insincere camouflage. Both readings insult his intelligence and trivialize a fundamental problem. Quesnay refused to jettison all sanctions on human action, just as he refused to reduce humans to their material components. He believed that by identifying God with Reason he could explain the extraordinary quality of human intelligence without falling into a mechanical deification of man.

Temperamentally, Quesnay leaned strongly toward material determinism, but reality had no meaning for him apart from its apprehension by reasonable men. In this ambiguity lies the core of his dualism: reality exists both independently and as known through human consciousness and can be shaped by human will assisted by divine reason. It could be argued that he deified reason itself, that he interpreted God as the ultimate rational explanation, or as the full consciousness of reality. This deification, however, did not entail bringing God down into the world and making Him, as Reason, a property of human minds. Reason in Quesnay's thought remained in the heavens as the standard against which the partial efforts of men could be measured. Material reality itself only represented the embodiment of divine wisdom. Quesnay's God did not fall into the role of a diffuse, general providence. He retained all the majesty of the Old Testament prototype, as well as the benevolence of the New Testament variant. Unlike material reality, intelligence in essence could not be derived from a grain of wheat. Quesnay's dualism saved him from ever viewing man as an exclusively economic being, completely determined by his material conditions.

As Quesnay turned from medicine and metaphysics to economics, he carried the legacy of his early work with him. From the start, his bias as a practical scientist led him to focus sharply upon the technical problems of agricultural production. In his hands, the fashionable preoccupation with grain became a serious investigation of the state of agriculture, and ultimately a science of wealth. His metaphysics enabled him to explain the process of economic development itself. His analysis of economic process, his diagnosis of economic illness, and his prescription for cure developed apace.

If Quesnay's peasant background led him to respect agriculture and those engaged in it, his residence at Versailles encouraged him to view the agricultural sector primarily as a source of royal revenues. Always fascinated with technical details, he avidly pursued the work of the burgeoning agronomic movement that was slowly infiltrating the French elite. Captivated by the examples of the English agricultural revolution, many of the court circle, including close associates of Quesnay like Le Roy, sought to reproduce its successes upon their own and the king's estates. The technical preoccupations of the *agronomes* who sought to diffuse new methods of cultivation, introduce new crops and livestock strains, and through the miracle of the Norfolk method raise the output of French agriculture, always appealed to Quesnay's delight in the specific. He closely followed the publications of Henri-Louis Duhamel de Monceau, the leading proponent of the new system, and never tired of discussing crops, manures, or agricultural techniques. He even bought a large estate in the Nivernais for his son, and it became, according to Henri Patullo, one of the showpieces of French agricultural innovation.[36]

Quesnay also read extensively on nontechnical questions. He diagnosed a serious economic crisis in the collapse of agricultural prices. The work of Labrousse shows that Quesnay mistook a

36. ADY, "Inventaire," shows that Quesnay owned most of the works of Duhamel de Monceau. Cf. Kuczynski's introduction to Quesnay, *Oekonomische Schriften,* xl–xli, and her excellent discussion of the library, 493–98. See also Henri Patullo, *Essai sur l'amélioration des terres* (Paris, 1759), 77–78; EMHL, Winterthur MSS, group 2, series B, "Observations sur une partie du Nivernois par M. Quesnay de Beauvoir"; and André Bourde, *Agronomie et agronomes en France au XVIIIe siècle,* 3 vols. (Paris, 1967), I, 180. On the influence of English farming methods, see André Bourde, *The Influence of England on the French Agronomes, 1750–1789* (Cambridge, Eng., 1953), esp. 22, 24–25, 51, 53, 68–69; and David J. Brandenburg, "Agriculture in the *Encyclopédie:* An Essay in French Intellectual History," *Agricultural History,* XXIV (1950), 96–108.

cyclical drop in a movement of steadily rising prices for a secular collapse, but his reading had already directed his attention to the need for a "good" price. Following Vauban and Boisguilbert, he saw the connection between the pitiable state of agriculture and the perilous state of the royal treasury and he argued for the support of high prices. Like Vauban, he sensibly concluded that a healthy agricultural sector required rational taxation. Like Boisguilbert, Herbert, and the Gournay circle, he insisted that a healthy economy, and particularly a healthy agriculture, presupposed complete freedom of circulation. From the beginning, he instinctively gravitated towards liberal policies as the best means of redressing the collapse of national wealth.[37]

Quesnay's commitment to free trade has frequently been traced to his medical practice, in which he preferred letting nature take its course to the problematical intervention of ignorant practitioners. This respect for the workings of the natural order characterized all his thought, and his reading of Mandeville, Shaftesbury, and Hume would have encouraged him to extend his attitude to economics. He had, however, probably also read Vauvenargues, whose discussion of human motivation would only have confirmed Quesnay's healthy respect for the destructive effect of human passions. His continuing preoccupation with the range of freedom in human choice also reappeared in his economic theory, in which the simple workings of nature, once

37. Ottomar Thiele, "François Quesnay und die Agrarkrisis im Ancien Régime: Dargestellt auf Grund Zwei Briefe," *Vierteljahreschrift für Sozial- und Wirtschaftsgeschichte*, IV (1906), 515–62, 633–52; and Ernest Labrousse, *Esquisse du mouvement des prix et des revenus en France au XVIIIe siècle*, 2 vols. (Paris, 1933), I, 103–4, II, 624. See also Eugene Daire, *Economistes financiers du XVIIIe siècle* (Paris, 1843), which contains selected works of Vauban, Boisguilbert, Jean Law, Melon, and Dutot; Pierre le Pesant, sieur de Boisguilbert, *Testament politique de monsieur de Vauban, maréchal de France* . . . , 2 vols. (n.p., 1708); INED, *Pierre de Boisguilbert, ou la naissance de l'économie politique*, 2 vols. (Paris, 1966); and Claude Herbert, *Essai sur la police générale des grains, suivi du "Supplément" à l'essai par Montaudouin de la Touche (1755–1757)*, publié avec notice et table par Edgar Depître (Paris, 1910), esp. Depître's introduction, xi, xxxiv–xxxv.

defined to include human actions, can result in catastrophe rather than the realization of divine purpose.

Quesnay's wide reading in mercantilist and neomercantilist economic theory convinced him that even the best theorists could favor erroneous policies. He corresponded with Forbonnais and cited both him and Melon in his arguments. He knew the work of Dutot and of the farmer-general and economic theorist Claude Dupin. His use of statistics reveals the debt to Petty acknowledged in his references. His association with Gournay had probably led him to study the work of the English free-trader Josiah Child. He showed great respect for all who tried to introduce scientific precision into the study of wealth. His library contained two of the more important new economic journals that had emerged from the critical climate of the late 1740s and early 1750s, *Bilan de l'Angleterre*, to which he referred in print, and the *Journal oeconomique*, which frequently published French translations of the English political and economic theorists, including Charles Davenant, of whose arguments, if not name, he took note. His considerable debt to Hume emerges from barely disguised borrowings in the economic articles. Although he disagreed with Locke, he had read him carefully.[38]

The list of Quesnay's intellectual debts could be extended further without more precisely defining their nature. Retrospectively, scholars have been able to refer to an imposing "mouvement pré-physiocratique," but without Quesnay the collection of names could hardly have been united under a single heading. The one name requiring specific mention is that of Richard Cantillon, the Irish banker whose *Essai sur le commerce* appeared in 1755. Georges Weulersse would not even consider Cantillon as a precursor, because he "belongs to the history of the school itself, as a *demi-adept*, and almost implicitly, under the

---

38. See "Deux lettres de Quesnay à Forbonnais," INED, I, 295–300; Hecht, "Vie de Quesnay," 252, on Quesnay's letter to Hume's translator, Abbé Le Blanc; and ADY, "Inventaire." As well as those of Hume, Quesnay owned works of Locke, Cumberland, Bacon, and Hobbes.

auspices of the marquis de Mirabeau, as a sort of co-founder."[39] Particularly in "Hommes," an early *Encyclopédie* essay, and in the early Tableaux, Quesnay's economic thought does bear the stamp of his running dialogue with Cantillon. As Schumpeter says in words that might well be taken as a judgment on his own relationship to Marx, "Affinity is obvious, differences being not less revelatory of it than are agreements: For a man may learn from another by criticizing him just as well as by accepting his teaching, and some of Quesnay's views look indeed as if they had been derived from Cantillon by the former method."[40] But as Schumpeter himself points out, even Cantillon does not account for Quesnay.

Ironically, the scholarly mania for intellectual pedigrees has neglected one of Quesnay's major interests. The catalogue of his library reveals that his medical collection accounted for half his volumes, but that dictionaries, geographies, and histories made up the major portion of the remainder. Those who have considered his work on China have been quick to identify the sources he used, if only to criticize their misuse. His interest in China like his interest in the Incas is usually portrayed as a typically ahistorical and uninformed Enlightenment sally designed to hold a corrective lens up to the French. This interpretation, if true in part, nevertheless obscures an important dimension of Quesnay's thought.[41]

39. "Le mouvement préphysiocratique en France," *RHES*, XIX (1931), 272.

40. Joseph A. Schumpeter, *History of Economic Analysis*, ed. Elizabeth Boody Schumpeter (New York, 1955), 217–18.

41. [François Quesnay], "Analyse du gouvernment des Yncas du Pérou, par M.A.," *Les éphémérides du citoyen*, I (1767), 35–47, and "Despotisme de la Chine, par M. A.," *Les éphémérides du citoyen* (1767), II, 5–88, IV, 5–77, V, 5–61, VI, 5–75; Vergile Pinot, *La Chine et la formation de l'esprit philosophique en France, 1640–1740* (Paris, 1932), and "Les Physiocrates et la Chine au XVIIIe siècle," *Revue d'histoire moderne et contemporaine*, VIII (1906–1907), 200–214; Adolf Reichwein, *China and Europe: Intellectual and Artistic Contacts in the Eighteenth Century* (London and New York, 1925); and Louis Rougier, "La Chine, les physiocrates, et la Révolution française," *Annales franco-chinoises*, no. 10 (1929), 1–10.

Quesnay especially prized his reference works as the source of raw data for a picture of historical development. Confronted by royal censorship, he used foreign lands as models for the analysis of French problems and shaped the foreign case to fit the French need. He had, however, read more of Montesquieu than the *Lettres persanes,* and despite his rejection of Montesquieu's system of classification and explanation he had learned that governments change according to material environment. His sociological models of an agricultural kingdom and a commercial republic reflect his debt to Montesquieu, although they propose a different set of laws. Like Montesquieu, Quesnay investigated the nature of societies in a historical perspective.

Quesnay's obsession with political discretion, as well as his early economic method, help explain his lack of recognition as a historian. The early economic articles, like the Tableau, address themselves to abstract problems of analysis and the curing of current ills. From the beginning Quesnay sought to avoid the painful political and social choices attendant upon the process of development and to cast his analysis as an absolute law. But the early articles were concerned more with the establishment of an economic than a natural law, and their economic analysis was primarily concerned with the problem of development.

Modern economists focus on the relationship of Quesnay's economic model to economic development. They chiefly debate whether the Tableau depicts a static or a dynamic equilibrium— whether Quesnay sought to rationalize an existing level of economic performance or to promote growth. Most economists recognize that he favored at least as much limited growth as a stationary state could sponsor.[42] But their emphasis upon his attitude toward future growth misses a decisive point. Quesnay's entire economic analysis rested upon his understanding of past

42. For example, Michel Lutfalla, *L'état stationnaire* (Paris, 1964); Nicole Moës, "Y a-t-il une théorie de croissance chez François Quesnay?" *RHES,* XL (1962), 363–76. For the more technical economic literature on physiocracy as an equilibrium model, see Chapter 7.

growth, and his economic program required radical economic transformation as a prerequisite. His sense of historical development colored everything he ever wrote.

In varying degrees the early economic articles all implicitly compare the historical development of England with that of France. Taken together they afford a startlingly modern discussion of the progress of societies beyond a subsistence level and of the different levels of progress attained by England and France respectively. In them Quesnay betrays his own keen awareness of the relationship between feudal and modern forms of sociopolitical organization and between seigneurial and capitalist modes of production, as exemplified by the historical development of those two countries. Even as Quesnay formally accepted the French government as modern, he exposed the French agricultural system as antiquated. By the time he had formulated his first Tableau, he had assimilated Mirabeau's ideological concerns, and with him had attempted to work through a history of the French state. The insurmountable obstacles to French progress which this investigation revealed pushed him to cast his work in ever more abstract and ahistorical terms. But the original analysis, which remained the core of physiocratic economics, derived directly from the historical analysis of English economic progress.

Quesnay was among the first to discuss the role of capital in agriculture, to analyze the structure of English agricultural production, and to focus on the problem of the social surplus. Cantillon had already argued that land rent sustained nonproductive classes, and both England and France supported ruling classes that did not work for their living. Quesnay, seeing that England enjoyed a greater surplus (net product) than did France, ascribed it to a qualitative difference in the mode of production. He did not immediately consider whether the economic transformation he advocated might entail a concommitant social and political readjustment. He attributed to France as great a material potential as to England, which, his metaphysics led him to believe, could be realized by the enlightened action of men. The state itself could do the job.

Quesnay's epistemological method, as laid out in "Evidence," held that men had the power to analyze material reality according to the laws of science. He always translated his economic thought into numerical examples in order to prevent that useless disagreement which arises from abstract speculations. On this level he presented his economics as an abstract or invariable law, but he maintained that his conclusions followed an investigation of the historical development of the social production of wealth. He insisted in his study of economic development, as he had in "Evidence," that false ideas can lead men astray. While the English and French started as equals at some point in the past, at a crucial juncture Frenchmen succumbed to the notion that social wealth resulted from the possession of gold and silver or the capturing of foreign trade. Fortunately, their error could be corrected.

3

Quesnay—The Emergence
of an Economics

Quesnay hammered out the substance of his economic analysis in the four economic articles that he wrote for the *Encyclopédie* between 1755 and 1757. In "Fermiers" and "Grains" (published in volumes VI and VII, in 1756 and 1757, respectively) he laid the foundations of his analysis of capitalist production. In "Hommes" and "Impôts" (also written in the same years, but not published at the time because the royal approbation of the *Encyclopédie* had been rescinded), he attempted to move from economic analysis to political economy.[1] He did not, however, elaborate a coherent political economy at this time. Accepting the reigning polarity between the absolutist state and "feudal" privileges, he firmly cast his lot with the state. The security of this ideological perspective permitted him to make the innocent assumption that the progress of economic science would serve the needs of that state. It had not yet occurred to him that his

1. All references for these four articles will be to INED, II. Quesnay wrote two additional articles (besides "Evidence") for the *Encyclopédie*: "Fonctions de l'âme" and "Intérêt de l'argent." We do not know why the former was not published. The original manuscript has never been found, but in 1760 Quesnay published a four-page pamphlet, *Aspect de la psychologie* (Versailles, 1760), which appears to be an outline or résumé of "Fonctions," See INED, II, 683–85; and Jacqueline Hecht, "La vie de François Quesnay," in INED, I, 253. "Intérêt de l'argent" (INED, II, 763–70) appeared during Quesnay's lifetime as "Observations sur l'intérêt de l'argent par M. Nisaque," *Journal de l'agriculture du commerce et des finances*, LV (Jan. 1766), 1st pt., 151–71.

economic analysis presupposed the existence of a market society that did not prevail in eighteenth-century France, and he had not yet reached the analytic certainty that would permit him to argue that the state should obey the dictates of the market economy—even if such obedience entailed reforming the society upon which the state rested. The progress of his work does point toward the Tableau, but the development of physiocracy cannot be understood on the assumption that the early articles had inevitably to arrive at the most abstract version, the "Analyse de la formule arithmétique du Tableau économique" of 1766, much less to end with the mature formulation of physiocratic doctrine.[2]

The early articles cannot be ascribed to a clearly defined school of political economy: they represent initial gropings toward a completely new concept of political economy itself. Adam Smith first pointed out the opposition between mercantilism and physiocracy, but his insight blurred a decisive stage in the development of economic thought.[3] Smith, in emphasizing the free-trade aspects of physiocratic thought in contrast to the regulatory predilections of the mercantilists, neglected the many common features of the two doctrines, particularly their strong statist bias. Mercantilism, the political economy of the emerging modern state, offered policies designed to strengthen the state irrespective of its political and social base. Hence, mercantilism influenced states with radically different philosophies. So much emphasis has been placed on mercantilism as the economic arm of national aggression, or on mercantilism as the protection of national interest, that many recent critics have dismissed the very idea of mercantilism on the grounds that all states, in all historical periods, pursue power and plenty.[4] Mercantilism, however, as

2. See Lars Herlitz, "The Tableau Economique and the Doctrine of Sterility," *Scandinavian Economic History Review*, IX (1961), 3–51. Louis Salleron's editing of the articles, INED, II, emphasizes those aspects of them which prefigure the Tableau, cf. 427n.
3. *An Inquiry into the Nature and Causes of the Wealth of Nations* [1776], Mod. Lib. Ed., ed. E. Cannan (New York, 1937), 627–52.
4. Cf. Jacob Viner, "Power versus Plenty as Objectives of Foreign Policy

Quesnay and Smith knew, corresponded to a particular stage of historical development and represented a phase not only of national but of class development. Or to put it differently, mercantilism constituted the rationale, in national terms, for the primitive accumulation of capital. The mercantilists, despite frequent assertions that the trading interests supported the crown, did not usually cast their arguments in class terms. On the contrary, they proclaimed that their policies fostered the best interests of the entire community. Nevertheless, merchant and finance capitalists emerged as the great beneficiaries of the panoply of regulations protecting shipping, colonies, and national manufacture; and entrepreneurs who pursued economic production on a national scale emerged as the great beneficiaries of the attack on guilds, municipal autonomy, private tolls, and other obstacles to national economic unification.[5]

Mercantilism, although flourishing under traditional systems of social organization, helped establish the necessary preconditions for a modern class society. Once traditional systems had given way before a national market and a unified government, mercantilism had served its purpose. Mercantilist economic assumptions, as well as policies, came under increasing fire. First physiocracy and then liberal political economy developed more sophisticated forms of economic analysis and more clearly bourgeois visions of social organization. For although mercantilism arose in a period of transition from a traditional to a class society, it never concerned itself directly with the problem of social organization. The mercantilists presented the state as an entity in order to avoid discussion of its internal composition, whereas the liberal political economists conceived of the state as a system.

in the Seventeenth and Eighteenth Centuries," in D. C. Coleman, ed., *Revisions in Mercantilism* (London, 1969), and A. V. Judges, "The Idea of a Mercantilist State," *ibid.*

5. Eli Hecksher, *Mercantilism*, trans. M. Shapiro, 2 vols., rev. ed. (London and New York, 1955). Cf. also, Thomas Mun, *England's Treasure by Forraign Trade* [1664] (Oxford, 1959), Lionel Rothkrug, *The Opposition to Louis XIV* (Princeton, 1963), and Smith, *Wealth of Nations*, 226.

In the words of J. J. Spengler, the mercantilists "were usually concerned with aggregate output, rather than with output per head, often conceiving of the state or nation as an entity or organism."[6]

Liberal political economy—including mature physiocracy—differed from mercantilism not over the specific question of protection but in favoring the increase in per capita real income rather than national aggregate income.[7] This distinction does not mean that the classical political economists did not wish to promote national growth, but merely that they saw the nation as an organic system of free individuals. Only the increase of per capita wealth could, in their eyes, increase aggregate wealth. Viewing society as a system, they reduced the state to a simple emanation of a larger social system. Mercantilist thought, which postulated the state as the natural repository for wealth and power, reflected the course of political and economic development within a traditional rather than a market framework. In the absence of politically recognized individual rights, individuals who had outstripped their traditional role turned to the state, upon which they depended for recognition and privilege. Capitalism developed in pre-Revolutionary France, however slowly, primarily under the aegis of the state, which provided much of the push toward economic rationalization.[8]

6. "Mercantilist and Physiocratic Growth Theory," in Bert Hoselitz, ed., *Theories of Economic Growth* (London and New York, 1960), 26–27, 62. See also Pierre Struve, "L'idée de la loi naturelle dans la science économique," *Revue d'économie politique*, XXV (1921), 468–69; and Carl Landauer, *Die Theorien der Merkantilisten und der Physiokraten über die oekonomische Bedeutung des Luxus* (Munich, 1915), esp. 117–27.

7. See Alfred Bürgin, "Ein Streiflicht auf die Anfange der National-Ökonomie in Frankreich: Colbert und Quesnay," *Kyklos*, XX (1967), 249–69; Martin Wolfe, "French Wealth and Taxes," in Coleman, ed., *Revisions in Mercantilism*, 481; and J. Faure-Soulet, *Economie politique et progrès au "Siècle des Lumières"* (Paris, 1964), 7.

8. Spengler, "Mercantilist and Physiocratic Theory," in Hoselitz, ed., *Theories of Growth*, 43; Charles Cole, *French Mercantilism, 1683–1700* [1943] (New York, 1971); Pierre Léon, *La naissance de la grande industrie*

Eighteenth-century French absolutism can be traced back to the medieval origins from which it never decisively broke. Nevertheless, it derived more directly from the efforts of its great seventeenth-century architects, who, sobered by the potential chaos revealed in the Wars of Religion, sought to establish the monarchy on a strong and independent base. Richelieu, followed by Colbert and Louis XIV, had worked to make a reality of that sovereignty whose nature and necessity Bodin had chronicled in the midst of the sixteenth-century maelstrom. Their effort entailed, in essence, adapting Machiavelli's insight into the *sui generis* claims of the political to the higher principles of Christian morality and to the fundamental constitution of the French realm.[9]

None of the great state builders ever intended to jettison the most venerable accomplishments and theoretical pretensions of the medieval state. Nor could they completely abolish the essentially feudal structure of post-medieval society. Their task lay in transforming old theoretical commitments into a modern theory of absolute government befitting a major European power. They had much to draw on. The judicial function and the juridical theory of the monarchy had been solidly established. The time-

---

en Dauphiné fin *XVIIe–1869*, 2 vols. (Paris, 1956), esp. I, 24; Herbert Lüthy, *La banque protestante en France de la révocation de l'Edit de Nantes à la Révolution*, 2 vols. (Paris, 1961), esp. II, 595; Samuel Hollander, *The Economics of Adam Smith* (Toronto and London, 1973), 34–35; Jacques Proust, *Diderot et l'Encyclopédie* (Paris, 1962), 168.

9. See Julian H. Franklin, *Jean Bodin and the Rise of Absolutist Theory* (Cambridge, 1973); and Felix Gilbert, *Machiavelli and Guicciardini: Politics and History in Sixteenth-Century Florence* (Princeton, 1965). Machiavelli's appreciation of the nature of the political is not identical to his notions of political morality. This discussion of the absolute state is based primarily on the following works: William Church, *Richelieu and Reason of State* (Princeton, 1972): John B. Wolf, *Louis XIV* (New York, 1968); Martin Wolfe, *The Fiscal System of Renaissance France* (New Haven and London, 1972); A. Lloyd Moote, *The Revolt of the Judges* (Princeton, 1971); Julian Dent, *Crisis in Finance* (New York, 1973); John C. Rule, ed., *Louis XIV and the Craft of Kingship* (Columbus, 1969); and Roland Mousnier, *La vénalité des offices sous Henri IV et Louis XIII*, 2d ed. (Paris, 1971).

honored Christian mission of the prince served to underscore his unique position in the state. The claims to absolute power had been laid down long before Richelieu set about implementing them. That the claims existed, however, did not prevent recalcitrant nobles, towns, or peasants, from seeing their implementation as revolutionary.

After the work of William Church, none can reasonably doubt that Richelieu took his religious principles seriously. The monarchy never sacrificed its sincere commitment to the service of God. To have done so would not only have entailed a thoroughgoing cynicism not easily reconcilable with the convictions of the age, but worse would have jeopardized the sacred authority of the monarch as the deputy of God. Thus Bossuet, that great legitimizer of the historical fact, must be taken at face value when he affirms that the state finds its incarnation in the person of the prince whose power knows no limits other than those of his own interest or his obligation to God, which Bossuet, like Richelieu before him, accepts as identical. For all the great royal servants, divine and political necessity had to converge in the person of the prince. For the prince, as the pinnacle of society and the representative of divine purpose, alone enjoyed the ideological sanction requisite to building political power. Thus, however strong the state became and however bureaucratic and independent its administration became, the Christian foundations of monarchy and the special quality of nobility remained secure.[10]

These commitments did not prevent Richelieu and his successors from systematically assaulting all political pretensions of church, nobility, and other privileged groups. Their work, however, in its success promoted the distinction established by Bodin between political and civil society. And that distinction in turn served to strengthen the notion that civil society existed to further the interests (usually warfare) of the prince. The absolute state rested upon the contention that all subjects, whatever their rank,

10. Church, *Richelieu*, esp. 190–91, 454, 494; J. B. Bossuet, *Politique tirée des propres paroles de l'Ecriture Sainte*, ed. Le Brun (Geneva, 1967), I.

are equally subjects of the monarch. Once they had made good this claim, however, the royal ministers and their propagandists did not press the advantage to the extent of redefining civil society itself. Thus privilege—distinctions of rank, status, locality—did not succumb to the statist program. Society retained much of its "feudal" superstructure and its corporate framework. How could it have been otherwise so long as even the most modern "reason of state" derived so much of its legitimizing force from Christian and hierarchical principles?[11]

The evermore perfected absolute state did not triumph without opposition and many of its critics fashioned their arguments from the arsenal of traditional Christian and social norms. As a group, the critics, particularly those of the closing years of the reign of Louis XIV, insisted that society must constitute an integrated system and that the state must function as the ultimate guarantor of society's underlying principles. These critics rejected the notion that the state could have its own purposes and principles that must command the unquestioning obedience of society even at the price of the distortion or corruption of society itself. They had a point that would subsequently be cited as the governing principle of political life by classical liberalism, but at the dawn of the eighteenth century it did not seem compatible with a modern, effective state. For like the statists, the critics accepted the norms of hierarchy and saw authority as an emanation from superior to inferior; and unlike the absolute monarchy they had no means of guaranteeing the unity of the kingdom, much less its pre-eminence in the international arena.

Some of the critics, like Fénelon, drew upon the venerable *dévôt* tradition to hold the mirror of true Christian piety up to the actions of the sovereign. The royal defense rested upon the

11. See Herbert H. Rowen, "Louis XIV and Absolutism," in Rule, ed., *Louis XIV*, 302–16; E. Lousse, *La société d'ancien régime*, 2d ed. (Louvain, 1952), I, and "Absolutisme, droit divin, despotisme éclairé," *Schweizer Beiträge zur Allgemeine Geschichte*, XVI (1958); and J. C. Timbal, "L'esprit du droit privé au XVIIe siècle," *XVII siècle*, nos. 58–59 (1963).

assurance that the king, as deputy, realized the will of God. The Christian critique replied with reminders of Christian prescriptions of charity and morality to which the king's interpretation of the divine purpose clearly did not correspond.[12] Others, including royal servants, protested the departure from social responsibility—particularly to the poor and the visibly overtaxed peasantry. Colbert himself had boldly raised the issue in a communication to his royal master: "As all alliances between great kings always have two principal ends, one their particular glory and sometimes the joining of their interests, either to conserve or to acquire, . . . and the other the advantage of their subjects. . . . And although in the order of division, that of the advantage of their subjects is the last, it is still the first in the mind of good princes." Increasingly, toward the end of the great reign the implications of divergent interests inherent in Colbert's remarks took clear shape, particularly in the insistence of Vauban and Boisguilbert on agricultural improvement and reform of taxation. In addition, a stream of criticism arose condemning the degradation of the "ancient" Constitution of France and demanding an increased share in government for the traditional Orders. For a long time these demands for participation found their greatest response among the more reactionary elements of the nobility whose ablest spokesman, Montesquieu, clearly intended to buttress the traditional social order.[13]

Nobles, clergy, *parlementaires*, townsmen bent on defending corporate privilege, all contributed to the critique of impending

12. Church, *Richelieu*, 511–13.
13. Jean-Baptiste Colbert, "Dissertation sur la question quelle des deux alliances de France ou de Hollande peut être plus avantageuse à l'Angleterre," Mar. 1669, cited by Viner, "Power versus Plenty," 69; Cole, *French Mercantilism*, 231–35; Martin Wolfe, "French Views on Wealth and Taxes from the Middle Ages to the Old Regime," *Journal of Economic History*, XXVI (1966), 481–83; Franklin L. Ford, *Robe and Sword: The Regrouping of the French Aristocracy after Louis XIV* (Cambridge, Mass., 1953); Elie Carcassonne, *Montesquieu et le problème de la constitution française au XVIIIe siècle* [1927] (Geneva, 1970), 95; and Louis Althusser, *Montesquieu: La politique et l'histoire* (Paris, 1959), 100.

tyranny. They did not, however, point the way to a modern state. The most progressive opponents of the ancien régime, such as Gournay, Herbert, Forbonnais, Voltaire, and even the young Diderot, looked to the absolute monarchy to reform society. To suggest in the 1750s that society should determine and limit government would have been to call for a restoration of feudal anarchy. Social peace and economic growth required strengthening the state, not abolishing it.

The absolute state of the eighteenth century rested upon an impressive record of success, but it had developed as an independent institution rather than as a direct emanation of society. Royal ministers, with their mushrooming bureaucracy, had succeeded in subjecting many of the vital resources of society to the needs of the king, but in so doing, they had insisted upon the direct relationship of each individual or *corps* [constituted body] to the king. They had not effected a comparable rationalization of society itself. True, the state had succeeded in drawing many of the vital social forces into its own orbit, as with the sale of offices, but that pattern merely reinforced ancient privileges.

When Quesnay began his economic articles, he unquestioningly accepted the statist point of view: divesting the state of its hard-won power and authority never figured among his intentions. Quesnay struggled with the problems of a state that through the policies of Sully, Richelieu, and above all Colbert had assumed the task of whipping France along the road to economic development without relinquishing its role as protector and director of the traditional seigneurial social order.[14] This central contradiction plagued not only Quesnay's work but that of all eighteenth-century French social and political theorists and accounts for the

14. Georges Weulersse, "Sully et Colbert jugés par les physiocrates," *RHDES*, X (1922), 234–51, esp. 248; Henri Hauser, *La pensée et l'action économiques du Cardinal de Richelieu* (Paris, 1944); Church, *Richelieu*, esp. 173–282; A. D. Lublinskaya, *French Absolutism: The Crucial Phase, 1620–1629* (Cambridge, 1968), esp. 220–71; David Buisseret, *Sully* (London, 1968), 170–78; and Roland Mousnier, *L'assassinat d'Henri IV* (Paris, 1964), 237–66.

slow development of a coherent French liberal theory. For capitalist development and political participation, however restricted, were not understood as complementary phenomena. The economic liberals assumed that reform consisted in a rationalization of production and circulation that could be effected by the state. Furthermore, their experience proved that commerce and industry could make remarkable progress through the agency of the state itself. Quesnay, while sharing their confidence in the effectiveness of state action, broke sharply with them on the latter question of economic analysis. In many respects the idea of the state presented in Quesnay's economic articles is the logical successor to that of the mercantilists: his thought cannot be understood apart from the historical development of the French monarchy from the time of Richelieu, for at least initially it quarreled with mercantilist methods, not goals.

Quesnay's early articles represent a transition from mercantilism to mature physiocracy. Quesnay's stated purpose in 1756 does not differ significantly from that of Colbert; and he even risks a misreading of his economic work by identifying his program with that of Sully, who had also favored agriculture as a base on which to raise soldiers and taxes for the crown and to encourage frugality. Richelieu, and more dramatically Colbert, had turned to commerce and manufacture to accomplish the same goals. Quesnay attacked Colbert's economic analysis, and reinforced his own agricultural bias with a new economic analysis which carried deeper implications than he had initially recognized. Colbert had encouraged the growth of a mercantile and financial sector within the interstices of the seigneurial system. Quesnay, contrary to general opinion, never denied the necessity for commerce or manufacture, but he did repudiate the existing forms of merchant and finance capital as parasites upon an archaic system of production. These early articles retain a series of analytic confusions, however, about the possible economic value of labor, commerce, navigation, and manufacture. From the start he wished to foster the growth of a prosperous commercial France. His micro-economic analysis of agricultural production convinced him that agriculture itself must become capitalist, but he could not immediately translate this conviction into a coherent macroeconomic analysis. Cantillon seems to have provided the decisive impetus. By the time Quesnay had finished all of the articles, he had become convinced that previous theorists had erred in favoring a large population. Quality of population, he claimed, mattered more than quantity, and by quality he meant independent, nonseigneurial inhabitants who would constitute a free labor force.

The crucial differences between mercantilism and physiocracy do not emerge clearly from the early articles. Quesnay's statist—or aggregate—perspective still colors much of his thought and would even leave its imprint on the early editions of the Tableau. But his deeper commitments ultimately forced a break from the mercantilist tradition. When Colbert spoke of economic growth, he meant maximizing the output of the existing seigneurial economy. For Quesnay, growth meant the qualitative transformation of the existing system into a capitalist system. Physiocracy constitutes a watershed in the history of economic thought precisely because of this analysis of capitalist production.[15]

Deploring the apparent stagnation of French agriculture and the manifest increase of merchant and finance capital, Quesnay sought a more rational and humane means of filling the royal coffers. His extensive reading in English and French economic theory and his association with the *agronomes* had familiarized him with the magnificent performance of English agriculture. Drawing upon his own scientific training, he set out to analyze that success and rapidly became convinced that capitalist agriculture was the cure to France's economic ills. In all good faith, he believed his new science could better fulfill mercantilist goals than the traditional policies, and he offered it to the crown as the infallible guide to redressing its own fortunes.

15. Cf. Robert V. Eagley, *The Structure of Classical Economic Theory* (New York, 1974), 10–21.

"Fermiers," the first of the economic articles, begins: *"Fermiers (Econ. polit.)* are those who lease and exploit the goods of the countryside, and who procure the wealth and the resources, the most essential to the support of the State; thus the use of the *farmer* is an important subject in the kingdom and merits the attention of the government." Farmers, that is, are a prime economic agent; they cultivate land and procure wealth that serves the state. The second clause clarifies the meaning of "state" to include a territory, the kingdom, and an administration or government. Thus the first sentence of Quesnay's first work on political economy addresses itself to the needs of the state and introduces the farmer as a means to providing those ends.[16]

Quesnay goes on to describe the farmer as a rich man who cultivates large plots with horses, a modern entrepreneur sharing nothing in common with those destitute peasants or sharecroppers who eke out a precarious subsistence from small-scale cultivation. The article then calculates the superior profitability of large-scale enterprise and leaves no doubt that profit alone matters.[17] Peasants who cultivate wheat with their own hands would never be able to reimburse themselves for their own labor. "Only a large harvest can yield some profit." And the greater costs of producing such a harvest are insignificant compared with the monetary price it would yield in a free market. Only a free market would assure a price high enough to cover costs, furnish a surplus, guarantee greater and steadier returns for its producer, and raise

16. "Fermiers," 428. Another article, "Fermiers (économie rustique)," was written by Le Roy, "Intendant des chasses du parc de Versailles." See also, David J. Brandenburg, "Agriculture in the *Encyclopédie*: An Essay in French Intellectual History," *Agricultural History*, XXIV (1950), 96–108; Weulersse, *Mouvement*, I, 36–37; and Arthur M. Wilson, *Diderot* (New York, 1972), 135.

17. On the physiocrats' distinctions between large- and small-scale cultivation, see Charles Rebéyrol, *De la grande et de la petite culture chez les physiocrates* (Paris, 1912); and du Pont's unpublished memorandum on the subject of peasant property, EMHL, Winterthur MSS, group 2, series B, "Mémoire sur la question proposée par la société économique de Petersbourg."

the general standard of living of the citizens who "in paying a little more for the livre of bread, will spend less to satisfy their needs." A misguided policy of favoring the urban populace by maintaining a low price of bread can only destroy the country-side—"the true source of the wealth of the State." Quesnay not only questions such mercantilist policies as price-fixing and export restriction, he also argues that large farms rationally exploited with a heavy capital outlay would yield commensurate profits in a free market. The farmer acquires importance as a factor of production, and by the accumulation of wealth which when re-invested in the process of production, re-emerges as a monetary return in the form of its market price.[18]

The farmers "must be rich in their own right," and it behooves the government to pay close attention to their condition. To those who would argue that what such farmers produced would be too expensive, Quesnay replies: "It is true that if one examines only the profit of the cultivator, it would be necessary to subtract the costs; but by envisaging these objects relative to the State, one perceives that the money employed in these costs remains in the kingdom, and the entire product is augmented by them." The re-establishment of *grande culture* will yield an enormous increase in wealth. "This wealth will spread out among all the inhabitants; procure them better food; satisfy their needs; make

18. "Fermiers," 445–47. See Lars Herlitz, "Trends in the Development of Physiocratic Doctrine," *Scandinavian Economic History Review*, IX (1961), 136–40; Meek, *Economics*, 282–83; Hollander, *Economics of Adam Smith*, 459; G. F. Le Trosne, *La liberté du commerce des grains toujours utile et jamais nuisible* (Paris, 1765). The capitalist thrust of Quesnay's thought has long been recognized. See Karl Marx, *Theories of Surplus Value*, 2 vols. (Moscow, 1969), I, 64–65; Friedrich Engels, *Anti-Dühring: Herr Eugen Dühring's Revolution in Science* [1939] (New York, 1970), 269–71; Joseph A. Schumpeter, *History of Economic Analysis*, ed. Elizabeth Boody Schumpeter (New York, 1954), 273: "He introduced capital into economic theory as wealth accumulated previous to starting the production under consideration." Cf. also Bert Hoselitz, "Agrarian Capitalism, the Natural Order of Things: François Quesnay," *Kyklos*, XXI (1968), esp. 657; and Meek, *Economics*, 395–97.

them happy; increase the population; increase the revenues of the proprietors and those of the State."[19]

At the first reading this passage sounds like Cantillon, and on the level of political economy it reflects typical populationist and neomercantilist concerns. At the same time, however, it diverges from them by proposing larger economic units, rather than a larger population, as the proper means of achieving the traditional goals. As macro-economic analysis, the passage is hardly sophisticated, particularly in its failure to deal with the mechanism of circulation. Quesnay had developed an original micro-economics, but he remained content to plug it into the most platitudinous macro framework. In micro terms, capital, applied to agriculture and rationally administered, yields a profit above and beyond simple reproduction. Quesnay then argues, in a general fashion, that the individual economics of scale will yield a greater revenue for the state. He has not, however, made up his mind in analytic terms how the transition from micro- to macro-economics should be effected.[20] The ultimate process of economic growth must be to enrich the state. Undoubtedly, such development will also benefit society at large, for the people will achieve a higher standard of living: the higher cost of production will in part reflect a higher return to the producers and laborers. But the main point remains that by using farmers to cultivate the kingdom, revenue is increased beyond the costs of production, and the resultant surplus accrues ultimately to the state.

Twice in "Fermiers" Quesnay associates the proprietors of land with the state as beneficiaries of the economic miracle he advocates, but this association can almost be read as accidental. He also speaks of "subjects" in a similar way. At no point does he spell out the proprietors' interest as distinct from that of the state, nor does he accord them any rhetorical emphasis to justify the view that they constitute a particular object of his attention. Possibly, he simply took the term, together with the economic

19. "Fermiers," 448, 451, 452.
20. Cf. *Ibid.*, 456, 457.

concept it embodied, directly from the English literature, without at this juncture subjecting it to any particular investigation. On the other hand, he mentions the state twenty times in thirty-one pages, exclusive of the numerous references to government, sovereign, or kingdom. Poor cultivators are "of such small use to the State"; commerce contributes little to the "force and prosperity of the State"; but the return of capital to the countryside "would be much more advantageous to the State"; and encouragement of an indigenous textile industry would constitute a "pure profit for the State" while fostering an increase in population, particularly in the countryside, which "would contribute no less to the force and wealth of the State." Finally, the last sentence of the article, echoing the first, recapitulates the message: "Thus in removing all the other causes prejudicial to the progress of agriculture, the strength of the kingdom will slowly recuperate through the increase of men and by the growth of the revenues of the State."[21]

He does not, however, explicitly discuss his idea of the state. He does not mean the government, as he makes clear by his juxtaposition of the two words: the government can only tax commercial wealth "by means onerous to the State." Nor does he mean the kingdom, which is always used in a sense suggestive of territory and on occasion specifically identified with France. The strength of the kingdom, he argues, will increase with the increase of the revenues of the state. "A kingdom rich in fertile lands" enjoys an indisputable advantage over one which is not, "but to profit from this, it is necessary to remove those causes" which lead to the desertion of the countryside. Implicitly, some entity other than the kingdom profits—namely, the state.[22]

Nation and sovereign pose more difficult problems. Quesnay rarely uses either in this piece, and when he does he does not

21. *Ibid.*, 455, 454, 455, 452, 458.

22. *Ibid.*, 455, 458. Cf. 439, where he explicitly identifies the kingdom with France, 448, where he speaks of retaining grain *in* the kingdom, and 449, where he speaks of reviving agriculture *in* the kingdom (my ital.).

capitalize them as he does state. In one instance he argues that the richer the farmers become, "the more they increase by their facilities and the product of their lands the power of the nation. A poor farmer can only cultivate to the detriment of the State." The difference, if more than rhetorical, is subtle. Later he asserts that "it is the sale of the surplus which enriches the subjects and the sovereign." And at the end of the same paragraph devoted to an attack on merchants, *rentiers* and the like, he adds, "agriculture is the patrimony of the sovereign."[23] A first reading might infer the intrusion of a new element. Agriculture belongs to the sovereign with the emphasis on possession—a traditional, dynastic emphasis on the primacy of the ruling house. In context, the sentence should probably be read "[It is] agriculture [which] is the patrimony of the sovereign." Quesnay has treated his audience to a rhetorical flourish to underscore his conviction that agriculture, the noble art—as opposed to base and secretive commerce—particularly deserves royal patronage, for it is the only form of economic activity that can be taxed without cost to the state.

Quesnay's failure to define the state, which played such a pivotal role in his scheme, reflects the central paradox of mid-century French political life. The definition could be taken for granted, the state existed; but the monarchy's diminishing credibility prompted both specific criticism and theoretical speculation, to which Quesnay's own work belongs. His imprecise terminology reflects the deeper confusion characteristic of an age of profound transformation. No small part of the intellectual achievement of the eighteenth century lay simply in defining and redefining words. The process of definition did not proceed easily, and during its course it gave more than one meaning to many words. The historical agents of this transformation were not always conscious of the direction of their work and did not label their thoughts for the benefit of modern commentators.

The key words in Quesnay's vocabulary include kingdom,

23. *Ibid.,* 441, 455.

government, sovereign, subject, and nation. The state holds dominion over the kingdom—its territorial base—which the government administers with responsibility for its prosperity or decline. Quesnay suggests that the sovereign bears a close relationship to the state, but he stops short of equating them. Occasionally, he uses the word nation as a synonym for the state.

In Quesnay's early work the state appears as the ultimate beneficiary of the economic surplus, and the government as the sole administrator of the national patrimony. Because of its responsibility for the increase or decrease of the surplus, the government must carefully favor the wealth of the farmers "to raise an estate so essential in the kingdom."[24] Quesnay argues, in effect, that certain material factors operate in all times and places to determine men's reproduction of the bare minimum necessary to their own survival, but he also insists that such subsistence agriculture results only in loss for the state. The wealth and power of the state depend upon the revenues of commercial agriculture, but the creation of such an agriculture depends upon the activity of the government. Economic development results from the policies of government, not the workings of nature. Thus Quesnay resisted the more mechanistic formulations of the materialist doctrine to which he was committed. In the economic sphere he endowed the state with a role comparable to that with which he had endowed man in his metaphysics.

At this juncture Quesnay thought only of criticizing the policies followed by the monarchy, not of developing a critique of the nature of the state. He did not attempt to translate his commitment to individualism into political terms. Nor could he accept the feudal nobility as a serious alternative to the state. He merely divested the state of dynastic overtones and made it the agent of society. For Quesnay the state was the depersonalized, concrete embodiment of a specific society based on a specific national territory. Quesnay's state not only surpassed its component members, but transformed their subjective human realities into an

24. *Ibid.*, 448.

objective entity. It could not be a collection of individuals, for individuals have conflicting interests, whereas the state enjoys unity and purpose. Similarly, the state could not be identified completely with the sovereign, who could easily manifest the irrationality of any individual. Implicitly, Quesnay rejected the purely dynastic idea of the state; instead he expected it to foster the maximum development of the kingdom, France, to the benefit of society at large.

Quesnay's depersonalization of the state reflected both the actual gulf between state and society under the ancien régime and his own positivist bias. To create a science of society and a political economy, he needed a specific beneficiary of the economic process. In the state forged by the French monarchy, he found one ready at hand; but he never clarifies whether he created his economic model to serve the state, or adapted the state to fit the needs of his economic model. His discussions suggest correspondence rather than causation, and it is possible that he wished to avoid any imputation that his economic analysis raised dangerous questions about the existing political and social organization. Certainly, his own previous scientific training and his attempt to apply its method to the study of wealth encouraged his instinct to depersonalize social categories in general, and the state in particular. This early work still takes for granted the hegemony of French absolutism and of mercantilist statism. Quesnay understood that the demands for political participation frequently were euphemisms for the perpetuation of reactionary special interest, but he did not yet perceive that his own growing concern with a free market for labor would lead to the question of individual freedom, and therefore to a challenge to the absolute monarchy. The state could shelter the growth of commercial and finance capital within the seigneurial system, but it could not possibly sponsor the capitalist rationalization of that system itself without calling into question its own existence. In the absence of a national market, economic development and social position both depended heavily upon royal privilege, whether time-honored or newly conferred. Even property derived directly or indirectly from the crown.[25]

In "Fermiers," Quesnay avoided questioning this reality and argued simply that state favor should be more rationally deployed. Again an ambiguity highlights his thought. The word proprietors, which was to assume such significance in physiocratic doctrine, was used infrequently and variously. Proprietors appear as large landowners, corecipients with the state of the surplus, but also as those holders of land too poor to employ more than a few oxen in its exploitation. Not once does he use the word property, nor does he suggest that its nature might give rise to discussion. A reader of "Fermiers" would never suspect that the social organization of feudalism determined its level of production. Quesnay's presuppositions resemble those of his mercantilist predecessors, and if his English authorities undoubtedly had a different concept of property, they did not discuss it. Quesnay therefore could read them without recognizing any problems of transposition.[26]

One aspect of "Fermiers," however, does suggest contradictions that would push Quesnay toward the formulation of an economic theory and the elaboration of a liberal ideology. While France undeniably remained his political model, England provided his model for economic growth in a society in which the farmer was protected, the price of grain high, the raising of livestock flourishing, the textile industry prospering. The English wool trade alone produced more than 160 million livres. "There is no single other branch of commerce which can be compared to this single share of the produce of livestock; the slave trade, which is the principal object of the external trade of this nation, rises only to about 60 millions: thus the share of the cultivator

25. See Lüthy, *Banque protestante,* II, 16–19, on the relationship between the feudal property structure and the monarchy. See also Lucien Goldmann, *Sciences humaines et philosophie* (Paris, 1952), 122–27, and Charles Morazé, *La France bourgeoise XVIIIe–XXe siècles* (Paris, 1946), 156–57.

26. "Fermiers," 455. See Struve, "Idée de la loi naturelle," 296.

infinitely exceeds that of the merchant." But the profits of agriculture depend on access to the market in which its produce can command a monetary price. In his discussion of England, Quesnay does not talk of political institutions, religious freedom, or other subversive nonsense. Yet he had read some Locke, and his admiration for England extended beyond its balanced government so much praised by reactionary *parlementaires* to its national market.[27] His commitment to that institution ultimately led him from the strict confines of economic theory to the development of a liberal ideology.

If "Fermiers" provides a clear picture of Quesnay's initial preoccupations as a political economist, the succeeding articles, "Grains," "Hommes," and "Impôts," begin to develop his doctrine. According to du Pont, "The word *Fermiers* presented some of the germinal (*mères*) ideas of a great science. In the word *Grains* we see this science formed and almost complete." He attributes this decisive advance first, to the explanation of the difference between the mean price of commodities for their initial sellers and consumers, and second, to its distinction between the total product and the net product of cultivation. In addition, "Grains" contributes the original set of maxims, "Maximes de gouvernement économique," which, while still far from the later versions, reveal the positivist direction of Quesnay's thought.[28] "Hommes," after a

27. "Fermiers," 440, 448, 455. Cf. Ford, *Robe and Sword;* Althusser, *Montesquieu;* and Jean Egret, *Louis XV et l'opposition parlementaire* (Paris, 1970), esp. 230.

28. See Herlitz, "Trends in Physiocratic Doctrine," for the best single discussion of the development; also Stephan Bauer, "Zur Entstehung der Physiokratie, auf Grund ungedruckten Schriften François Quesnays," *Jahrbücher für National-Ökonomie und Statistik,* N.F. XXI (1890), 115, "L'article 'Hommes' de François Quesnay, publié par Etienne Bauer, professeur à l'Université Bâle," RHDES, II (1908), 4, and "Studies on the Origins of the French Economists," *Quarterly Journal of Economics,* V (1890), 101. See also Louis Salleron's notes to the INED text for internal contradictions in Quesnay's thought both within the article and between the article and the Tableau. See also Auguste Onken, *Geschichte der National-Ökonomie* (Leipzig, 1902), I, 369–71; Meek, *Economics,* 231–62;

confused beginning, argues that wealth produces population, and it should be read as a refutation of the populationists and of Cantillon.[29] Finally, "Impôts" argues for a rational system of taxation based so far as possible upon the net product of agriculture.

The opening section of "Grains" lays out the problem nicely: grain, together with wine, spirits, salt, flax, linen, wool, and livestock, forms "the principal object of trade in France." Industries transform these raw materials, thereby enhancing the value of the raw materials themselves and assuring the livelihood of many men. But for a long time now "luxury manufactures have seduced the nation." Their false promises have lured men out of the countryside into the cities, where the need to provide cheap labor has compelled the lowering of the price of grain. The vain hope of attracting gold and silver into the nation has in fact reduced agriculture to a pitiable state of subsistence. Tariff barriers have been raised against other nations who have quite naturally retaliated. "By this policy we have extinguished the reciprocal commerce between them and us which was completely to our advantage. . . . To gain a few millions by the manufacture and sale of beautiful materials, we have lost billions on the produce of our lands and the nation, decked out in gold and silver cloth, believed itself to be enjoying a flourishing commerce." This illusion has blinded France to her true interests. The consumption of the subjects provides the revenues of the sovereign, and "the sale of the surplus abroad increases the

Gustave Schelle, "Quesnay et le Tableau économique," *Revue d'économie politique*, XIX (1905), 520–21; and du Pont, "Notice abrégée," in Onken, *Oeuvres*, 150. (Du Pont is wrong; "Fermiers" does contain the notion of the mean price.) Weulersse, *Mouvement*, I, 46, barely mentions the articles.

29. See Adolphe Landry, "Les idées de Quesnay sur la population" [1909], in INED, I, 16–18; Edmond Cocks, "The Servitude Theory of Population," *American Scholar*, XLIII (1974), 472–80; Jules Conan, "Une fantaisie démographique du docteur Quesnay," in INED, I, 51–54. Despite the alphabetical sequence, it is more than likely that "Impôts" was drafted simultaneously with or even before "Hommes." Cf. my "A Physiocratic Model: The Transition from Feudalism to Capitalism," *Journal of European Economic History* (1975).

wealth of the subjects." Together they constitute the prosperity of the state, "but luxury consumption is much too limited to be supported by anything but real opulence." Ordinary men can only participate in such extravagant consumption "to their own prejudice and to the detriment of the State."[30]

Quesnay then argues at length the advantages of large-scale production and discusses the nature of pricing and the necessity of free trade for the maximum development of the national economy. Obviously familiar with the agronomic literature and the technical agricultural concerns of many of his contemporaries, Quesnay treats the realm of France as one vast estate and overlooks no managerial detail from field rotation to manure to choice of crop. Simultaneously, he lays the groundwork for a theoretical economics. These two aspects of his thought must be understood in conjunction: scholars have generally argued that his close attention to his own milieu reduces his economics, for all its theoretical brilliance, to a description and analysis of a given moment of historical development. They criticize him for his static picture of reality and suggest that by extrapolating a universal and invariable theory from a limited conjuncture, he implicitly denied the complexity of historical development.[31]

Quesnay's method, however, does not rely on a unidimensional dissection of the present. The present condition of France, he contends, resulted from an irresponsible disregard of economic principles in the past. Subsistence agriculture, he explained in

30. "Grains," 459, 460.
31. R. Reuss, *Charles de Butré: Un physiocrate tourangeau en Alsace et dans le margraviat de Bade* (Paris, 1887); Patullo, *Essai;* Proust, *Diderot,* 23, 176. ADY, "Inventaire," lists La Salle de l'Etang, *Prairies artificielles,* and Vivens, *Observations sur l'agriculture de la Guienne.* See also Bourde, *Agronomes,* esp. I, 220. Leo Rogin, *The Meaning and Validity of Economic Theory* [1956] (New York, 1971), 5; Pierre Goubert, *L'ancien régime* (Paris, 1969), 55–56; Lüthy, *Banque protestante,* II, 16–19, and "Les contours du siècle de Louis XV," in *Le passé présent: Combat d'idées de Calvin à Rousseau* (Monaco, 1965); Michel Bernard, *Introduction à une sociologie des doctrines des Physiocrates à Stuart Mill* (The Hague, 1963), 21–22; and Meek, *Economics,* 392–98.

"Fermiers," constitutes the normal condition of mankind in any time or place. "When France," he continues in "Hommes," "was divided among several great vassals of the crown, . . . each one, having possessions in sovereignty to defend, was occupied only with the cultivation of his lands, and the profession of arms." Since the French provinces have, however, been united under a single sovereign, and since laws now assure the rights of possessors, France has become by its unity and position a "truly maritime, commercial and agricultural State, for its wealth and its power could only sustain themselves and grow by the production of its lands, by its merchant marine and by its navy."[32] So the state arose at a specific historical moment, presumably at the beginning of the sixteenth century when Brittany passed finally to the crown. And from the moment of its birth, its government required broader aims than the mere perpetuation of population. In the absence of rational cultivation, autarchy could persist indefinitely and there would be no net product. "A poor man who draws from the land by his own labor only crops of small value, like potatoes, black grain, chestnuts, etc. who nourishes himself on them, who buys nothing and sells nothing, works only for himself: he lives in misery; he and the land he cultivates yield nothing for the State."[33]

The government, therefore, must overcome national underdevelopment, but few early officials realized this. For Quesnay, Sully's great merit lay in his favoring agriculture, complete with free export of its produce, and in encouraging the woolen industry, as well as in his understanding that the needs of the state dictated heavy capital investment in agriculture and the reduction of labor used on the land. "Cost and the labor of men," he wrote, "are only profitable to the State to the extent that their products renew and increase the wealth of the nation. Land

32. "Hommes," 525. Cf. Herlitz, "Trends in Physiocratic Doctrine," 134–41.
33. "Grains," 498. See J. Letaconnoux, *Les subsistances et le commerce des grains en Bretagne au XVIIIe siècle* (Rennes, 1909), 342.

must not only nourish those who cultivate it, it must supply the State with the largest part of its subsidies, procure tithes for the clergy, revenues to proprietors, profits to farmers and gains to those they employ in cultivation."[34] This capital accumulation— he cites Cantillon—creates cities and their attendant commercial life.

Unfortunately, France did not pursue this course. Colbert, hypnotized by manufacturing, had sense enough to attempt to decrease the *taille* and to advance capital to agriculturalists, but "he was unable to reconcile this with the needs of the State."[35] He never understood that the essential task should have been to rationalize the *taille* and free the grain trade. "Agriculture was neglected, the wars were continuous, the militia which devastated the countryside diminished the revenues of the kingdom; the *traitants* [private businessmen who contracted to do some business for the crown] by their perfidious aid became the supports of the State."[36]

Quesnay provides a plausible and in some ways surprisingly modern analysis of the historical development of France and Western Europe generally. He associates the autarchy of the medieval period with local feudal government, which eventually gave way to the absolute state and the re-emergence of trade, increase in national wealth, and expansion of governmental responsibilities. During the late seventeenth and early eighteenth centuries, this society underwent a severe crisis manifested in a falling population and the collapse of agricultural revenues. Quesnay's acute sense of periodization derives from his flair for economic history and prefigures the most recent interpretations. His interpretation of causation, however, derives from his metaphysics.[37] According to his analysis, the state, from the time of

34. "Grains," 481.

35. *Ibid.*, 482. See Weulersse, "Sully et Colbert," 239, who argues that Sully understood no such thing.

36. "Grains," 473; "Hommes," 549. See Ernest Lavisse, *Histoire de France depuis les origines jusqu'à la Révolution* (Paris, 1910), VII, 263.

37. Eric J. Hobsbawm, "The General Crisis of the European Economy in

its formation, had assumed responsibility for economic development. He thus falls into the profound but unrecognized dilemma that was to plague the remainder of his work. On the one hand, he presents the economy as the determining force in society; on the other, he charges the state with complete responsibility for the economy. He has, that is, announced that the economic base of society is the motor force of history and then held the state, defined as superstructure, responsible for the implementation of that force.

Quesnay's dilemma emerges more clearly in his treatment of England in these three *Encyclopédie* articles. If number of references is any indication, he has the English example more firmly in mind than he had in "Fermiers." First he celebrates England as the home of a prosperous agriculture that enjoys the benefits of free export and a high price for grain. In such a land it is this primary wealth, ever renewed, "which supports the other estates of the kingdom, which activates all other professions, which causes commerce to flourish, which favors population, which animates industry, which supports the prosperity of the nation." The English example demonstrates how a normally high price of grain, stabilized by free access to foreign markets, prevents the *disettes* [dearths] which plagued France. Excessively high prices "occur only through the lack of freedom of the grain trade," as was seen in 1709, when French prices soared to 100 livres a *septier,* and those in England never exceeded 43 livres—only double the ordinary price.[38]

Quesnay rounds off his discussion of England with the observation that its fundamentally sound economy guarantees English opulence; "the paper which there represents money has a value assured by trade and by the revenues of the assets (*biens*) of the

the Seventeenth Century," *Past and Present,* 5–6 (1954). See Trevor Aston, ed., *Crisis in Europe, 1560–1666* (Garden City, N.Y., 1967), esp. Pierre Goubert, "The French Peasantry of the Seventeenth Century: A Regional Example," 150–76; and Lublinskaya, *French Absolutism.*

38. "Grains," 474, 480, 494.

nation." So it cannot be the greater or lesser degree of monetary wealth that decides the true wealth of the state. "The English-man, always guided by his calculations, judges the duration of the undertakings of his enemies by their efforts in men and expenditures: he assures his success, by the successive fund of his wealth; he does not measure it by the mass of specie in the State."[39] Quesnay marvels at how consciously English political theorists see that the source of their wealth lies in agriculture. He quotes with approval a French translation of a composite of English thinkers intended to depict the English mentality: "We conduct ourselves as a rich landowner who has little ready cash, and who by his great income can always meet great expenditures." He applauds the pervasive commercial rationality that has convinced the English to dispense with a traditional army. Even English soldiers are brave for money—none of this nonsense about the elite of a military nation.[40]

In "Grains," Quesnay quotes Plumart de Dangeul's contention that as long as the English cultivated merely for their own subsistence they never had enough to meet their needs, but that since they made grain an object of commerce, their agriculture has increased to the point that a good harvest can feed the entire nation for five years.[41] In "Hommes" he returns to this issue and

39. "Hommes," 517. See C. B. MacPherson, *The Theory of Possessive Individualism from Hobbes to Locke* (London, New York, Toronto, 1962), 207.

40. "Hommes," 518. Quote from "Avis économiques d'Angleterre," *Journal économique* (June and July 1757). Although Quesnay does not identify the reference, it was to Charles Davenant. See Charles Whitworth, *The Political and Commercial Writings of . . . Charles Davenant . . .* (London, 1771), I, 13–16. The journal featured a series of translated extracts of English economists, particularly Sir William Petty. See his *Two Essays in Political Arithmetik concerning . . . London and Paris* [1686], in *Economic Writings of Sir Wm. Petty*, 2 vols., ed. Charles Henry Hull [1899], (New York, 1964), II, 501–13. Quesnay may well have known Petty's other essays in political arithmetic also.

41. "Grains," 493. Plumart de Dangeul published his work, *Remarques sur les avantages et les désavantages de la France et de la Grande-Bretagne, par*

after eulogizing the wealth produced by such an agriculture, draws attention to the wool trade, which has enjoyed the solicitous interest of the government since the fourteenth century and which now constitutes one of the principal branches of external trade. In stark contrast to such continuous growth, he raises the spectre of the Malthusian crisis hanging over France.

Among all men, who produce by their labors, those who consume only what they produce and all they produce, are the least profitable to the State; such are the peasants, the poor, who cultivate only a few niggardly-priced products, who nourish themselves from them, who sell nothing, who buy nothing, who are of no use to other men, and who are uniquely occupied in providing miserably and with difficulty for their own needs: these men, who multiply in proportion as those who govern them ruin them and ruin the State, finally perish, and the abandoned territory offers only wastes (*frîches*) for the domination of the sovereign.[42]

By this point such rhetoric has a familiar ring. But despite his reliance on England as a model of economic development, Quesnay damns the Navigation Acts and usually ignores English political structure. Beginning with his earliest economic work, he recognized the free market as the necessary prerequisite to England's sustained growth. Later he would come to understand that it was difficult to have the unfettered market without social, juridical, and maybe even political changes. Even in the *Encyclopédie* articles, however, his preoccupation with wealth sharply distinguishes him from the *agronomes*. Although like them he admired English agricultural techniques, he concentrated on the macro-economic implications of agricultural innovation in contrast to the more limited micro-economic concerns of the strict agronomists.

For Quesnay, agricultural production constituted the basic economic activity of society. Rationalization of production, to

---

rapport au commerce et aux autres sources de la puissance des états (Leyden, 1754), under the pseudonym John Nickolls.

42. "Hommes," 553. David Hume, "Of Commerce," in Eugene Rotwein, ed., *David Hume: Writings on Economics* (Madison, Wisc., 1955), 11.

do more than enable a finite number of agricultural workers to eke out a precarious existence, required heavy capital investment and a divorce of part of the labor force from the natural means of production. Men and land had formed a single unit. The English experience showed that a reduction in the number of those directly employed on the land would result in more efficient cultivation of the land and greater division of labor, together with greater diversification of output in society as a whole. The secret to this transformation was the concept of market price, which Quesnay made the basis of his attack on the populationists. Although their insistence upon the role of men and agriculture in the creation of wealth represented a significant advance over bullionism, they still aimed to raise the gross rather than the net product, and thus neglected the importance of market value. The government must never forget, Quesnay warns, "that the value of the products of landed properties and those of the gains of men can only be estimated by their price, that the State is wealthy only by virtue of that price, that the revenue of the king must also be regulated on that price and that in a commercial State the price is real only to the extent that it is accepted abroad." Any import or export duty which interferes with this price, he elaborates, threatens the wealth of society. He then explains that the total national wealth should not be confused with individual profits. While maintaining the mercantilist emphasis on aggregate output as the basis of the wealth of the state, Quesnay thus proposes a new means of determining that output —it is not enough to add up units of output, it is necessary to calculate the total surplus output.[43] Furthermore, the market price alone ascribes value to that output. Quesnay's analysis implicitly demands not only a free market in grain, but also one

---

43. "Impôts," 602. Cf. Spengler, "Mercantilist and Physiocratic Theory," 11; Thomas Hobbes, *Leviathan*, 11–13; and Cantillon, *Essai*, pt. 2, ch. 15 (see Chapter 4, note 26 below). Both Hobbes and Cantillon recognized that the pursuit of power and wealth in the aggregate might adversely affect the pursuit of individual welfare.

in labor, for the return cannot be measured in kind but must command a market value.

Traditional or paternalist societies, based on an essentially subsistence agriculture, have their own criteria for the social allocation of resources, and market societies have theirs. "Fermiers" reveals Quesnay's desire to create a full-fledged market economy in France. In "Hommes" he links the market operation to social organization: even in some imaginary nation which has no access to foreign markets, the realization of a market price for agricultural commodities would be necessary. Would not such a country still have a sovereign, landowners, cultivators, and workers of all kinds? It would, accordingly, be necessary there as in all other nations "that the annual revenue of this nation be distributed . . . to these different classes of men, by sales and purchases, in conformity with the venal value assigned to the annual productions, and to the works of labor."[44] But in eighteenth-century France, any number of vested interests were secured by that very state for whose benefit Quesnay wished to introduce economic modernization. Unconsciously, he had fallen into a dilemma which would plague all his work.

The more Quesnay became convinced of the necessity for a market price of commodities to secure revenues, the more he attacked the impediments to free circulation. "All duties on exports and imports, all prohibitions and all regulations which constrain internal and external commerce diminish the wealth of the State and the revenues of the sovereign; all imposition of duties prejudicial to commerce and the production of goods is destructive imposition."[45] The impersonality of Quesnay's tone

---

44. "Hommes," 535. In seventeenth- and eighteenth-century French usage, *vénal* meant that which could be obtained for money. In 1789 the *valeur vénale* was the value estimated in money. Quesnay uses the phrase as a direct substitute for market value. I have chosen to retain his word, for his failure specifically to equate value in money with market value reflects a typical eighteenth-century confusion.

45. "Impôts," 602.

might almost suggest that his argument speaks to a neutral question of national tariff policy which the state could rectify at will. In another passage he acknowledges that the troubles may lie deeper, for in insisting that the excessive *droits de rivière et de péage* [tolls] destroy the revenues of distant provinces and must be abolished, he adds that "those to whom these *droits* belong will be sufficiently compensated by their share in the general increase of the revenue and assets of the kingdom." But the obstructive tolls belong to specific individuals and these individuals might be presumed to have a stake in their retention. No, says Quesnay, they would profit more from free trade. It "is no less necessary to extinguish the privileges appropriated (*surpris*) by provinces, by towns, by communities, for their particular advantage."[46]

In practical terms the abolition of mercantilist monopolies, privileges, and tariff policies would threaten the commercial and financial community, whereas the abolition of feudal dues and tolls of all kinds would threaten the nobility. Quesnay handles these two questions differently. His economic analysis claims to prove the sterility of commercial and finance capital. Although he does not yet describe this group as a *classe stérile*, he concludes that monetary fortunes contribute nothing to the wealth of the state and that their protection actually destroys state revenues. Drawing on the vast fund of pastoral and nostalgic literature current in the early eighteenth century, he condemns the cities for their luxuries, corruption of morals, seduction of the honest peasantry, and assorted other evils. The true France is thus being ruined for an illusion.[47]

Diatribes pitting country against city formed the common stock of those who have been called the *économistes grands*

46. "Grains," 503.
47. See Jean-Claude Perrot, "Rapports sociaux et villes au XVIIIe siècle," *Annales ESC*, XXIII (1968), 241, 267; also Durand Echeverria, *Mirage in the West: A History of the French Image of American Society to 1815* (Princeton, 1957); Rothkrug, *Opposition*, 111–15.

seigneurs—for example, Mirabeau in *L'ami des hommes*.[48] But this literature aimed at returning men to the land, together with their natural lords, the feudal nobility, and its goal might be described as a "full employment" traditional economy. Quesnay's analysis, however, had already led him to prefer monetary revenues to feudal dues in kind, and much more important, to favor transforming dependent peasants into agricultural wage-laborers.

One could, perhaps, envisage those kingdoms where the peasants are serfs of the great proprietors and subject to working only for the profit of their lord, who reduces them to the barest minimum. But such a constitution which is no less contrary to the domination of the Sovereign than disadvantageous to the prosperity of a State, stifles all emulation and all activity: it is moreover incompatible with navigation and commerce: this feudal tyranny can never suit a maritime kingdom nor a truly monarchical government, it is liberty and individual interest which vivify States.[49]

Seigneurial tyranny, and therefore the feudal nobility, stand in the way of progress. Nevertheless, Quesnay has not committed himself to uprooting the traditional estates. Speaking of despotism in terms that echo Montesquieu and foreshadow Tocqueville, he argues that "one man cannot arbitrarily govern millions of men; sovereign, monarchical power can only subsist by the authority of laws and the equilibrium of the *corps* of the State reciprocally contained by each other; and by laws which concern their interest and which limit and assure their rights."[50]

At no other point in his work does Quesnay speak of an equilibrium of *corps*. His passing approval of the notion probably reflects his perception of the problem of disproportionate state power and his understanding that the nobility must, in some manner, be conciliated. But he displays no particular sympathy for the feudal sensibilities of the nobility when he proposes that

48. L. Cabantous, "L'ami des hommes et les économistes grands seigneurs," *Mémoires de l'Académie des sciences, agriculture, arts et belles-lettres d'Aix*, IX, pt. 2, 185–91.

49. "Hommes," 567.

50. "Hommes," 539–40.

the poorer members of the order be allowed to lease land like any tenant farmer in order to recoup their fortunes or merely earn their living.[51] In the *Encyclopédie* articles he does not directly challenge traditional social organization. But although his rhetoric spared noble pretentions, his analysis groped toward a justification for a new kind of ruling class.

Quesnay argues that a sovereign cannot raise one *corps* above the others in the state without incurring the danger of becoming too dependent on it. The increase of wealth and population—the only guarantee of state power—requires "that men be assured of their freedom and the possession of their wealth, because men do not attach themselves either to the sovereign or to the fatherland in a country in which they have neither protection, nor rights, nor property." A proprietor who enjoys security of possession "is a very profitable citizen for the State."[52] Quesnay waxes eloquent upon the role such a man can play in increasing the wealth of the kingdom. The reward for such services is a share in the net product; but the advantages entail distinct responsibilities. The proprietor who receives the revenue must spend it so that this wealth is distributed throughout the nation. "Without this distribution, the State could not subsist; if the proprietors retained these revenues, they would necessarily have to be divested of them; thus this sort of wealth belongs as much to the State as to the proprietors themselves; they only enjoy them to spend them." The proprietors are of no use to the state except through their consumption: "Their revenues relieve them from working; they produce nothing. . . ." The profits they draw from their lands "are thus the true wealth of the nation, the wealth of the sovereign, the wealth of the subjects, the wealth that underwrites (*subvienne*) the needs of the State."[53]

Quesnay had not at this time developed a coherent theory of property. In "Hommes" he even toys briefly with the notion

51. "Impôts," 608.
52. "Hommes," 540, 538, 560.
53. "Impôts," 582.

that "the proprietors can also be regarded as men who produce by their direction and improvement of their lands."[54] But he rejects this theory, much as he rejects the labor theory of value, and never returns to the concept of proprietor as entrepreneur again. Even in the early articles he grasps the need for security of possession to assure the workings of the market. At the same time, he has not divested himself of the governing myths of his society. He advances the claims of property but cannot yet sustain the advance. The conclusions of his economic analysis point to the need for secure property and show that the direct beneficiaries of his miracle of economic development would be the owners of land. The question of social responsibility, however, remained. What could insure that the entire revenue from the nation's labor would be put to a proper purpose? Here Quesnay falls back on the state, for which the whole program has been designed. If the proprietors should fail to meet their social obligations of spending, the laws themselves "would rise up against these men useless to society and withholders of the wealth of the fatherland."[55] State omnipotence was not, however, a solution he could live with, and even while provisionally advancing the claims of Leviathan, his mind sought other means of securing the market and fostering responsible behavior through enlightened self-interest.

Quesnay fully appreciates the role of individual interest in the commercial world and argues that all trade should be free precisely "because it is in the interest of merchants to attach themselves to the most secure and the most profitable branches of external trade."[56] But this same interest, which could assure a market value to agricultural products, has a less attractive side. A merchant's pursuit of his particular interest might run contrary to the general interest. Merchant profits being "so independent of any suitable order," merchants can multiply indefinitely

54. "Hommes," 559.
55. "Impôts," 582.
56. "Grains," 502.

and raise prices artificially by their multiplication of transactions over a single product without contributing a thing to national prosperity.[57]

The only men whose deeper intentions Quesnay does not viscerally mistrust are the peasants and agricultural workers. He pours out contempt and outrage against the argument that misery excites the poor to labor. On the contrary, "the state of well-being provokes work." Men become accustomed to the good life and work to preserve it: "The hope of success sustains their courage and success satisfies their tenderness and self-esteem." Honor, feeling, and ambition all contribute to the desire to maintain a decent standard of living. These reflections prompt Quesnay to a more general conclusion. "Motives founded on the possibility of increasing wealth by wealth are thus the true causes which excite men to work, which render them useful and which procure wealth for the State."[58] His words echo the traditional literature portraying the peasants as the force of the crown. The *grands* of society, ran the experience of early modern France, rise against the state and demand protection for their special interests. They can never be trusted and must always be individually bought off or intimidated.

It required Mirabeau's insistence upon an organic social order to awaken Quesnay to the idea that society as a whole should constitute a rational system. But only when the two men replaced the pivotal role they had previously assigned to the state with Quesnay's idea of the market did the disparate elements of physiocratic thought fall into place.

57. "Hommes," 565. See Hector Denis, *Histoire des systèmes économiques et socialistes*, 2 vols. (Paris, 1904), I, 102–3.
58. "Hommes," 541.

Mirabeau—"The Oldest Son of the Doctrine"

Noblemen were pulled down, which is the foundation of monarchy—monarchy soon after fell.

Marquis of Newcastle

Victor de Riqueti, marquis de Mirabeau, has never enjoyed a good press among the admirers of physiocratic liberalism. At most, he receives credit for having lent his services to the propagation of Quesnay's economic doctrine. Yet in 1757, while Quesnay's economic articles remained virtually unknown beyond a circle of specialists, Mirabeau's *L'ami des hommes, ou traité de la population,* was becoming a best seller. By 1760 it had run through twenty printings and earned its publishers, by their own admission, a profit of more than eighty thousand livres. Mirabeau's idiosyncratic reading of Cantillon's economics, combined with his equally idiosyncratic picture of an organic social order dominated by a full-fledged feudal nobility, had stirred a response in the public mind that Quesnay's independent work never achieved.[1]

1. René Gonnard, *Histoire des doctrines économiques* (Paris, 1943), 198; Weulersse, *Mouvement,* I, 53; Louis de Loménie, *Les Mirabeau: Nouvelles études sur la société française au XVIIIe siècle,* 5 vols. (Paris, 1879–1891), II, 136–38; and Lucien Brocard, *Les doctrines économiques et sociales du marquis de Mirabeau* (Paris, 1902), 4. *L'ami des hommes* (Avignon, 1756) in fact appeared in mid-1757. In all likelihood it had been printed in 1756 and its distribution delayed because of the tightening of censorship at the beginning of the Seven Years' War. See Auguste

Quesnay fully appreciated the charismatic force of Mirabeau's work, although he completely repudiated its conclusions, and he determined to secure for his economics the service of the marquis' pen. In July 1757, after reading *L'ami*, Quesnay invited Mirabeau to his *entresol* at Versailles. At the end of a stormy interview, the doctor had failed to convert the marquis. After some private reflection, however, Mirabeau returned to Versailles the same evening and embraced the new science. From the first meeting, in du Pont's version, Quesnay spared nothing in exposing Mirabeau's errors. "The docile soul of *L'ami des hommes* recognized the truth, and . . . that illustrious man, then the object of the infatuation of all others, became a school boy, haughtily and opinionatedly abjured his error, consecrated all the rest of his time and his work and devoted his celebrity to the publication of the science discovered by Quesnay."[2] Mirabeau can more easily be imagined "haughtily and opinionatedly" denying he made any errors than abjuring them; and there is no evidence of a docile soul in the man who terrorized his peasants and sent his own son to the dungeon of Vincennes. Yet all other accounts of the famous meeting substantially confirm du Pont's general description. It did take place, and did, in the words of Mirabeau himself, result in the cracking of the skull of Goliath.[3] Quesnay had acquired his first disciple, "the oldest son of the doctrine," and from their collaboration emerged the early outlines of physiocracy.

Traditionally, interpretations of the Quesnay-Mirabeau col-

Onken, *Geschichte der National-Ökonomie* (Leipzig, 1902), I, 280. All references to *L'ami des hommes* will be to the Paris, 1883, edition.

2. "Notice abrégée," in Onken, *Oeuvres*, 151–53.

3. Mirabeau to J. J. Rousseau, 30 July 1767, published by Mirabeau in his *Précis de l'ordre légal* (Amsterdam and Paris, 1768), 223–25. See Loménie, *Les Mirabeau*, II, 171; Carl Friedrichs von Baden, *Brieflicher Verkehr mit Mirabeau und Du Pont*, 2 vols., ed. Karl Knies (Heidelberg, 1892), I, cxxxvii; Weulersse, *Mouvement*, I, 53; and Meek, *Economics*, 16–18. Du Pont, in his account of 1773, "Discours pour la clôture . . . ," Knies, ed., *Brieflicher Verkehr*, II, 108, offers a particularly exaggerated account, even for him.

laboration have stressed the master-disciple relationship. By July 1757 Quesnay was well on his way to having formulated a coherent economic analysis, the principles of which Mirabeau was coming to understand only slowly. Accordingly, scholars have been quick to see Mirabeau as the forty-year-old schoolboy acquiring the rudiments of economic science at the knee of his tutor. Quesnay's authoritarian correction of Mirabeau's errors is taken as the model for the rest of their joint efforts. Those principally interested in the development of physiocratic economics have readily consigned Mirabeau to the role assigned him by du Pont and confirmed by Mirabeau's own enthusiastic account of his conversion.[4] Those whose works have been devoted to Mirabeau himself invariably confirm this view but regard it less as a salvation than a disaster. Mirabeau, his admirers maintain, had a profound and organic vision of society and of the proper relations between men. By sacrificing that vision to the authoritarian and bourgeois inclinations of Quesnay, he betrayed his own higher principles and helped undermine traditional French society.[5]

The superficial confrontation between these two interpretations obscures their central agreement on the respective roles played

4. Mirabeau to Rousseau; to Longo, cited by Loménie, *Les Mirabeau*, II, 171. See Henri Ripert, *Le marquis de Mirabeau: Ses théories politiques et économiques* (Paris, 1910), 251; Onken, *Geschichte der National-Ökonomie*, 318; and Weulersse, *Mouvement*, I, 57. This point of view emerges forcefully from Weulersse, *Manuscrits*, which continually shows Quesnay "correcting" Mirabeau. See also Meek, *Economics*, 15–18, 27, which implicitly takes the same line; and J. Conan, "Les débuts de l'école physiocratique, un faux départ: l'échec de la réforme fiscale," *RHES*, XXXVI (1958), 57, 59.

5. Ripert, *Marquis de Mirabeau*, 4, 261; Brocard, *Doctrines*, 230–31. Some more recent scholarship also favors the prephysiocratic Mirabeau, seeing in him the champion of more rational economic policies rather than the defender of a more organic social order. See Paul Chanier, "Le dilemme de Mirabeau, Cantillon ou Quesnay?" in *Les Mirabeau et leur temps* (Paris, 1968), 35; Jean Ehrard, " 'L'ami des hommes' et Paris," *ibid.* 43. For a far more perceptive and much less anachronistic reading, see Alexis de Tocqueville, *Oeuvres complètes*, ed. J. P. Mayer, vol. II, *L'ancien régime et la Révolution* (Paris, 1953), pt. 2, 440–44.

by Quesnay and Mirabeau: the interpretations present the same scenario with different evaluations, but neither seriously investigates Mirabeau's active contribution to the development of physiocracy. Karl Knies, who came closest to appreciating fully both the significance of physiocracy and the integrity of Mirabeau, unfortunately limited his catalogue of Mirabeau's contribution to technical points of elaboration.[6]

The widespread failure to understand Mirabeau's contributions derives, first, from Quesnay's indisputable leadership in economic analysis, and second, from subsequent physiocratic insistence that their political economy and ideology arose inexorably from the economic analysis—that is, that all social and political institutions must derive from their material base. Such a view implies that, in accepting Quesnay's economic analysis, Mirabeau accepted his political theory, including legal despotism. Quesnay's own thought, however, was still in flux, and he had not yet established a necessary relationship between his economic analysis and his political economy. Although Mirabeau dedicated himself totally to the understanding and propagation of Quesnay's thought, he was not one to prostrate himself before another man who had not yet developed a clearly articulated doctrine. Mirabeau was no economic genius, but he did have a clear and independent mind; and it would be rash to suppose that he sacrificed all his previous convictions at the snap of a finger.

Born in 1715, a generation younger than Quesnay, Mirabeau was the oldest son of a Provençal nobleman of middling fortune and ferocious temper. After a brief education with the Jesuits, he had been sent out to pursue the appropriate military career. But the ruggedly individualistic Riqueti temperament had not prepared him for the niceties of the Louis Quinzième court, and in 1735 he failed to gain the necessary approval to purchase his own regiment. This foreclosing of the only public career for which

6. *Brieflicher Verkehr,* I, cxlii–cxlvi, 387–89. Loménie, *Les Mirabeau,* II, 136n offers the most judicious appraisal.

he might have had training or inclination freed Mirabeau for a long and tumultuous private life. The story of his disastrous marriage, confrontations with his wife and children, and precarious real estate speculations and administration of his lands has been admirably recounted elsewhere.[7] In fact, Mirabeau's personality dominates the literature he has inspired. Unlike Quesnay, in whom the man seems to recede behind his own intellectual accomplishment, Mirabeau, in his enthusiasms, angers, prejudices, and commitments, rises above any single one of his own works. Where Quesnay proves, or claims to prove, with calm arithmetical demonstration, Mirabeau exhorts, cajoles, commands. His personality thus becomes a genuine element to be weighed in the appraisal of physiocracy. At the time he met Quesnay, whatever Mirabeau lacked in economic sophistication, he made up for in passionate ideological commitment.

Following family practice, in 1747 the thirty-two-year-old Mirabeau drafted his *Testament politique* for the instruction of his as yet unborn male heir. This literary form had served such illustrious figures as Richelieu, Colbert, Louvois, and Vauban as the vehicle of transmitting their experience and opinions in matters of government. But Mirabeau had no years of public service to furnish the justification for his views. He, in effect, adapted a public form to fit a private purpose, and his *Testament* remained unpublished. But if it qualified as an antiquarian curiosity within his own lifetime, it nevertheless constitutes the starting point of his political speculations and affords a glimpse of his original presuppositions. Loménie, the great historian of the Mirabeau family, describes that early vision as the marquis's "first utopia," a "plan for an aristocratic and even feudal restoration." He emphasizes Mirabeau's deep hatred for the central government, particularly the intendants, who used their superior knowledge of administrative technique to subject and humiliate the old

7. Loménie, *Les Mirabeau*, is still the best and most complete account.

nobility of race, and even to turn the lowly rural population against their natural lords.[8]

From experience Mirabeau had learned that the French state of the middle third of the eighteenth century had no place for him or those who thought like him. His father had reputedly lost two hundred thousand livres during the Law fiasco; his younger brother had failed to obtain desired posts, and he himself had been unable to secure so much as a regiment, the proper claim of one of his majesty's distinguished vassals. Like Montesquieu, whose acquaintance he had sought sometime around 1739 and whose example had convinced him "that the glory of letters is compatible with that of increasing one's revenue," Mirabeau opposed the trend toward despotism as the betrayal of an historic and organic alliance between sovereign and nobility.[9]

One year after Mirabeau wrote his *Testament*, Montesquieu published his *Esprit des lois*. What Mirabeau had tackled as a private grief, Montesquieu analyzed as a social ill. In 1769 du Pont adopted Montesquieu's work as the special precursor of physiocracy. Most subsequent students have dismissed his claim as a mere literary flourish. Nothing, they argue, could be further from Quesnay's legal despotism than Montesquieu's checks and balances. Quesnay's own early writings certainly bear no significant trace of Montesquieu's specific thought. Yet under du Pont's more grandiose claims for physiocracy as the logical heir of the best of previous thought lies the perception that Montesquieu's work inaugurated the fashion for the social sciences in French intellectual life and thus broke ground for physiocracy. Moreover, even those who doubt Montesquieu's influence on Quesnay do not question his profound impact on Mirabeau, who saw that the outdated claims of the declining castes might be bolstered by

8. *Ibid.,* II, 3, 101, 90–93.
9. Henry Higgs, *The Physiocrats* (London, 1897), 54; M. Rouxel, "Notice biographique," in *L'ami des hommes,* xxxix–xl; Loménie, *Les Mirabeau,* I, 405, which quotes from a letter Mirabeau wrote to his friend Vauvenargues.

the most sophisticated of modern sciences. Mirabeau brought this modernized traditionalism as his own special dowry to physiocratic thought.[10]

Quite probably, Montesquieu's success inspired Mirabeau's next project, which moved him from the private to the public arena. In 1750 he anonymously published a *Mémoire concernant l'utilité des états provinciaux*, which took up the cause of decentralization by advocating a strong role for provincial estates throughout the kingdom, including establishing them in provinces in which they did not exist. In the *Mémoire* he also argues for a reinvigorated feudal nobility that would embody the interests of the public weal. Mirabeau's extension of his claims to cover administration and larger social well-being entailed no significant modification in his point of view.[11] He proposes not to innovate but to restore, and in so doing follows the tradition exemplified by Fénelon and the duc de Chevreuse in the *Table de Chaulnes*. Mirabeau in his *Mémoire* acknowledges his debt to Fénelon's specific project of aristocratic reform and thus places himself squarely in that tradition which he thought had culminated with the administration of Henri IV and Sully. That administration had rested upon the legitimate support of peasants and nobility, rather than on townsmen and upstart financiers as in the recent bureaucratic absolutism.[12]

In the Estates of Languedoc, Mirabeau found the model of

10. Du Pont, "Notice abrégée," 145–46, and *Origine et progrès d'une science nouvelle* [1768], ed. A. Dubois (Paris, 1910), 7; and Mirabeau, *Lettres sur la législation* . . . , 3 vols. (Berne, 1775), II, 621. See also Weulersse, *Mouvement*, I, 38–39; and Elie Carcassonne, *Montesquieu et le problème de la constitution française au XVIIIe siècle* [1927] (Geneva, 1970), 312–25.

11. *Mémoire concernant l'utilité des états provinciaux, relativement à l'autorité royale, aux finances, au bonheur et à l'avantage des peuples* (Rome, 1750), esp. 252. See Ripert, *Marquis de Mirabeau*, 92–93, and Tocqueville, *Oeuvres*, II, pt. 2, 440–41.

12. Mirabeau, *Mémoire*, 86. See also AN, M 783, no. 7, "Eloge historique de Fénelon." Mirabeau wrote this eulogy in July 1772. Selections from it were published in Weulersse, *Manuscrits*, 117–19.

what he believed government could and should be. Such estates, established in all provinces, would not only raise the yield of taxation by uniform assessment based on the *taille réelle* (a tax on land rather than on persons) and by local collection and spending of revenues to save time and the expense of centralization of receipts in Paris. They would also facilitate royal borrowing at a low interest rate (5 percent instead of the usual 10) while avoiding recourse to the hated *Fermiers-généraux* (farmers-general, a company of tax-farmers who purchased from the crown the right to collect indirect taxes) or the *Caisse d'amortissement* (an independently managed fund for the extinction of the royal debt, rather like a sinking fund).[13] In addition, the estates, while promoting decentralization of the administrative apparatus, would actually strengthen the authority of the monarchy. Unlike the hated intendants, the estates would never interpose themselves between the king and his subjects and, because of their purely local interests, would not be tempted to meddle with taxation or questions of war and peace.

In fact, Mirabeau does not envisage the proposed estates as political bodies and thus departs from Montesquieu's vision of the Parlements. He accepts the sovereign as the very essence of the state. The estates will merely serve the lowly function of "raising the pence" and supervising certain aspects of internal *police* (local administration and enforcement). Actually, he argues, they should strengthen royal authority by providing the leading men of the province with a role in government and by playing them off against each other. Under a despotic government with no provision for the use of local talent, he warns, the least breath of revolt can enable a *grand* to take over, chase the intendant, rouse the people, and even invite the notables to form estates of their own.[14]

13. Mirabeau, *Mémoire*, 27–44. See also Tocqueville, *Oeuvres*, II, pt. 1, 253–61. Loménie. *Les Mirabeau*, II, 117, points out that Tocqueville got many of his thoughts on the role of the provincial estates from Mirabeau.
14. Mirabeau, *Mémoire*, 17, 26.

Mirabeau assuredly knew that the days of full-scale armed provincial rebellion had passed; erstwhile local magnates lured to Versailles had settled down as courtiers. He himself had even attempted to join their ranks. Much of the world he wished to restore had passed beyond recall. Yet Mirabeau, like so many of his contemporaries, felt that the growth of government had distracted the sovereign from his proper relationship to his nobility and violated the constitution of the state. These fundamental laws were based on the historical privileges of its component members: those of the king; of the royal blood, including "succession, rank, and distinction, recognized throughout the earth"; those of the different orders, "either founded at the same time as the Monarchy, or established by the Prince, with the assent of the other assembled bodies"; those of the different provinces, "seal of their reunion to the body of the State, price of the blood spilled and wealth expended for its defenses"; those of the towns; and of the "civil and particular laws of each country as they are authorized by ancient usage." All these discrete privileges must be honored as so many parts in that whole "which is the body of the State, for the Monarchy is the cornerstone that alone supports this edifice, but without the edifice, it would be hidden under grass and thorns."[15]

Of course the king is sovereign, but on what grounds could this sovereignty be defended? Hardly on age, since some other privileges can claim equal age. On public utility then? "I believe so," he answers, "but if one accustoms men to calculate all rights only according to their utility, (if you set them this example), what dangerous progress could not that cause in men's minds?"[16] The progress of such dangerous modern habits of thought may perhaps best be measured by the title of Mirabeau's own *Mémoire*. If he could fall prey to arguments based on utility, he indeed had reason to fear what his world was coming to.

15. *Ibid.*, 9–10, 11.
16. *Ibid.*, 11–12.

With only a trace of embarrassment, Mirabeau defends his specific class interests including noble privilege and tax exemption. But the *Mémoire* also transcends specific interests and advances an organic conception of society. At the time of its publication rumors circulated that it had been written by Montesquieu. But where Montesquieu sought to legitimize an emerging aristocracy of privilege and wealth that united the old ruling class of sword nobles and the new robe elite of ennobled, office-owning bourgeois, and to guarantee its economic predominance through traditional legal privilege, Mirabeau sought to restore an older order—and incidentally to return the robe nobles to the status of bourgeois. Whatever degree of special pleading for the nobility underlay the work of Montesquieu, he accepted the world as he found it and looked to the future. Mirabeau, insisting upon the religious and historical foundation of social relations, looked to the past.

Montesquieu and Mirabeau only appear to use the same vocabulary and to address the same questions. Like Mirabeau, Montesquieu may be charged, as the physiocrats later charged him, with not taking sufficient account of the deeper unity of political economy—of not grounding his principles of government firmly in social and economic reality. *Esprit des lois*, however, constituted a radical break with even the most sophisticated of previous political theory "in discovering and verifying this hypothesis, that the state is a real totality and that all the details of its legislation, of its institutions and of its customs are only the expression of its internal unity. . . . With Montesquieu what was an *idea* becomes a scientific hypothesis destined to take account of the facts."[17] But by no stretch of the imagination can Mirabeau be called a social scientist at the time he wrote the *Mémoire*. If by his moral and historical preoccupations, and particularly by his conception of the state as a social and political

17. Louis Althusser, *Montesquieu: La politique et l'histoire* (Paris, 1959), 42.

unit, he seems close to Montesquieu, he differs from him radically in his method and understanding.[18]

Where Montesquieu investigated the principles of a variety of governments and accepted a cultural relativism that placed different religions on a plane with different customs, Mirabeau sought to restore the true government under the auspices of the true faith. His advocacy of provincial estates aimed not at an increased voice for the most powerful subjects in the affairs of royal government, but at administrative decentralization and increased local authority for legitimate elites. Mirabeau continued his war against the intendants and the growth of royal administration but never attacked the sanctity of the royal will. He accepted government as an emanation from above.[19] Whereas his contemporaries increasingly sought the equivalent of a scientific mechanism in their discussion of the body politic, he clung to the traditional notion of moral or religious purpose as the mainspring of social organization. Mirabeau's rejection of utility as a justification of privilege demonstrated his alarm at the growing claims of the individual against society.

Mirabeau never succeeded in restoring the credibility of the monarchy and religion, let alone of a responsible feudal nobility, but his attempt assumes tremendous importance in his "conversion." Although his *Mémoire* displays little literary merit, political acumen, or sociological insight, it does express a deep traditional sensibility. Unquestionably, he felt a loss of harmony, a disintegration of organic relationships in society. As it dawned on him that he could not singlehandedly dismantle the administrative machine of the absolute monarchy (he had enough perspective to refer to himself on one occasion as a Don Quixote), he tried increasingly to bring his goals into line with intellectual

18. *Ibid.*, 57; Raymond Aron, *The Main Currents of Sociological Thought*, vol. I, *Montesquieu, Comte, Marx, Tocqueville . . .* , trans. Richard Howard and Helen Weaver [1960] (New York, 1965), 14–16; and Gay, *The Enlightenment*, II, 323–24.

19. Ripert, *Marquis de Mirabeau*, 101. See also Mirabeau, *Mémoire*, 11–12, and *L'ami des hommes*, 246.

currents of his time. Physiocracy as a whole is frequently pre-sented as more or less an attempt to restore a lost world. Such an interpretation slights the genuine innovation of Quesnay's eco-nomic analysis in its twin dimensions of restoration and renova-tion, but it captures exactly the spirit of Mirabeau's first interest in the economic process.

Whereas the *Mémoire* had reflected Mirabeau's desire to re-store the feudal monarchy, *L'ami des hommes*, when it appeared in 1757, addressed itself to the general well-being of mankind, specifically the economic interests of the French. Between the publication of the two works, Mirabeau had examined the current economic literature; and if economists have not usually taken Mirabeau seriously enough to identify the origins of his thought, no one can doubt the extent of his debt to Cantillon. Pierre Chanier has recently reduced Mirabeau's career as an economist to the dilemma of choosing between Cantillon and Quesnay, and argues that "it is in the margin of Cantillon's work that the thought of Mirabeau was formed."[20] Mirabeau did possess a copy of the manuscript of Cantillon's *Essai sur le commerce* from which he borrowed liberally. Mirabeau was also the first to signal the extent of his debt to Cantillon. In *L'ami* he quotes a passage that argues that the number of inhabitants in a state depends upon the means of subsistence, which in turn depend upon the use made of land. This use depends "principally upon the wills, tastes and modes of life of the proprietors of land, and it is clear that the multiplication or diminution of the people depends upon them." Mirabeau adds: "These words are drawn from the work of M. Cantillon, which was printed last year. He was, without gainsay the most adept man on these matters who has appeared."[21] As a measure of his respect, Mirabeau lifted the entire popula-

20. "Dilemme," 24. The text of the manuscript is in AN, M 779, no. 1. Cf. Richard Cantillon, *Essai sur la nature du commerce en général*, INED, lxvii–lxxiii.
21. *L'ami des hommes*, 94.

tion theory of *L'ami* from chapters 14 and 15 of part 1 of Cantillon's *Essai*. As he noted on the margin of Cantillon's manuscript, "This chapter and the following one are the entire key of my system." But despite his own claims, Mirabeau never followed Cantillon rigorously.[22]

At no point did Mirabeau claim originality as an economic theorist. He wrote Rousseau that before he met Quesnay, he was "no more an economist than my cat."[23] He always had trouble with the *zigzag* and the arithmetical calculations in which Quesnay delighted. He had a literary or historical rather than an analytic mind. The verdict of one of his greatest admirers that *L'ami* was rather a work "of social economy than political economy" is suggestive of the difference between Mirabeau and both Cantillon and Quesnay in this respect.[24] Mirabeau adapted the analytic advances of others to his own purposes, but created none of his own. His departures from Cantillon's analysis, therefore, are probably less the result of theoretical disagreements than of larger commitments. Mirabeau's ideology always took precedence over his economic analysis and must be seen as the most important single determinant of whatever political economy he produced.

In addition, Cantillon, being dead, could not explain his meaning to his "disciple," but Quesnay, as a living master, enjoyed that advantage, which underscores the qualitatively different nature of Mirabeau's relationship to him, even if it does not fully account for the differences. Quesnay's theoretical advances over Cantillon presented a total picture of the economy that not only

22. Cited by Chanier, "Dilemme," 29. See Joseph Schumpeter, *Economic Doctrine and Method* (London, 1954), 45; and J. J. Spengler, *French Predecessors of Malthus* (Durham, N.C., 1942), 128–36, for detailed discussions on Mirabeau's divergences from Cantillon.

23. *Précis de l'ordre légal*, 223.

24. Ripert, *Marquis de Mirabeau*, 139. Cf. AN, M 784, no. 70, a letter from Quesnay to Mirabeau, which has been translated by Meek, *Economics*, 115.

coincided with Mirabeau's ideological convictions, but even endowed them with the force of necessity.

The ambiguity underlying Mirabeau's relationship to Cantillon and such other economists as Melon, Dutot, and Hume, all of whom he cites, is forcefully revealed by his refusal to acknowledge the central thesis of their work, the importance of luxury to economic development.[25] For example, because Mirabeau understood only too well that the expansion of commerce had acted as the principal dissolvent of those organic, traditional bonds he so valued, he thoroughly mistrusted money. And yet Cantillon, a banker, had been so fascinated by the process of monetary circulation that he failed to develop a complete picture of the economic process in early eighteenth-century France because money had far from completely penetrated the social production of wealth. Mirabeau, more in touch with that agricultural base, would have preferred to reduce so far as possible the incidence of monetary wealth. So when Mirabeau adopted the concept of *vivification* from Cantillon, as Hume had adapted "enlivement," he used it for a different purpose. Instead of reflecting, as enlivement did in Hume's work, the awakening of all human attributes and the unlimited perspective of growth and diversification, Mirabeau's notion of *vivification* was designed to restore a stable and hierarchical natural order. Thus, while for Cantillon the pursuit of luxury had been the motive force of the economy and the incentive for the spending of the proprietors' incomes, for Mirabeau luxury became a symbol of moral decline to be avoided at all costs.[26] Yet Mirabeau did learn from Cantillon the

25. *L'ami des hommes*, 14–15, 276ff. for examples of Mirabeau's attack on luxury.

26. Richard Cantillon, *Essai sur la nature du commerce en général*, ed. and trans. Henry Higgs (London, 1931). All subsequent references will be to this edition. Cf. Chanier, "Dilemme," 26–27; and *L'ami des hommes*, 132, for a discussion of *vivification*, and ch. 5, "Luxury." Cf. David Hume, "Of Refinement in the Arts," in Eugene Rotwein, ed., *David Hume: Writings on Economics* (Madison, Wisc., 1970), 19–32; Cantillon, *Essai*, 229–33, and

language of economics, or a new way of describing social relations, which he applied to French society in *L'ami des hommes*.

Mirabeau opens *L'ami* with a discussion of man as an animal, albeit one who even in his most barbarous form has certain virtues. He cautions, however, that the social cultivation of innate human virtue requires tremendous effort. The first relationship between men of equal age and dignity terminated in murder. That event (Cain's and Abel's fratricidal quarrel) confirms the existence in nature of two contrary principles; one draws man towards his fellows and the other leads him to regard them as enemies and proves "that the laws concerning the division of goods must have been the first of all and the most indispensable." "In a word," Mirabeau insists, "the division of goods is the first law of society, and the trunk, so to speak, of all other laws."

And he dismisses in advance all objections based on a vision of community of goods among savages as a figment of the civilized imagination. Not only are savages like a family defending its territory against the incursion of others, but "the most brutal savages have *properties* recognized among themselves, bows, arrows, cabins, etc."[27] So property began with the first humans, existed in the most primitive social arrangements, and like anything else was subject to the abuses "of which inequality of fortune was an indispensable result." Mirabeau takes pains to explain how such seeming inequities occurred naturally: "Strength, industry, good fortune, thrift increased one heritage, the contrary faults diminished the other. It is thus that the entire territory of society passes into the hands of a small number and that all the rest live in a sort of dependence on this small number, either on its wages, or as the entrepreneurs of the managing of lands and their product."[28]

---

pt. 1, Ch. 7, "The Labor of the Husbandman Is of Less Value Than That of the Handicrafts-Man."

27. *L'ami des hommes*, 1–3.
28. *Ibid.*, 3.

Like Quesnay, Mirabeau recognizes two principles or elements at work in human action, but where Quesnay adopted a matter-spirit dualism, which he tried to resolve dialectically, Mirabeau, as a pure idealist, believed that moral considerations alone determined human behavior. His apparent dualism represented nothing more than his manichean vision of a struggle between good and bad.

From his discussion of property as the foundation of society, Mirabeau proceeds to round out the "exterior tableau" of population by describing the concentration of the people in villages, towns, and cities, a picture of human distribution that follows Cantillon exactly.[29] This surface fidelity, however, hardly prepares the reader for his conclusion that "everything here below goes by hierarchy and ranks, like the steps of a staircase which are equally necessary to the perfection, but of which the lowest . . . are destined to support the whole structure and, consequently, merit more attention as they approach the base."[30]

Mirabeau has taken Cantillon's conception of the proprietors as luxury consumers whose spending stimulates the economy and reversed it so that the proprietors serve as the guarantors of social hierarchy. He has also subordinated the economic role of the proprietors (as generators of economic activity, as the primary agents of exchange) to that of the lowly workers. Instinctively, Mirabeau may be denying a primary role to distribution and allocating it to production, but he lacks the analytic structure to express his preference. In effect, he is defending a primitive labor theory of value in a premarket context in which the primary goal remains reinforcing social stability rather than promoting economic growth. His position constitutes an implicit

29. *Ibid.*, 4. Cf. Cantillon, *Essai*, 9–19; and Pierre Dockès, *L'espace dans la pensée économique du XVIe au XVIIIe siècle* (Paris, 1969), 234–59.

30. *L'ami des hommes*, 4. Cf. S. Vauban, *La Dixme Royale* [1707], ed. Emile Coornaert (Paris, 1933), 6; and Schumpeter, *Economic Doctrine and Method*, 36.

repudiation of the spirit of early bourgeois, preclassical economics, even though Mirabeau himself sees that economics as a buttress for his own conception of society.

Ultimately, Mirabeau's most striking debt to Cantillon is his argument that property constitutes the basis of society. In the course of developing other arguments, he continues to insist that "the basis of the positive laws is the division of the goods and advantages of society, and the maintenance of the rights of each individual in this respect." But he also asserts that the basis of speculative law "is the direction of human anxiety and avarice towards sociability and truth and the continual care of diverting them from cupidity and illusion"—a task he assigns to the sovereign.[31] Mirabeau found Cantillon's conception of the proprietor as the mainspring of economic life congenial to his own vision of a feudal nobility. He saw no contradiction in the characterization of "advantages" as a fundamental right, but neither did he trust the working of unfettered self-interests. The sovereign must channel human natures to acceptable social ends. Only by turning a people towards sociability could a ruler enrich it.[32] The confusion of the moral and the economic could not be more complete, for Mirabeau saw sociability as a purely moral quality.

In L'ami des hommes, Mirabeau tries to use market economics to attack market society. His rejection of the market itself led to a faulty understanding and contradictory application of Cantillon's work. Mirabeau never decides whether population measures subsistance or subsistance population.[33] But then, he does not care as much about the theoretical problem as he does about having a large population securely tied to the land. He

31. L'ami des hommes, 11.
32. Ibid., 4.
33. The full ambiguity of his position is expressed in his statement, "The measure of subsistence is the measure of population." He also says that "population depends on subsistence," and that "true wealth consists only in population." (L'ami des hommes, 579, 13, 579). Cf. Spengler, French Predecessors, 129–31.

remains certain that although consumption in Cantillon's sense is desirable as an agent of *vivification,* it must be spread out among the largest possible number of consumers. "A great deal of consumption fostered by a small number of consumers is a continual and ever growing corrosion of the nerve of population." Cantillon never argued in this fashion, but Mirabeau seems to understand that a concentration of consumption implies a concentration of capital, which corrodes traditional social relationships. He maintains that Hume and other Englishmen who complain of the depopulation of their country fail to understand that it is due to an increase in wealth and an attendant increase in consumption.[34]

Englishmen may or may not have been right in thinking that their population was decreasing, but Mirabeau, accepting their diagnosis, associated wealth with consumption and believed that it led to depopulation. This destructive concentration of wealth may be avoided, he argues, by the maximum subdivision of the national territory: "It is this repartition, this difference *of thine* from *mine,* principal of all evils as the poets used to say, which makes all the enlivement (*vivification*) of the State." Or in one of his most frequently quoted lines: "The large pike depopulate the ponds; the large proprietors stifle the small." Small proprietors grant the land that loving attention and individual care which alone assure its maximum productivity.[35]

Subsequent commentators, concerned with their own views on the concentration of wealth, or in pursuit of the development of property theory, readily assume that Mirabeau's espousal of small property revealed, in the words of Tocqueville, "the invasion of democratic ideas in a feudal mind."[36] But, despite a certain respect for the small peasant, Mirabeau betrays little interest in democracy. His thought does have a quality that makes him appear in retrospect like a sort of spiritual predecessor

34. *L'ami des hommes,* 20, 25. Cf. Cantillon, *Essai,* 85.
35. *L'ami des hommes,* 45–46, 47.
36. Tocqueville, *Oeuvres,* II, pt. 2, 440.

of the "red tories"; and it is surely not without significance that he attracted Tocqueville's careful attention. Unfortunately, Tocqueville's copious notes on Mirabeau have been lost; but Loménie, to whom he gave them, incorporated many in the text of his history of the Mirabeau. The final seal on the Mirabeau legacy was set by Loménie's grandnephew, Beau de Loménie, who earned his reputation as a "Marxist-Legitimist" by cataloguing every sin and shady parliamentary combination of those bourgeois dynasties which destroyed traditional society and led the French nation irretrievably astray.

Tocqueville and the Loménies were weighing Mirabeau's ideas against a world in which bourgeois concepts of property had triumphed, and they assumed that when Mirabeau wrote about small property, he meant independent ownership in the context of a market economy. But at this point in his career, Mirabeau had given little if any thought to the meaning of property. His brief discussion of savages at the dawn of civilization shows that he understood property to include personal effects and private dwellings and assumed that his contemporaries would share his understanding. Yet he never defines the word, and since he argues that property constitutes the basis of social relations, his modern readers must grapple with peculiar problems.

Mirabeau favors landed property as a counterweight to social mobility, which he equates with social disintegration. Similarly, he opposes monetary wealth as a solvent of social bonds. He does, however, understand that the two forms of property have become inextricably entwined as the "fief" has become more a source of income than a means of fulfilling a personal service. The rise of commerce and the quest for luxury have further undermined the independent role of the land as an end in itself. Modern practice includes encumbering landed property with rents, contracts, and mortgages which slowly transfer ownership to the owners of capital. Yet these new owners, not living on the land, have no moral sense of property, no love for the land, no desire to improve it. Money thus undermines "real" property, although as Mirabeau recognizes with dismay, it is also a form of property. As his argument becomes more confused, Mirabeau begins to recognize that his private distinction between legitimate and illegitimate property could threaten his defense of the sanctity of property per se and lead to further embarrassing questions about social order, rank, and privilege. Hastily, he retreats, protesting that he intends no subversion of existing society.[37]

My political principle, if it were in me to have one, would be to so respect public law, that all title of property, even the worst acquired as to the past, should be a peaceable and assured possession; that all engagements, even the most burdensome and forced, be sacred in society, and that it is only by just and gentle means that I should wish to engage each individual to voluntarily divide his own fortune to procure himself more precious and esteemed advantages. Here it is, therefore, no question of the title, but of the usufruct only.[38]

Mirabeau has reached a theoretical impasse that prefigures the dilemma later faced by physiocracy. He believes that society should conform to a moral imperative; he also believes that recent developments in France have undermined the social fabric. He would even like to argue that the spread of merchant and finance capital is not only contrary to moral norms, but also contrary to economic well-being. To do so, however, he has to repudiate economic growth entirely and advocate a simple return to a healthier past. At the same time, he so values social order, even when based on false practices, that he prefers preserving it to contemplating the revolutionary transformation (dispossessing *rentiers*) that would bring the present configuration more in line with his moral imperative. Both morality and economic well-being depend upon the preservation of social order. Established property must be held sacred.

Mirabeau unquestionably understood that even property in land, the true basis of his society, had two separate aspects— seigneurial and absolute. His support for multiple subdivisions

37. *L'ami des hommes,* 134–37.
38. *Ibid.,* 137.

recognizes the peasants' thirst for possession of the land they worked and managed, and endorses a common eighteenth-century practice. Peasants no longer worked the lord's demesne, but rather an individual plot that more or less supported their family and yielded a quitrent (*cens*), frequently in kind, for the lord. Having become accustomed to passing their land on to their children, they regarded it as theirs.[39] Mirabeau approved this sense of possession as a motivation for sound agricultural practice and good moral behavior. "What a difference," he insists, "between the fertility of a small domaine that furnishes the subsistance of a laboring family and that of these vast countrysides given over to passing farmers or lazy or self-interested agents, charged with contributing to the luxury of their masters, immersed in the presumptuous ignorance of cities."[40] One is struck, however, at the way he sidesteps the question of the quitrent and other seigneurial dues. Although he castigates the farmers and agents who collected dues for absent owners, he does not object to resident nobles drawing such dues, which constituted the second component of landed property. Legally, the peasant did not own the land and had no title to its surplus. Instead, the surplus constituted part of what Mirabeau euphemistically called the lord's "advantages" and derived from his property rights in the land.[41]

39. Cf. Marcel Garaud, *Histoire générale du droit privé français (de 1789 à 1804)*, vol. II, *La Révolution et la propriété foncière* (Paris, 1959), 15–16; and Philippe Sagnac, "L'agriculture et les classes rurales en France au dix-huitième siècle," *Revue de synthèse historique*, XII (1906), 133–51. See Jean Meyer, *La noblesse bretonne au XVIIIe siècle*, 2 vols. (Paris, 1966), II, 734–77, on the special *domaine congéable* and *complaint nantais*.

40. *L'ami des hommes*, 43.

41. Garaud, *Revolution et propriété foncière*, 7, 17–109; Philippe Sagnac, "La propriété foncière et les paysans pendant la Révolution (1789–1793)," in Emile Faguet, ed., *L'oeuvre sociale de la Révolution française* (Paris, n.d.), 219–71; Loménie, *Les Mirabeau*, II, 18–34; Albert Soboul, "La communauté rurale (XVIIIe–XIXe siècle): Problèmes de base," *Revue de synthèse*, LXXVIII (1957); Martin Göhring, *Die Frage der Feudalität in Frankreich* (Berlin, 1934), esp. 9–38; and Meyer, *Noblesse bretonne*, II, esp. 777–805. For the most recent general overview, see Labrousse *et al.*, 473–81.

Mirabeau understood this aspect of property; his own income depended on it. He heartily defends feudal law and even argues that that law bears a direct relationship to the control of land, which always confers "a sort of luster and rank, independently of the preeminence and jurisdiction of fiefs over their inhabitants: invention which, although gothic is no less admirable.⁴² No other form of property can carry with it the same combination of pecuniary advantage and moral authority. "The proprietor of land naturally has a jurisdiction of dependence over the cultivators, a consideration and a natural rapport in the country-side, whereas the possessor of contracts is known only to the prosecutor who watches out for the conservation of his mortgage; and the man whose fortune is in houses, has no other relation on that account than with his entrepreneur, the mason and the notary who draws up the leases."⁴³ And finally, the material advantages of landed estates must not be neglected, for there are always "profits and good returns in lands." He knew whereof he spoke.

Mirabeau recognizes that the feudal nobility enjoyed a kind of property in its honors, jurisdictions, and economic perquisites. He ignores the possible conflicts between the interests of that small property, over which he waxes so sentimental, and those of the large estates, which he finds grounded in feudal law. He would prefer to see all conflicts as clashes between mobile and landed property, and thus he offers a clash of systems rather than of classes. Agriculture, he assures us, should not only be preferred because of its superior moral qualities, but also because it affords "more certain and more considerable profits than those of maritime commerce, even than the search for gold."⁴⁴ But his real point is that it offers a dependable, stable, and sociably acceptable profit.

Mirabeau does not share Quesnay's view that agriculture should be a source of capital accumulation; he prefers to see it simply as

42. *L'ami des hommes,* 55.
43. *Ibid.*
44. *Ibid.,* 36.

a source of revenue. He has no use for the farmers whom Quesnay praises so highly as the vehicle for maximizing returns by economies of scale. Nothing could be further from Mirabeau's mind than separating the laborer from the land. Where Quesnay intuitively recognized the growth and implicitly praised the advantage of a market in free labor, Mirabeau repudiates it completely, together with all other commercial intrusions into the social relations of traditional agriculture.

Although Mirabeau learned his economics from men reared in and committed to the commercial world, he appropriated their language without accepting their world view. He discusses commerce at some length, including questions of foreign trade, but he reveals his deep mistrust of the process when he states that it should be limited to "the exchange of the necessities and commodities of life, [and] in no way [include] . . . properties."[45] He even deplores the modern habit of changing the furnishings of a house and rejects the argument that it serves a positive economic function by providing work for many. Old castles, in which the furnishings have been cherished and handed down from generation to generation, he insists, contain much greater wealth. The chateau is the proper home of the surplus. There furniture accumulates, whereas the town houses of Paris foster only transient conspicuous consumption, and the pretentious change of furnishings only provides a livelihood for rogues (*fripons*).[46] The passage echoes the language of last wills and testaments of a traditional society in which such furnishings accounted for a significant portion of family wealth, and it completely repudiates the deepest insight of Cantillon's defense of luxury.

Mirabeau pursues his attack on mobile wealth and claims he can prove "that the continual transfer of goods and fortunes is not an advantage for commerce." It has undermined the solid

45. *Ibid.*, 100. The whole third part of the work is devoted to commerce.
46. *Ibid.*, 101.

traditional hierarchy, because everyone wishes to make his son a noble. So the peasants forsake the useful profession into which they were born, while the true nobility, assaulted by money on all sides, can barely provide for its own. This social disintegration can only be halted by guaranteeing fiefs and letting others make their properties an object of commerce if they so choose. In order to prevent profits from disturbing the true life of society, all intermarriage between classes must be prohibited. Society would benefit enormously if everyone married within his own estate, or better yet, within his own occupational grouping. Misalliances destroy the social fabric.[47]

Although Mirabeau protests that his interest lies in economics, not politics, he admits, "I cannot prevent myself from saying in passing that the respect for the old stock, all other things being equal, supports subordination and order among the inhabitants of the countryside."[48] Peasants are never fooled by an *anobli;* they have long memories and never forget that the recently ennobled are no better than they. The old nobles may have vexed their peasants on occasion, but at least as resident landowners, they vexed them in person, "which is certainly better" than vexing them by proxy. In the past, nobles of character actually contributed to the well-being of their peasants. "The poor, the sick were succored at the castle; the orphans found their subsistence there and became domestics. There was, in a word, a direct rapport from the lord to his subject and, in consequence, more ties and fewer irritants on one side and the other."[49] Mirabeau does his best to reinforce this paternalistic tradition with an economic argument clearly derived from Cantillon. He compares the proprietor to a river.

If he is at the head of production, of which he should naturally be the soul, and in which no one has a greater interest than he, he

47. *Ibid.,* 102–7.
48. *Ibid.,* 64.
49. *Ibid.,* 62. Cf. Lawrence Stone, *The Crisis of the Aristocracy, 1558–1641,* abr. ed. (Oxford, 1967), esp. 105, 143.

assures and enlivens the whole canton, he protects the isolated agriculturalist; or, if the rusticity of the country deprives him of such honest and enlightened views, which is only too much to be feared today, at least by the necessity of his position he will accomplish a part of the good one should expect from him. If, on the contrary, he is at the center of consumption, he is the low and swampy stream and contributes to drowning a territory already too damp on its own.[50]

Once again, Mirabeau gets his economics backwards, or rather, since he was by no means stupid, willfully turns it upside down.

Mirabeau understands that his defense of the nobility might occasion some demurs, but protests that his nobles are the custodians of the national honor and the general interest. When they reside on their estates and play their proper role, they guarantee that "particular interest instead of harming the public interest serves it. The more a man exploits his lands and multiplies their productions, the more men he makes live, the more he increases the subsistence of the State."[51]

Mirabeau's reading of Cantillon and Hume cannot begin to compare with Quesnay's in analytic sophistication, but he did share with him a general understanding that particular or special interest, as heretofore manifested in French society, might require some taming—not to say coercing—before it could be relied upon to promote the public weal. Mirabeau and Quesnay differ, however, on how this domestication should best be accomplished. Quesnay's argument for large-scale agriculture and an attendant divorce between land and labor implicitly sacrificed the traditional community to economic growth, no matter how much he sought to guard against that result. Mirabeau implicitly sacrificed economic growth to the preservation of community, complete with its resident nobility, no matter how much lip service he paid to market economics.

All that Mirabeau wants is that "everyone live" by his own

50. *L'ami des hommes*, 81. Cf. the difference of emphasis in Cantillon, *Essai*, 59.
51. *L'ami des hommes*, 87.

work. The larger the population, the less expensive life will be. But inequalities of wealth hinder the growth of population, and "like all other vices of a State are a consequence of prosperity and power."[52] The whole trouble derives from the abundance of gold, the most serious consequence of which has been to undermine all traditional authority and values. "Respect, consideration, authority, preeminence, etc. are goods precious, in all times, to human opinion; but these goods are only gradually distributed over the surface of a state, gaining as they are spread out, and losing as they are accumulated. Gold, on the contrary, once put in the place of all these things, only gives a false appearance, only draws forced homages to itself, puts nothing in order, even insinuates disorder everywhere."[53] Mirabeau, describing the effect of merchant and finance capital upon a traditional society, judges the price too high. In the interests of restoring social harmony and an orderly community, he urges the state to relinquish all pretensions of grandeur and return to its traditional role. He does not, however, ask it to sacrifice its authority, but rather its misguided pursuit of wealth that has undermined its legitimate power. For him, throne and altar remain essential to social order.[54]

Mirabeau never doubts that religion constitutes the indispensable cement of an ordered society. He defies anyone to show him a direct attack on religion that "does not at the same time carry this spirit of discussion of the rights of sovereigns." In their talk of contracts, the "blind," "liberal" philosophes rival the most odious tyrants in ignoring the "coeternal contract between authority and dependence," established by the Creator for "protection and surety on the part of authority, . . . obedience and service on the part of dependence, and above all . . . respective love on one side and the other." Since religion is "without contradiction the first and most useful brake on humanity, . . . the

52. *Ibid.*, 144, 145.
53. *Ibid.*, 145.
54. *Ibid.*, 20–23. He even defended monarchism and church property as constructive contributions to social order.

first mainspring of civilization," its priests deserve every respect. This spiritual force must have that political embodiment as a duly constituted estate which it has earned. "Without religion, the assemblies of men would never have taken the form of society." Those enemies of the clergy who wish to deny them their legitimate political role fail to understand how dangerous it would be for the ministers of the faith to have no part in government. To pretend that they can be reduced to the spiritual realm alone "is to relegate them to imaginary spaces. Independent of their rights to temporal administration, as possessors of fiefs, jurisdiction and other goods, as the national guides of morals, everything is of their province in the capacity of consultation."[55]

Both Quesnay and Mirabeau saw that property was central to the issues with which they were grappling, but neither came to grips with the problem in their early work. Mirabeau never shared Quesnay's doubts about property, but then, he did not try to define it either. He unquestionably wished to preserve noble property—the fief—as an inviolable right; but he did not approve of large noble estates and explicitly denounced their proprietors and their commercial counterparts. Part of his abhorrence of large estates derived from his knowledge that many of them had passed out of the hands of the old nobility and into those of tax-farmers or recently ennobled merchants. In addition, he opposed the use of agents or farmers to collect the rents or exploit the lands. Yet he never condoned unmanageably large estates for the resident nobles either. His preference for the noble producer over the noble consumer (presumably courtier) suggests his opposition to large accumulations of wealth for any member of society. He states plainly that the essence of property rights in a fief lies in its "advantages," its honors and distinctions, its right of command. Such rights lend themselves only with difficulty to marketplace exchange—the higher their mobility, the

55. *Ibid.*, 246, 149, 150, 151.

less their moral authority. For that reason, Mirabeau opposed all aristocratic involvement in market transactions, and sought, rather, to defend the nobility's position as an estate or caste even at the sacrifice of its economic interests.[56]

At no point does Mirabeau explain the source of noble income beyond attributing it to land. His talk of châteaux, furnishings, and charity to subjects leaves no doubt that he envisaged noble income as substantial, however much he deplored excess. Since he hardly intended to work his fields himself, he clearly expected his revenue to come from seigneurial dues and *cens*. Despite his enthusiastic support for small peasant property, he was no Tom Paine or Rousseau. His peasants were to own their land only in the sense that peasants generally owned land in eighteenth-century France. They were to enjoy secure life tenancy with the possibility of succession for their offspring; but their title would remain one of usufruct, not outright possession. On the face of it, such an arrangement would differ little from the long-term English tenant leases Quesnay and the *agronomes* so much admired. But the lord's traditional title to the economic surplus that accompanied his eminent domaine and the seigneurial rights did make a difference which the peasants fiercely resented. Without access to their surplus, they had no way of making the capital investments requisite to sustained economic growth, but that problem Mirabeau ignored.

Where Quesnay had understood that a market in labor would accelerate capital accumulation and economic transformation, Mirabeau also understood that it would destroy the social system. He therefore urged the necessity of binding men to the land in ever greater numbers, since land put to any other use than the creation of human subsistence ipso facto detracted from its gross output and therefore retarded population growth. One horse, that is, takes the place of four men by consuming the produce necessary to their survival.[57] Never did he admit the possibility

---

56. Cf. Tocqueville, *Oeuvres*, II, pt. 2, 442, and Labrousse *et al.*, 473–78.
57. *L'ami des hommes*, 95. Cf. Cantillon, *Essai*, 75.

that if the horse took the place of men in the process of production and produced, say, four times what it consumed, it would in fact assure the subsistence of sixteen men. The gap between Quesnay's and Mirabeau's understanding of the function of labor can be seen clearly in their attitudes towards China. Where Quesnay saw only the piteous waste of millions of human beings eking out a scant livelihood from a disastrously labor-intensive culture, Mirabeau saw a wondrously wise people who, being "persuaded that from the use of land depends . . . the means of subsistence which one extracts from them, that the extent of the means of subsistence is the exact measure of population, and that population is the only true wealth of the State, regard as a crime the use of land for houses or gardens of pleasure, as if by them one defrauded men of their nourishment."[58]

In *L'ami*, Mirabeau betrays no understanding of Quesnay's distinction between the gross and the net product. In fact, Mirabeau probably did not merely fail to understand, but actually did not favor economic growth. His desire to increase the output of agriculture and the national population was aimed at the realization of existing French economic potential, which he took to be finite. He advocates maximizing the return from traditional agriculture, but believes that what his contemporaries took for economic progress—the increase of monetary wealth derived from various commercial undertakings—would actually undermine the nation's economic health. In this hatred for merchant and finance capital he does approach Quesnay's perspective, particularly when he argues that the only legitimate commerce is that of the proprietor who "exchanges the excess of the product of his land for the things which it does not furnish him and which he needs." In words that might have come from Quesnay's own pen, he distinguishes such commerce from that of "the mercenary who traffics the product of others and who finds his subsistence and frequently fat profits merely by being the inter-

58. *L'ami des hommes*, 67. Cf. Cantillon, *Essai*, 67–69.

mediary of the exchange."[59] But if Quesnay and Mirabeau agree that the development of trade and neglect of agriculture destroy national wealth, they remain a world apart in the analyses underlying their common judgment. Mirabeau had no interest in the price mechanism—when he mentions prices at all, it is to argue that they are too high—or in the profitable marketing of agricultural produce. He even sees monetary circulation more in moral than in economic terms.

Mirabeau's preoccupation with the restoration of a state of traditional well-being and harmony also emerges from his discussion of the state. No more than Quesnay does Mirabeau set out to write a treatise on political theory, but his various references to the state suggest a definition quite different from that which Quesnay apparently had in mind. According to Mirabeau, "The entire body of society" is "what we call the State." Society, being ridden with the conflicting principles of cupidity and sociability, requires direction, and Mirabeau holds the sovereign responsible for this task. At another point he argues that man cannot possibly assure himself of "the subsistence and commodities of life, if his work is not protected against the cupidity of his neighbors by a universal and superior regime. This superior regime is what we call *the Government*." But, he continues, the preservation and security of the individual also require that each individual be necessary to the public of which he is a member, and adds that "the territory which this public occupies is what we call the *State*." The state, he specifies, is a generic name also used "to express the mass and the body of the public thing."[60]

Mirabeau sees the relations between state and society as inextricably entwined. "The surety, the work, and the ease of individuals alone constitute the veritable prosperity of a State. . . . But . . . it is up to the State to procure for individuals the surety, the work and the ease of which it receives the fruits." To Mirabeau this relationship once again proves that "everything

59. *L'ami des hommes*, 175.
60. *Ibid.*, 178–80, 8.

makes a circle here below"; and he maintains that this "paternal distribution is, in the divine decrees, as well as by human prudence, the only object of what we call Government." Anything which exceeds its just distribution "must be called abuse"; and he shows that historically the sovereign power has offered protection for the individual members of society while they, in turn, have supplied the sovereign with the tribute necessary to provide that protection. Originally this exchange was effected in kind, more recently it has been effected by money payments; but the same principle operates in both cases. The money that circulates between sovereign and subjects is merely the sign of their mutual dependence.[61]

Mirabeau displays none of the mercantilist zeal to enrich the state. Exchange between state and society can be no other than that which should govern all commercial relations—equal value received for equal value rendered. Furthermore, Mirabeau takes pains to refute, as tactfully as possible, the absolutist pretensions of the Bourbon monarchy perfected by Louis XIV. While, he maintains, "it would be difficult to prove . . . that all France does not belong to the king, as the king belongs to France; there is only, in this respect, to understand one another." Those who suppose that Louis XIV thought his royal authority extended to the private properties of individuals also "suppose him crazy, and never was a man less so."[62] In these words Mirabeau, who included traditional rights and privileges within his definition of property, set substantial limits to his sovereign's power.

Starting from the same historical experience, Quesnay and Mirabeau arrived at different concepts of the state. Although they both rejected the mercantilist claims for the contribution of commercial wealth to national power, they differed in their notions of national well-being. Quesnay's interest in political economy was the product of his preoccupation with economic analysis. Fascinated by his vision of the net product, he more or

61. *Ibid.*, 171–72.
62. *Ibid.*, 185–87.

less accepted the mercantilist or absolutist concept of a unitary state, distinct from the society over which it presided. He did not totally ignore the claims of society, for he did favor such reforms as a more equitable taxation and relief from militia service for the peasantry; but he never undertook a systematic investigation of the social system. Obsessed with the production of a net product, Quesnay studied economic rather than social relations, and the state figured in his thought as the monolithic unit which received the surplus product of the national economy.

Mirabeau always remained concerned with the state as a part of a larger social system. He placed it at the summit of a hierarchy that it must guarantee in order to preserve its own legitimacy. The production of wealth serves both state and society in their common pursuit of prosperity, but never emerges as an end in itself or as the special perquisite of the state. Mirabeau repeatedly emphasized the necessity for distribution and circulation of goods as the means of assuring the perpetuation of an existing and time-honored system.

Mirabeau's strong preference for agriculture over commerce differs from Quesnay's in that Mirabeau saw agriculture as the foundation of a stable social system, which commercial wealth was threatening with destruction. He thus opposed creation of a *noblesse commerçante* on the grounds that such a modification of the existing social order would "tend to overthrow . . . the fundamental principles of the monarchy." Quesnay, however, simply argued that agriculture rather than commerce provided the true source of wealth and accepted the state as the logical beneficiary of economic growth. For Mirabeau the state was nothing other than "a collection of individual homes," with the implication that increased prosperity should accrue equally to all.[63] Thus Quesnay postulates a unitary state as beneficiary of his economic system, whereas Mirabeau postulates a state presiding over the social system of which it remains a part. But the conceptions of both remain riddled with ambiguities. From

63. *Ibid.*, 115, 173, 101.

separate perspectives they criticized the path taken by the absolute monarchy since the reign of Louis XIV even as they defended the coherence it had brought to the national life of France.

Both men, in their separate ways, failed to extricate themselves from the tradition in which had been reared, and yet each attempted to impart a new content to that tradition. For Quesnay and Mirabeau alike, economic analysis offered the most promising new method of social discourse. During the same short span of years they both read and were deeply influenced by Cantillon and Hume, whose insights they tried to apply to their own society. In the realm of economic analysis Quesnay far outdistanced Mirabeau and laid the foundation for a revolutionary theory. But Mirabeau, in his attempt to integrate Cantillon's analysis into his own ideological framework, pointed the way to the development of a comprehensive view of society. His very insistence upon organic social relations, combined with his inclination to reduce the state to an emanation of society as a whole, opened the door to a central—as opposed to merely tactical—role for economics in the larger social system. It remained for Mirabeau to convince Quesnay of the importance of the social dimension of any political economy, and for Quesnay to convince Mirabeau that his specific social commitment could only be realized by the sacrifice of its historical form and the translation of its moral force into a new economic language.

Quesnay and Mirabeau
Confront the Monarchy

Mirabeau's "conversion" after the stormy first interview at Versailles inaugurated a period of intense collaboration between himself and Quesnay. On the face of it, the two men could not have had less in common. To this day, their respective intellectual partisans remain fiercely divided. Quesnay, an upwardly mobile, recently ennobled professional, had firmly identified himself in his economic articles with the tradition of the great royal ministers, and had implicitly advocated a kind of "enlightened despotism." However much he differed with some specific policies, he enthusiastically adopted the perspective of the crown, complete with the bureaucracy and intendants necessary to impose the royal will. Mirabeau, scion of a provincial noble house, had with equal firmness taken his stand among the most unreconstructed elements of the aristocracy. In defense of what he believed to be the traditional French community (resident nobles and serfs), he was prepared to dismantle not only absolutism but also the robe nobility and to do away with the use of money.

The two men thus embodied, in their lives as well as in their intellectual perspectives, two profoundly contradictory interpretations of the proper nature and role of the monarchy. But their collaboration, which took the form of an extraordinary and sustained dialogue, ultimately resulted in the formulation of physiocracy. Neither Quesnay nor Mirabeau, however, approached their common effort as physiocrats, nor even as conscious innovators, much less as consciously radical opponents of the official ideology of their own society. Both had independently established themselves as critics of recent monarchical policies, but neither intended to challenge what they understood to be the deeper principles of monarchical hegemony. They did not set out to forge a new ideology; they set out to restore an old one. Yet the confrontation of their ideas on the essence of monarchy, within a context of mutual respect and shared purpose, resulted in a radically new interpretation of the constituent elements of legitimate government. Together, by a complex process of mutual criticism, they effected a revolution in the conception of the relationship between state and society.

Neither Quesnay nor Mirabeau started as liberals. Had either been more fully integrated into the avant-garde of Parisian intellectual life or more fully identified with the actual workings of the regime, they might never have developed their unique and cogent perspective. Surely neither, working alone, would have formulated physiocratic theory. As it was, however, beyond their shared commitment to revitalizing the monarchy—as each envisioned it—they brought to their work a particularly powerful alliance of opposing talents, sensibilities, and political traditions.

The confrontation between Quesnay and Mirabeau must be understood as the confrontation between the two most important strains of political thought developed under the ancien régime, the statist versus the "feudal" (or social) interpretation of the nature of authority. Both were designed, from different perspectives, to buttress the traditional, hierarchical model of society. Quesnay and Mirabeau did no more than add systematic economic analysis as a variable of the debate, or as a new language in which to pursue it. Yet when Quesnay and Mirabeau fought out their differences through the history of the French monarchy, the resolution of their confrontation produced an ideology that implicitly repudiated that monarchy and the principles upon which it rested.

The published results of Quesnay's and Mirabeau's initial

collaboration appeared under Mirabeau's name, and at his risk, as parts 4 (1758) and 5–6 (1759) of *L'ami des hommes*. That public record, however, remains incomprehensible if divorced from Quesnay's and Mirabeau's prior and strictly private investigation of the monarchy. The elaboration of physiocratic doctrine must be followed through the manuscripts that shadow the published work. In them lies a clear account of an almost unique example of intellectual partnership. Along with some letters, this collection includes the drafts of Mirabeau's unpublished as well as published work, many of them extensively annotated in Quesnay's hand, as well as Quesnay's projects including the first two editions of the Tableau. Quesnay's numerous corrections of Mirabeau's drafts contribute to the common assumption that the one molded the other's thought. But during these years Mirabeau did all the writing except for the most technical economic analysis, for which he accepted Quesnay as undisputed master. And even in relation to the economic analysis one tends to forget that Quesnay had to make Mirabeau understand it, if Mirabeau were to defend it coherently. No one has ever suggested that Mirabeau provided the actual impetus for the construction of the Tableau, but since the first edition appeared in December 1758, seventeen months after the two met, it seems at least possible that Quesnay first devised it in part to instruct his disciple.[1]

Scholars have invariably concentrated upon Quesnay's contri-

1. AN, M 778–785. The first two editions of the Tableau and the accompanying letters are in M 784. See Weulersse, *Manuscrits*. Meek, *Economics*, 65–68, 108–25, also provides selected translations from the economic manuscripts although the second group, entirely devoted to the Tableau, has in part been superseded by his and Marguerite Kuczynski's *Quesnay's Tableau*. Cf. also Quesnay to Mirabeau, December 1758, announcing the first "edition" of the Tableau, M 784, no. 70. This letter has been frequently reproduced. Cf. Stephan Bauer, "Quesnay's Tableau économique," *Economic Journal*, V (1895), 1–21; Gustave Schelle, *Le docteur Quesnay* (Paris, 1907), 389–90; and Meek, *Economics*, 108. For the most authoritative treatment of the problems of dating, see Meek's "Introduction," *Quesnay's Tableau*. See Chapter 6, note 1, for full citation to the additions to *L'ami des hommes*.

butions to the economic manuscripts. Even Weulersse, in introducing his excerpts from Mirabeau's unpublished "Traité de la monarchie," admitted that it was "not the draft itself of this unpublished treatise that struck us as interesting, but certain of the notes which Quesnay put on it." Henry Higgs, in his review of the collection, confirmed Weulersse's judgment, declaring "that it was altogether useless to publish what Mirabeau himself—the man of the hand of bronze . . . who so tired the printers—had not judged worthy to see the light of day."[2] The justification for this interpretation, if there is any, would surely be that Quesnay's observations have a ring of bourgeois "modernity" totally lacking in those of his disciple; but in fact nothing in his early work foreshadows that radical critique of the pre-Revolutionary social or political system which now attracts scholars to his comments on Mirabeau's manuscripts. To take those comments as direct harbingers of a new radical vision can only distort their nature, for in the realm of political economy Quesnay's thought, unlike Mirabeau's, remained unsystematic.

Mirabeau and Quesnay served each other well as catalysts. Quesnay's economics and metaphysics destroyed the premises of Mirabeau's ideology, but Mirabeau, after his own fashion, had repaired the damage, and in so doing had showed Quesnay the unity and coherence his own thought still lacked. Mirabeau demonstrated not only that policy recommendations would not suffice, but that Quesnay's economics urgently required an integral formulation that described and legitimized social organization as forcefully as the traditional vision had. Quesnay's disagreements with Mirabeau reflected the seriousness with which he took Mirabeau's insistence on the elaboration of a coherent system of social and political life. His rejection of Mirabeau's outmoded prejudices and pretensions never implied a rejection of Mirabeau's commitment to the systematic formulation of their views of

2. Weulersse, *Manuscrits*, 20; Higgs, quoted by Weulersse in his introductory remarks to "Bref état," 177 (full citation, note 5 below).

human experience. Quesnay's frequently aphoristic comments delight but they remain ad hoc objections. Mirabeau laid out the problem, Quesnay criticized the specifics, and then Mirabeau reorganized his proposals and Quesnay's criticisms into the final argument. Over a period of time, this dialectic procedure led both men to search for principles and forms that would guarantee the stability of a complex community.

Shortly after Mirabeau encountered Quesnay, he embarked upon the series of projects that developed into the revised and enlarged editions of *L'ami des hommes*. At Quesnay's instigation he began with a revision of his *Mémoire concernant l'utilité des états provinciaux* published in 1750, which involved not only overhauling the original text but also drafting a preliminary discourse and a "Traité de la monarchie." Although the treatise passed through a number of drafts in response to Quesnay's scrupulous criticism, it never reached the public, not because of its persisting weaknesses but because of its incredible political indiscretion. Mirabeau seems not to have understood the danger, and in 1760 he would go to prison for the much milder *Théorie de l'impôt*. Quesnay possessed a much larger measure of political realism, but neither saw any contradiction in a proposal that a monarchy should radically reform the system on which that monarchy depended. Their failure revealed not so much the limits of their intelligence as the central dilemma of the ancien régime itself. Quesnay and Mirabeau had both independently inaugurated their investigation of political economy with a critique of the course of the absolute monarchy since the reign of Louis XIV. Quesnay's economics led to their common desire to increase the royal revenues, and Mirabeau's sociology to their attempt to establish a satisfactory basis for the social allocation of resources and the adequate protection of society from impingements of the state. Like Montesquieu, Quesnay and Mirabeau regarded the monarchy not merely as one form of government among many but as the form of government generic to a landed kingdom, with all other forms no more than corruptions of this ideal.[3] But as the French monarchy of their day was unfortunately prey to just such corruption, they proposed to set it back on its true course.

Practically from the moment of their first meeting Quesnay must have impressed upon Mirabeau the need to increase the financial resources of the monarchy, for sometime between 1756 and 1760 Mirabeau drafted a "Bref état des moyens pour la restauration de l'autorité du roi et de ses finances." Weulersse, who first published the "Bref état" in 1913, refrained from dating its composition precisely. Yet both the title of the work and additional internal evidence point conclusively to the period immediately following Quesnay's and Mirabeau's first meeting and prior to their collaboration on the "Traité de la monarchie." Indeed, Mirabeau must have offered the "Bref état" to Quesnay as the first proof of his conversion. The initial limits of the conversion, however, emerge clearly from the title, format, and contents of the work.[4]

As the title clearly states, Mirabeau remains wedded to restoring the authority of the king, by which he means the traditional authority derived from a properly religious and feudal society. He tacks on finances, obviously to please Quesnay, as something of an afterthought, and thereby implies that fiscal needs can be handled within, and without jeopardy to, the traditional social

3. AN, M 778, no. 1, "Traité de la monarchie," sec. 1, esp. 6; and *Théorie de l'impôt* (n.p., 1760). Bibliothèque de l'Arsenal, Fonds de la Bastille, no. 12, 101 contains papers pertaining to Mirabeau's detention at Vincennes, 15–24 December 1760.

4. AN, M 783, no. 2. In his introductory remarks to the "Bref état," 177, Weulersse places the date between 1757 and 1760. In his *Manuscrits*, 5, he places it at "around 1757 or 1758." As I shall argue below, I think the nature and level of the arguments advanced strongly indicate that it was composed before the "Traité." Cf. Jacqueline Hecht, "La vie de François Quesnay," INED, I, 258, who places the date of Quesnay's annotations "very shortly after [he] met Mirabeau."

context. Mirabeau chose to interpret royal finances as dependent upon the entire activity of society, and Quesnay confirmed his judgment in marginal annotations almost as long as the text. Mirabeau did not yet, however, understand that increasing fiscal yields along the lines proposed in Quesnay's economic analysis might entail altering the structure of the society he cherished.

The substantive positions of both Quesnay and Mirabeau as advanced in the "Bref état" recur in more extended and interesting form in the "Traité" and do not require separate treatment. The format, however, deserves attention. Unlike the "Traité" or the "Introduction" to the revised version of the *Mémoire concernant les états provinciaux*, which constitute essentially theoretical discussions, the "Bref état" is cast as a manual for the prince, much like Quesnay's numerous sets of "Maximes." Mirabeau adopted that format, characteristic also of much earlier political writing, as a vehicle for persuading the monarch to restore the traditional order. His chronicle of rules to be observed includes sections pertaining to the rites of the court, religion, morals, laws, *police*, agriculture, industry, commerce, and finances, and represents the sum of his and Quesnay's interests rather than an integration of the two. He particularly insists upon the need to reinstitute strict religious observances and social distinctions which he deems every bit as important as sound administration and finances to royal authority.

Quesnay's marginal comments never suggest that he, any more than Mirabeau, regards religion as irrelevant to royal authority, but he does not share Mirabeau's passion to restore the traditional order by fiat. The political pretensions of the church, the imposed religious uniformity, the legislation of morals, all strike him as dysfunctional anachronisms at best and veritable hazards at worst. Quesnay, in the role of critic of Mirabeau, emerges as the most rational and modern of men, no longer accepting institutionalized religion as the foundation of, and justification for, social organization. He objects to that fanaticism which, on such occasions as the Revocation of the Edict of Nantes, deprived the kingdom of valuable subjects, and to those political ambitions which threaten the unity of the state. He also instinctively rejects a rigid social structure. But for all his brave talk of concern for individuals as the criterion for the utility of laws, the utility of individuals as the guarantee of their status, the considerations prescribed by natural law, and the spontaneous public order, he has not welded these notions into any coherent world view, let alone reconciled them with the realities of his own world. Furthermore, his professed tolerance evaporates completely when he turns to economic questions or to the role of financiers.[5]

Every bit as much as Mirabeau, Quesnay sought a higher authority that would unilaterally justify his program and anchor society. Like Mirabeau, he wanted a necessity that would command the obedience of sovereigns. Unlike Mirabeau, he did not expect the old religious and feudal world view to do the job; but neither did he believe that the philosophes had provided a viable alternative. Those "moralist-political philosophers," he wrote, lacked any a priori basis for their opinions and had accordingly "built on sand." If a philosopher is to have any hope of convincing a prince to behave in conformity with the true principles of monarchical government, he must have more than opinions in his arsenal. "It is not enough to propose rules to monarchs; it is necessary to make these rules obligatory by a sanction."[6]

At this point Quesnay is arguing passionately that good government requires the whip of necessity, and his understanding of the nature of that necessity differs surprisingly little from Mirabeau's. Although he rejects Mirabeau's attempt to resurrect the

---

5. "Bref état des moyens pour la restauration de l'autorité du roi et de ses finances," ed. Georges Weulersse, *RHES*, VI (1913), 177–211, esp. 187–88. This edition is identical to the manuscript version (including Quesnay's notes) except that, with good reason, it omits the first section, "Les rites de la cour," which shows Mirabeau at his most pretentious and banal. See also *Quesnay's Tableau*, app. A, n.p.

6. AN, M 778, no. 116, closing note.

idealist necessity of traditional society, as well as its embodiment in church and hierarchy, he does not yet know what to replace it with. Despite his rejection of many of the specific forms of traditional society, his tacit assumptions about the principles of social organization still derive from the traditional vision of a corporate community under God. Mirabeau's "Traité de la monarchie" provided both men with the chance to work through the history of the monarchy to find those principles which they regarded as the essence of good government. Breaking free of the ideological constraints of the society in which they were reared, however, cost a degree of effort that indicates the tremendous difficulties of formulating a new way of perceiving and justifying the purposes of society. Locke, Mandeville, and Hume had at least the advantage of elaborating their theories of property and government in terms of a newly reordered society.

Sometime toward the end of 1757, or more likely the beginning of 1758, Mirabeau informed Quesnay of his intention to revise his manuscript of the *Mémoire concernant les états provinciaux*— a project he claimed he might never have undertaken without Quesnay's request and promise of assistance.[7] Mirabeau's revision

7. I believe like Weulersse, *Manuscrits*, 2, that the letter (AN, M 778, no. 4, "Lettre") was addressed to Quesnay, although there are problems of attribution that Weulersse does not raise. A slightly revised version of the same text appears as "Lettre à M. de S. C.," a preface to the "Introduction" to the revised "Mémoire sur les états provinciaux" as it appeared in the new volume 4 of *L'ami des hommes* in 1758 (Vol. II, 69–70, of the 1760 edition). (For the revised edition, Mirabeau dropped *concernant l'utilité des* for *sur*.) The M. de S. C. in question might have been Bigot de Sainte-Croix to whom Mirabeau addressed a long, unpublished letter on the grain trade around 1768 (AN, M 784, no. 10, cotte R). No other commentator has even raised the problem of attribution. In fact, it is likely that the address on the published version simply conformed to a literary convention while respecting Quesnay's jealously guarded anonymity, and that the original draft was indeed intended for Quesnay. The manuscript version contains a passage, omitted from the published version, in which Mirabeau describes a preamble he intends to write on "public law" and the nature of the French kings which strongly suggests that the letter originally formed part of his and Quesnay's dialogue on this subject.

bears certain marked similarities to its original, but it also introduces a fundamental shift in perspective. If Mirabeau still regards hierarchy as the essence of fundamental law and still insists upon the entire obedience of the subjects to the monarch, he also displays a growing preoccupation with the need for "fixed and respected laws" that would transcend both the will of the king and the selfish interests of individuals. Moreover, if in the revision, as in the original, he pledges himself to the service of the general good rather than that of particular interests, his understanding of the nature of that general good has changed, and he proposes to reorganize the *Mémoire* accordingly. Whereas in the original he had discussed the utility of provincial estates relative to royal authority, to finances, and to the happiness of the people, he now will reverse the order and speak first of all of the happiness of the people.[8] He does not repudiate hierarchy as the proper articulation of the social space, but in shifting its locus from the apex to the base of the social order, he is, perhaps unwittingly, allowing for the possibility of a different principle of social organization. Quesnay undoubtedly contributed to this shift of perspective, but given Mirabeau's original preoccupations in *L'ami des hommes*, Quesnay cannot be held entirely responsible. Mirabeau's perception of the corruption of traditional society and government (that is, the monarchy) in his own time led him to question the historical functioning of his ideal traditional order, and to address himself increasingly to the nature and causes of the crisis of the ancien régime.

According to Mirabeau's ideal, the interests of sovereign and people are one: the need for social unity and hierarchy transcends petty self-interest and welds the discrete members of society into a social community that, to the extent possible for humans, implements the divine will on earth. Mirabeau recognizes that the interests of the people are not always well-served by the prince and his ministers. He does not, however, believe that the

8. AN, M 778, no. 4, "Lettre."

unfortunate activity of some criminal ministers who wish to separate "the interests of the prince from those of his subjects" vitiate his analysis of the body politic. "It is true that the people rarely knows its own true interests, [and] that the prince who does not see everything can very often be mistaken," but "nothing [is more important than the] relationship of the subjects and the sovereign . . . which alone can guarantee order if both parties remain true to the principles of their function." Legitimate authority in its natural structure differs markedly from tyranny, which "by oppressing everything, degenerates in the wink of an eye into anarchy."[9]

The most portentous feature of Mirabeau's analysis lies in his discussion of tyranny. The principal characteristics of this perversion of true monarchy, he argues, are the divorce between the interests of the prince and his people, the favoring of those who merely possess wealth, and the despotic leveling of all subjects. Moreover, both he and Quesnay, from their different points of departure, had arrived at the conclusion that the first two symptoms of tyranny prevailed in France in the 1750s, and despite the persistence of legal privilege, even the third seemed to be threatened by the action of Mirabeau's hated intendants. Initially, Quesnay did not share Mirabeau's alarm about the state. He wanted its power put to more enlightened uses, but he did not deplore its growth per se until his disciple directed his attention to its threat to the organic community.

Mirabeau's principles of organization, being hierarchical and religious, did not allow much space for the individual beyond the limits of his corporate existence, and he could imagine no alternative manner of maintaining the unity of the community. Yet we can reread Mirabeau's description of the structure of the relations between society and the state, and by substituting the marketplace for traditional authority, come out with a coherent statement. Such a procedure would jettison some of Mirabeau's

9. AN, M 778, no. 4, sec. 1, "Relative au bonheur des peuples," and sec. 2, "Relative à l'autorité royale."

most dearly held principles—or prejudices—since he could not himself envision traditional social values as separable from a coherent social order. Nor could he envision any need to justify the rejection of the reigning principles of social and political organization. Even Quesnay, who did not share his concerns about religion and nobility, only wished to eliminate the divisive political pretensions of these traditional institutions and had no coherent alternative system in mind. He did, however, propose to Mirabeau a new, common agenda: the systematic historical and theoretical analysis of the monarchy. That project, so obligingly undertaken by Mirabeau, was to lead to a paradoxical but decisive recognition that historical process could not be reversed. Mirabeau's cherished dream of a restoration of the true monarchy had to give way, since to preserve the idea of a natural rather than an arbitrary structure of society entailed the acceptance of a new organic development, not the return to an irretrievable past. But such considerations do not figure among the initial intentions of Mirabeau's "Traité de la monarchie," apparently drafted during 1758, which proposed merely to investigate the nature and history of the monarchy in order to discover where it had gone wrong.[10]

The form of the "Traité" follows a historical progression in four sections: "Origines de la monarchie," "Progrès de la monarchie," "Perfection de la monarchie," and "Abus de la monarchie." The term monarchy carries throughout the dual meaning of government in the generic sense, and the specific government of France. Reflecting this fundamental dualism, the argument swings back and forth between political theory and historical reality, leaning ever more towards a systematic critique of French institutions as it approaches the present. As Mirabeau seeks the origins of government in the dawn of society and attempts to establish the priority of the community (in its

10. AN, M 778, no. 1. Henceforth, "Traité."

feudal trappings) over the state, Quesnay scrutinizes the growth of absolutism in the light of its current, unifying role. But as the whole point of the exercise is to understand the abuses of the present in relation to a general theory of social and political organization, Mirabeau begins his treatise with a discussion of the origins of society.[11]

He uses this discussion to establish the social facts that will serve his subsequent theoretical justification of the monarchy, which, he believes, is only legitimate to the extent that it corresponds to social needs. Nature itself, he argues, by creating man with needs, creates his essential dependence. Could a man forego, at birth, the assistance of others, he would be born free and could claim the right to maintain himself so. But all of us are born dependent upon material care, and thus grow "under the shadow of paternal authority." Through our dependence upon our fathers, Mirabeau argues, we are equally dependent upon the arrangements of society, which include the rights of citizens to whatever they possess. Mirabeau underlines this identity between paternal and sovereign authority and insists that each individual moves necessarily from dependence upon the father to dependence upon the suzerain. "Such is the law which renders us subjects at birth without our oath of fidelity being required."[12]

In going over the text, Quesnay crossed out the words following "law" and substituted "which reunites the obligations and the authority of the sovereign, the needs and the dependence of the subjects."[13] The slight change beautifully exemplifies the process of intellectual transformation. Quesnay does not challenge Mirabeau's hierarchical assumptions; he questions the specific form of the feudal oath. Dependence was as much a fact of the life of the absolute state as it was of feudal society, and hence, from both points of view, inescapably part of the social condi-

---

11. *Ibid.*, sec. 1, 1. Each of the four sections begins with p. 1.
12. *Ibid.* Cf. *Locke*, "Of Paternal Power," in Sir Ernest Barker, ed., *Social Contract* [1947] (London, Oxford, New York, 1970), 30–45.
13. "Traité," sec. 1, 1.

tion of the eighteenth century. Yet while retaining the traditional paternalistic concepts of authority and dependence, Quesnay also introduces those of obligations and need, which, by shifting the emphasis to survival were to become the pivot of physiocratic theory.[14] Furthermore, Quesnay added a lengthy marginal annotation aimed at integrating the notions of dependence and authority into the framework of his own metaphysics, as if to reaffirm how deeply he, like Mirabeau, envisaged human order as a reflection of divine will.

Mirabeau argues that paternal care derives from instinct, which accounts for its existence even among those who, like the savages of North America, have poorly developed faculties of reason. Quesnay agrees that in animals physical instincts replace a moral sense, but he insists that both the physical and the moral "derive essentially from divine justice which is itself the author of all sensate beings." Primitive needs would be the cause of serious evil if divine providence had not provided for them by the institution of paternal care. The care that delivers infants from the misery attached to their birth must, therefore, be "infallible in the physical or instinctive and essentially obligatory in the moral." Thus, as filial dependence is founded in need, so is paternal authority founded in obligation. Quesnay concludes that there can be no dependence or superiority which has any principles other than dependence and authority themselves, even if the positions of authority and dependence do not seem to be established on any equitable foundation. Only that divine law which, as Quesnay argued in "Evidence," guarantees human reason can dictate dependence and authority. Human institutions thus find their sanction in the divine will so that everywhere human authority is no more than "the obligation of a judge charged with rendering the justice attributed and intimated to all men by the author of nature, and dependence is only the submission

14. Cf. Quesnay's formulation of 1765, "Observations sur le droit naturel des hommes réunis en société," INED, II, 729–42.

to the immutable order decisively indicated by his justice."[15]
Quesnay's remarks, in echoing the metaphysics of "Evidence,"
demonstrate the danger of counterposing too sharply his alleged
materialist determinism to Mirabeau's idealism.

Although Quesnay and Mirabeau agree on the centrality of the
paternal relationship, Mirabeau warns against the error of believ-
ing that government preceded society. After all, however important paternal authority, the formation of the first family
resulted from the voluntary free association of a man and a
woman as the necessary prerequisite for paternity itself. Although
hardly his most sophisticated proposition, this one does permit
Mirabeau to argue that society precedes the authority of its
ruler, and further, that "the inalterable administration of justice,
which constitutes the entire essence of the government of a
nation, is superior to the sovereign authority because it embraces
and composes all its essence." Quesnay demonstrates general
agreement with Mirabeau's basic train of thought in an editorial
emendation that deleted the words following "because" and
replaced them with "it is known and prescribed as clearly to those
who must obey as to those to whom it is granted to command."
His change, however, also introduces the notion heretofore
embodied in Bourbon absolutism, that a disorderly society must
be unified by a superior force that implements the fundamental
social principles. The path to legal despotism has been opened:
"The force of a state, the fundamental original and natural force,
consists in the consent and in the power of a nation; but the
most regular, the most fixed, the most absolute and the most
prompt exercise of this force is monarchical authority regulated
by the laws."[16]

Mirabeau is in a sense still trying to solve the problem posed
for the subjects of absolute monarchy at its birth by Jean Bodin,

15. "Traité," sec. 1, 2.

16. *Ibid.*, 2–3. Cf. Locke, "Of Paternal Power," 31, and [Simon-Nicolas-
Henri Linguet], *Théorie des loix civiles, ou principes fondamentaux de la
société*, 2 vols. (London, 1767), I, 88–89.

just as he is still trying like so many of his contemporaries to break out of its imprisoning formulation by Bossuet. The nation, he recognizes, is subordinate to the monarch, but, as Quesnay keeps reminding him, the monarch is subordinate to natural and positive law. The hegemony of the law, they agree, means that the king cannot be the proprietor of the nation, "nor of that which belongs to the nation." He may be the conservator, even the supreme and unique director of the nation, but "the constitutive authority of the government subsists in the nation and by the nation." Only the active authority which, following Quesnay's qualification. "is founded on the very authority of the laws," resides in the monarch and in him alone. In a good government, these two authorities do not conflict, indeed their mutual reinforcement constitutes the "essence of monarchical government considered in terms of natural law or in the very essence of Justice." Should the balance be destroyed, the government would degenerate into a regime that Quesnay describes as so "violent and transitory that [it] cannot subsist by monarchical power and that is more or less disordered and more or less near a revolution."[17]

Quesnay's and Mirabeau's joint efforts slowly pushed them into a serious re-examination of the monarchy. As they explored its origins and practices, they increasingly came to think that it could not provide its own legitimization if it failed to remain true to its principles. As Mirabeau writes: "Everything in the universe is subjected to a natural order and this order is well enough known to us to disclose, by universal analogy, the fundamental laws which form the entire system of a good government." The arbitrary power of one man, he continues, can hardly meet these conditions; nor can it even succeed in domination without the consent and cooperation of society. One cannot, therefore, derive the origin of society from the power of an individual.[18]

17. "Traité," sec. 1, 3.
18. *Ibid.*, 4.

Mirabeau, at this point, embarks upon a historical investigation of government among the Medes and the Persians, because, as he apologetically admits, his weak metaphysics has closed him into a circle of banalities. The banalities for which he begs forgiveness are nothing less than an attempt to show that, since the first need of any society is subsistence, and since men only cultivate the land if they are assured of the harvest, any nation that made rapid historical progress must have had a good government. He means, of course, a government that guaranteed property. But he cannot quite make the jump from the feudal theory of property to the bourgeois theory that was to form the essential core of subsequent physiocratic theory.

Quesnay, commenting in the margin, tries to draw him back from historical detail to metaphysical analysis, particularly to the discussion of natural law, which he insists is not, as superficial political theorists would lead us to believe, "an ideal being." Experience shows that natural law has been neglected by even the least enlightened nations only at great peril. History proves, Quesnay states, "that truly monarchical society and the natural law enunciated by the positive laws are so co-essential that one has never been able to subsist without the other." Dissolute or arbitrary authority invariably weakens the monarch who can only support his position by increasingly illegitimate measures which eventually destroy his own authority. It is therefore impossible "to treat the monarchy without speaking of natural law which is its most essential component." He adds that had he been speaking of despotism he might have settled for an irresistible force which subjugated prince, sovereignty, and nation; but with a truly monarchical government he has "sought the principles and the constitution in the very nature of this divine government."[19] Throughout this discussion, Quesnay is as concerned with formulating a social science as he is with formulating a political theory. The coincidence of vocabulary should not obscure the multiple and as yet undifferentiated meanings it cloaks. Natural

19. *Ibid.*, 5.

law contains all the ambiguity of eternal checks on monarchy and the scientific law of social development. That confusion between the attempt to make the monarchy conform to its historical tradition and the implicit attempt to develop an accurate science of social behaviour plagues all physiocratic thought. Quesnay and Mirabeau never completely disengaged the notion of law as norm from that of law as obligation. At this juncture, both men have come to see the monarchy as a vital part of a larger social system rather than as a force above society. They have taken the first step towards a new integration of state and society, but they still cannot define that force of necessity which Quesnay deems indispensable.

In his second section, entitled "Progrès de la monarchie," Mirabeau sets out to discover the principles that legitimize the state. On the surface his text still follows a historical sequence. Having discussed the origins of government, he now proceeds to examine its establishment, but, as throughout the entire treatise, the theoretical analysis breaks out of the chronological mold. He must be permitted, he insists, to take "the first construction of any state as giving form to the raw material of society. . . ." His formulation constitutes the most explicit and deceptive statement by any physiocrat about the relations between state and society— one that could apply to their later concept of legal despotism as accurately as to his discussion of the monarchy with Quesnay.[20] For the raw materials in question are human beings, complete with their interests and passions.

The first of these interests, for Mirabeau as for subsequent physiocrats, lies in private property. For each man, he argues, the desire to assure his own property to his own family leads him naturally to come to terms with the properties of others. Any head of state, even the most violent conqueror, must respect his subjects' fundamental commitment to property or else entertain no hope of perpetuating his dominion. Thus the principles

20. "Traité," sec. 2, 2.

of good government reside not in the criminal violence of the conqueror but in justice, "and the essence of justice is in the observation of the laws that men prescribed freely among themselves for their reciprocal security and for the conservation of their possessions." Mirabeau then introduces the idea that was to form the physiocrats' materialist justification for absolute private property. The laws that sanctify property, he asserts, "have as their foundation the natural order requiring each man to conserve himself and to satisfy his needs under pain of suffering, the first law of which ceaselessly cries vengeance against the barbarism of tyrants."[21]

Government, according to Mirabeau, begins not with the conqueror, but with his successor, who establishes the laws and who will consider legislation—or in Quesnay's superimposed word, authority—independent of such accidents as climate, genius, or people. In a pointed contradiction of Montesquieu, he insists that in any climate "man is capable of all virtues and susceptible to all vices." Climates can lend nations different inclinations, different physical qualities, different characters, but different governments exercise an infinitely more powerful influence than climate upon the people's conduct and their morals.[22]

Some governments, such as those of nomadic or conquering tribes, never escape from their primitive state of barbarism—a prospect that causes Mirabeau to shake his head in despair and proceed directly to his discussion of true monarchical government. His remarks also prompt Quesnay to interject his own thoughts on the differences between nomadic and settled peoples and their governments. His comments relate Mirabeau's earlier statement about subsistence constituting the basis of human existence to the different kinds of government. Nomadic tribes "are simply collections of men who have no ties binding them together other than the common purpose of providing for their subsistence" by living off the plundering of others. "Sub-

21. *Ibid.,* 4–5.
22. *Ibid.,* 5–6.

sistence," he adds, "is the primary object of all societies. This object must never be lost sight of in the constitution of governments: everything else is only modification." All social characteristics, Quesnay continues, whether disorder, cruelty, heroism, domination or order, politics, courtesy, humanity, the sciences, the arts, even economic government, legislation, and the assured possession of property, constitute no more than "the means and the results of different forms of society employed in different ways in satisfying, more or less abundantly and with more or less difficulty, their needs."[23]

Quesnay's remarks develop Mirabeau's thought by arguing for the direct relationship between the form of government and the society's means of providing for its subsistence. They should not, however, be read as implying more than that, certainly not that the means of providing for subsistence determine the form of government. Quesnay once comes close to proposing that the character of production determines the form of government, but he is not prepared to maintain such an uncompromising position.[24] His metaphysics point to the conclusion that man, to the extent that he is a free agent, realizes his own possibilities and those of the divine will. His further observations show him that governments rarely correspond to the optimal economic organization of societies and indeed frequently compromise it. This indecision plagued most of his assessment of the relationship of means of production to morals and ideology, much as it seemed to have influenced his conclusion that social characteristics can be both the cause and results of different forms of society.[25]

This ambiguous character of Quesnay's approach to the shaping of society emerges clearly from a lengthy dialogue with Mirabeau

23. *Ibid.*, Meek, *Economics*, 66–67, reproduces Quesnay's entire marginal comment. I have used his translation. As the rest of this chapter shows, I consider it misleading to use this passage as a completely typical example of Quesnay's thought at this time.

24. *Ibid.*, translated by Meek, *Economics*, 68.

25. *Ibid.*, 6. Cf. Hume, "Of the Original Contract," in Barker, ed., *Social Contract*, 147–66.

on religion. Mirabeau repeats his favorite arguments that social order requires the protection of institutionalized religion. Quesnay counters by pointing out that modern governments can ill afford such luxuries, whether or not the religions they support are true. The many published excerpts from Quesnay's annotations of the "Traité" have tended to distort his thought by overly emphasizing this skepticism about the political claims of institutionalized religion. Quesnay never did work out his own thoughts on religion. If he doubted the practicality of linking the fate of government to that of the ministers of a specific faith, he never doubted that all authority—including that of legitimate governments—required a religious guarantee. Only an absolute truth, external to society and unassailable by selfish human whim, would serve to anchor social order and to decide decisively conflicts between individuals. His ambiguity does not result from hypocrisy, but from his considered refusal to entrust human affairs, which require an objective standard, exclusively to humans, whose perspective is by definition subjective.[26]

The third section of the "Traité," "Perfection de la monarchie," deals with the social and political institutions in their historical context. Mirabeau turns to the monarchy's greatest period and tries to extrapolate a universal formula for political success. For a monarchy, the first condition of perfection lies in the stability and duration of the reigning house.[27] And a royal line rarely inaugurates its career except by conquest. "From conquest derives the spirit of the property of sovereignty and that of heredity." To the extent that the right of conquest derives from that of war, it can be considered the "rear vassal of equity"; but its rights only extend to those who wage war and who since the time of the transmigrations have been only princes, not peoples. "From which it follows that a Prince can conquer sovereignty and *political property* from another ruler; but *civil property*

26. "Traité," sec. 2, 8–19 *passim.*
27. "Traité," sec. 3, 2.

remains to those to whom it legitimately belongs and who have not deserved to lose it."[28]

Mirabeau admits that his seemingly metaphysical distinction between political and civil property—so clearly derived from Bodin—will hardly save conquered peoples from a miserable spoliation, but he staunchly defends it on grounds that the rights of a sovereign to appropriate a conquered state cannot legitimately extend to that of dispossessing its subjects. That sovereign has "only conquered the real rights which constitute a portion of the state and not the entire state." The political property legitimately conquered by the victorious prince becomes his in full title and may be passed on to his heirs. Mirabeau holds that his analysis limits neither the right of princes nor that of their subjects; it merely describes that equitable law which, in Quesnay's words, "assures and distinguishes" both sets of rights.[29]

Quesnay notes in the margin that Mirabeau has a tendency to confuse theoretical arguments with historical facts, but adds, "The fact should serve to elucidate the law." Then Quesnay himself tries to resolve some of the contradictions by drawing a distinction between kings (mere conquerors) and monarchs (true sovereigns). "I believe," he argues, "that one could find hardly any monarchs at the origins of states, but the kings, as the first and most powerful finally become such, and the nations imperceptibly devote themselves to them." The principle of conquest alone, however, does not suffice to legitimize the monarchy, which "will always have another principle, . . . namely the fundamental laws and the tacit or explicit consent of the nation. From that results not only the natural law of peoples but also their positive laws." Quesnay therefore also insists upon the distinction between the law of conquest and the natural law of society as the best guarantee for the nation. He offers Denmark as the example of a state ruled by an absolute

28. *Ibid.*, 4–5.
29. *Ibid.*, 5.

monarch who derives his rights from the nation as proof that "the right belongs by the most legitimate and most incontestable title to the Sovereign." Finally, he explains that the Holy Scripture teaches that sovereignty is by divine right and that monarchy cannot enjoy the exclusive claim to divine sanction since sovereignty can with equal legitimacy reside in the nation, as it does in republics. These principles, he concludes, are vital to a proper understanding of the nature of sovereignty.[30]

Both Quesnay and Mirabeau are groping for a definition of sovereignty adequate to maintaining the rights of the state and those of its subjects, and in so doing they have introduced a dualism into the heart of their political and social theory that would have been unacceptable to either of them earlier. Quesnay seems to have shed many of his earlier assumptions about the nature of the state, in particular its omnipotence, but he has yet to fashion a coherent or necessary theory of social and political order. Clearly, he is allowing increasing importance to the claims of society as against those of the state. Yet both he and Mirabeau still hold firmly to their commitment to society or the nation as a body without yet examining the possible claims of the individual against the collective order. It is Mirabeau who raises the pivotal question of property, its nature and its social guarantees.

He dismisses as extravagant the claims of princes, "those first Louis," to absolute possession of their kingdoms. Following the principles of equity, he insists that not only princes but also ministers, magistrates, and all who govern can only be proprietors by convention: "In reality we are all *usufructiers*. We owe an account of our administration to society to the good order of which we must all contribute." The idea of absolute and arbitrary property could not be more illusory. Mirabeau then explains, in a telescoped account of the origins and corruption of the feudal system, that men, in order to avoid the continual redistribution

30. *Ibid.*, Cf. Locke, "Of Paternal Power," 52.

of usufructs and to assure order to daily administration, entered into a convention to "call properties the alimentary portions and the assured possessions of citizens with the power to sell them, to engage them, and to designate a successor for them." Nature and conscience, however, protest "against the extension of these unlimited attributions," and deny that we should "envisage these arrangements of human institution as a real truth." For "*relative to the essence of good order*," no truth is absolute "unless it be eternal."[31]

Mirabeau, with Quesnay's full concurrence, has trapped himself in the contradiction between the reality of the ancien régime and his own theoretical inclinations. In his attempt to invalidate the more presumptuous claims of absolutism (that the kingdom is the property of the prince) and to avoid the pitfalls of proprietorship of public office, he has been led into repudiating property altogether. In its place he proposes the medieval notion of usufruct as a means of guaranteeing the responsible conduct of property-holders. And yet when not discussing property theory per se, Mirabeau relies heavily on property—implicitly absolute personal property—as the foundation of society. His dilemma reveals the difficulty inherent in reformulating an entire theory of social and political relations. The proprietary rights of the prince must be circumscribed in order to permit legitimate recognition of the political claims of society at large and in order to protect the rights of its members. At the same time, the property rights of individuals, still perceived as parcels of sovereignty, must be circumscribed to ensure larger social responsibility, even while the individual's commitment to his property—that divine distinction of *thine* from *mine*—is perceived as the foundation of society in the first place. To carry him over the shoals of contradiction. Mirabeau introduces the notion of a social contract or convention to explain the limitations of property rights. In so doing he retains the traditional concept of property

31. "Traité," sec. 3, 7–8.

as a right granted by society.[32] This theory would shortly become anathema to both him and Quesnay, but for the moment neither of them had succeeded in formulating an alternative concept of property as a natural and innate economic right.

Mirabeau's confusion of innate and externally conferred social roles emerges most forcefully from his discussion of the nobility. As in *L'ami des hommes*, he persists in his devotion to the nobility as a caste or legal estate. His rhetoric echoes that of his earlier work when he insists that noble wealth should not disproportionately exceed that of other members of society. In the past, nobility has been defined as "perpetuated wealth," but he favors "hereditary consideration." Nobility should not be regarded as an exemption from social responsibility, but rather as an obligation to the rest of society. In a word, nobility should close the doors of wealth and leave only the choice between virtues. To establish order in society requires unity among the different classes of citizens, which can never truly occur if they are not linked by reciprocal esteem and respect. Mirabeau fears for the position, and above all for the legitimate claim to position, of the nobility, should they not be able to justify their existence by a sufficient cultivation of virtue to command the allegiance of their fellow citizens.[33] The attempt of this convinced *feudataire* to find new support for the legitimacy of his order further underscores the disintegration of the ancien régime.

Quesnay fully shared Mirabeau's perception of the widening gap between the form and the substance of society. Mirabeau, however, because of his mistrust of disproportionate wealth, proposed jettisoning the material progress of society and refounding the old order on a new basis of virtue, while Quesnay looked to the material progress itself for a sounder justification for social dis-

32. Cf. A. Gurevic, "Représentations et attitudes à l'égard de la propriété pendant le haut Moyen Age," *Annales ESC*, XVII (1972), 523–47; Pashell Larkin, *Property in the 18th Century with Special Reference to England and Locke* (Cork, 1930), 1–20; Franco Venturi, *Utopia and Reform in the Enlightenment* (Cambridge, 1971), 70–94.

33. "Traité," sec. 3, 13, 16.

tinctions. There is even a hint of personal pique in the ennobled physician's insistence that the inheritance of talent—and consequently the merited consideration—cannot be guaranteed to particular families for all time by mere legislation. But he develops his position well beyond the personal when he argues, much as Tocqueville would a century later, that wealth and nobility are inseparable. Hereditary nobility originated, he insists, among the wealthy. "Because of their rank, the first nobles commanded a larger share in the conquered wealth," and their descendants as a result still enjoyed great power "because wealth is power." Even today, wealth and illustriousness form the high nobility of great magnates and proprietors. In other words, both wealth and personal talent are essential characteristics of the aristocracy, and no laws can guarantee that these properties will either exclusively or regularly descend in one family. The institution of nobility must be recognized as a necessary vice that will always prevail over heroic virtue, which at best is a rare and individual phenomenon. Quesnay nonetheless justifies nobility as "a pious fraud" which must not be so loudly questioned as to cause people to open their eyes. On the other hand, "one must not so falsify ideas as to veil the essence of things." Virtue, he warns Mirabeau, cannot be legally guaranteed: privileged social position certainly requires some moral justification to make it acceptable, but such a formal justification should not obscure the realities of wealth, which constitute the true basis of power and prestige.[34]

In discussing the nobility with Mirabeau, Quesnay articulates yet another aspect of that contradiction which so deeply pervades their thought. On the one hand, they have no desire to attack the social system, while on the other, they increasingly suspect that it does not adequately correspond either to the realities of their world or to their own sense of social and political legitimacy. Mirabeau concedes that the power of the nobility derives from the military origin of the state. Here again he merges a historical

34. *Ibid.*, 18. Cf. Alexis de Tocqueville, *Oeuvres complètes*, ed. J. P. Mayer, vol. II, *L'ancien régime et la Révolution* (Paris, 1953), 441.

and a theoretical argument, by bringing the nobles onto the historical scene at the moment of conquest and in the company of the conquering prince. This historical primacy accounts for their original role which, because they have persisted in it, has been translated into a theoretical primacy as well. This argument approaches that of Boulainvilliers and others who accepted the original Frankish conquest as a sufficient rationalization of the ancien régime; but Mirabeau also recognizes that military—or feudal—government does not constitute a true monarchy. Monarchy requires law to guarantee the stability of the civil regime and laws require judges to enforce them. To ensure proper respect for the laws, the judges who are their depositories cannot be too pure or too respected—their jurisdiction too complete; they must in short be sovereign. Here, he maintains, begins the subordinate republic, which in his mind constitutes the stability and perfection of the monarchy. While for the three orders and all else that emanates from the military power the rule of one man constitutes an appropriate governance, for the laws and all that concerns the civil power, the participation of many is required.

Mirabeau repeatedly returns to the need for pluralism because, he insists, absolute authority in civil society repudiates its very essence by reducing all men to slavery, a "state against nature" which contradicts the essence of monarchy. Domination that is not exercised over fully independent human beings, he continues, can only be called despotism and has little use.[35] Reverence for the sanctity of the laws alone can prevent this despotism, for the laws, properly understood, tend to forge a unit "of general property from an infinity of particular properties, and to subordinate the right of the particular proprietor which is the state." And as Mirabeau hastens to add, the state knows only one master, the king, who need not fear any potentially divisive implications of the laws since public utility takes precedence over private interests (utility). The law teaches us that in a monarchy public

---

35. "Traité," sec. 3, 23, 33.

utility has only one representative, the king—or as Quesnay adds, "the absolute sovereign."[36]

The more deeply Quesnay and Mirabeau reflected, the sharper the contradiction at the heart of their thought became. As they slowly worked through the surrounding problems, they clarified one issue after another; but their progress only deepened the ravine separating the two major aspects of their theory. Mirabeau incorporated even larger doses of his contemporaries' political speculation into his own work, and thereby allowed an ever larger role for that republican side of the monarchy which he insisted upon as the component that distinguished monarchy from despotism. He continued, however, to restrict the republic to civil society; and neither he nor Quesnay ever advocated republican institutions for the political structure of the nation. They both demanded a single central authority capable of enforcing the public interest—a sure indication of how little they trusted public interest. At the same time, they displayed united confidence in the monarch's respect for private interests and tended to fall back on immutable laws as a mediating force between public authority and the private citizen.

Mirabeau's insistence upon this pivotal role of law both foreshadowed the physiocratic theory of legal despotism, and in one decisive particular, differed from it. At this time, Mirabeau, and Quesnay as well, lacked a consistent theory of the nature of law. Mirabeau understood law as an emanation of divine justice the implementation of which was dictated to man from above. He thus retained the idealist political language of traditional society. Quesnay, while no less certain that law derived from a divine source, was inclined to accord greater importance to the material base of society as an inescapable determinant of human activity. His materialism, however, was tempered by his commitment to the power of the human will and his conviction that the optimum material order was indicated by the natural law that derived from God. At this juncture not even he had constructed a theoretical

36. *Ibid.*, 32.

link between society and the state which would permit the anchoring of a new theoretical system.

By the time they had completed their discussion of the monarchy, Quesnay and Mirabeau had assembled practically all the elements of their future doctrine save one—absolute property. Despite their lengthy discussion of property, they had been unable to disengage its essence, to use their favorite word, from the feudal context of its historical development. They continued to regard it at once as the indispensable guarantee of the individual against society, his parcel, as it were, of the public weal, and as a possible source of the fragmentation of the social polity. They thus retained the residual mistrust of social individualism that had plagued Quesnay's early articles. Mirabeau seemed at least to glimpse a new explanation of the institution when he wrote that the best means available to the prince of assuring his domain and furthering its prosperity "is to assure the property of our goods";[37] but neither he nor Quesnay pursued the insight. Quesnay actually closes the third section of the "Traité" with a long note warning Mirabeau against "the usurpation of the rights of monarchical power" by ministers, clergy, military bodies, nobility, tribunals, and provincial estates. He does not advocate weakening the different orders of the state but calls for determining the limits of their jurisdiction and preventing the arbitrary use of authority so that "they mutually depend the ones on the others."[38] Quesnay has learned from Mirabeau to respect social pluralism, but quite naturally in terms of his own view of society. At the same time he retains his visceral mistrust of constituted bodies. Only when he and Mirabeau grasped that potential of private property to which Mirabeau had alluded would they be able to construct a system to reconcile individual and public, as well as social and monarchical, interest in the pursuit of economic prosperity.

In the final section of the "Traité," significantly entitled *Abus*

37. *Ibid.*, 32.
38. *Ibid.*, 44.

de la monarchie, Mirabeau and Quesnay address themselves to a thorough critique of the eighteenth-century French state. Here their joint efforts draw heavily upon their earlier separate work, recapitulating their independent criticism, and formulating a radical indictment of the ancien régime. Theoretically, however, they add little to the analysis they had constructed in the first three sections of the treatise. Instead, they set out to apply their insights systematically to their immediate historical situation. In the process they formulate their individual positions more sharply, producing a confrontation that generated the ultimate synthesis of physiocratic theory.

Mirabeau argues that the despotic tendencies of the monarchy have only been exacerbated by palliative measures and are leading straight to social anarchy. Quesnay warns him against the loose use of that "great" word which "signifies nothing or at most the disorder of a revolution." And "revolution" itself conveys little meaning unless defined carefully, for it can lead to military, feudal, or ecclesiastical despotism, or to a republican, aristocratic, or mixed government, or simply to a change in the reigning house. A revolution is much less likely to produce a monarchical government, which ordinarily only develops over the centuries. In France the monarchy won out over feudal despotism, and the religious wars provided a diversion from the progressive abuse of monarchical authority. Unfortunately, during the last 150 years, the abuses have progressed rapidly. Clearly, Quesnay concludes, "a monarchy rapidly passes its goal and falls into ruin."[39]

Mirabeau agrees that, once it is strong enough to avoid surprise attacks, a monarchy reaches its optimum development, and with its legal power solidly established, lets the state take care of itself. But this equilibrium is possible, Quesnay adds, only so long as "the authority does not break the constitutive bonds of the monarchy." Unfortunately, the French monarchy in its scramble for money has done exactly that. It has sold offices, oppressed the

39. "Traité," sec. 4, 2.

peasantry, and pursued the chimera of mercantile wealth. The only viable solution to these problems is for Frenchmen to return to their venerable principles because "a state in decadence, like a building in ruins, can only be shored up by its foundations."[40] For Mirabeau, such a return must begin with a return to religion, a claim that revives the standing debate between him and Quesnay over the proper role for ecclesiastical authority. Natural law, Quesnay insists, must guide the morality of states, and the sovereign has but to invoke it in the preamble to his acts to place them squarely in the moral sphere. This insistence on natural law, Quesnay explains, does not deny Mirabeau's conviction that all political authority must derive from a moral base, but serves to warn that political morality must derive directly from God without the intervention of the ministers of any church and must provide its own justification.[41] He assuredly does not propose to advocate the secularization of social and political life but to transpose moral obligation from the institutionalized churches to the social unity. But he hardly reinforces his position by the naive claim that the sovereign need only invoke the natural law at the beginning of his edicts to ensure their morality.

Mirabeau, in keeping with his position in *L'ami des hommes*, argues that all property no matter how dubious its origin, must be treated with respect. And reflecting the influence of Montesquieu and others, he maintains that the specific protection of fiefs constitutes one of the central responsibilities and bulwarks of the monarchy. Quesnay objects that a feudal state lacks clear sovereignty, for the proprietors of the great fiefs tend naturally to appropriate the regalian rights to their own considerable rights and powers, and indeed to establish parity with the monarch.[42] For the first time Quesnay himself has joined the issue of the conflicting claims of the monarch and his vassals. He is no longer concerned with the theoretical nature of property, but rather

40. *Ibid.*, 4, 6.
41. *Ibid.*, 8.
42. *Ibid.*, 23.

with the dangers of appropriated regalian rights. While he still insists on wealth as the true basis of nobility, he now draws the lines of his argument so sharply as to reject the political property of the nobility completely. He does not, however, begin to face the practical dependence of the monarchy on its nobility. Instead, he reinforces his commitment to the indivisibility of sovereignty, at the same time leaving nobility unchallenged as an hereditary legal status and aristocratic distinction, albeit shorn of its historical justification.

Quesnay denies the special constitutive rights of the first two estates in order to assure the integrity of monarchical sovereignty, and thus beats a reasoned return to his own early but tacit assumptions of the power and centrality of the state. He has still not succeeded, however, in establishing a necessary check upon the misuse of that power by the state, and in the succeeding pages he and Mirabeau chronicle its corruption and economic errors at length. While Mirabeau struggles to integrate his moral outrage at the ruin of agriculture and the proliferation of moneyed fortunes into his growing understanding of Quesnay's economics, Quesnay adds running marginal instructions in the fine points of that science.[43]

For the first time in the course of their long dialogue, Quesnay presents his analysis of the necessary economic order and describes its mechanism with assurance. Together, he and Mirabeau develop the argument that agriculture alone assures the wealth of the state, and they demonstrate that the French monarchy has completely undermined its own property by its constant search for new sources of income. In its irresponsible pursuit of expedients the monarchy has created a parasitical social system, dependent upon itself but upon which it also depends. So long as the state needs money, it will not be able to free itself from its own creatures, particularly its bankers. Worse, their abuses will affect not only the physical but also the moral realm, because by their pursuit of wealth and favor they undermine all natural social

43. Weulersse, *Manuscrits*, 28–29, provides a typical excerpt.

order.[44] The government's cupidity has made the entire life of the state mercenary.

Mirabeau has yet to assimilate the full implications of Quesnay's conviction that agriculture constitutes the principal source of capital accumulation and can produce more wealth than commerce or banking. Instead, he still sees the cure of monarchical decadence in moral terms, and not surprisingly argues that to cure the current evils "one must not seek remedies of detail," but rather return to the "unique remedy" of the constitutive orders, their essence, their strength, their terrain, and their authority. *"All government consists in the conservation of property, . . . all tyranny and anarchy is nothing but the alteration of properties,"* and that, needless to say, includes feudal property.[45]

Quesnay does not openly dispute Mirabeau's declaration. Having reviewed the economic disasters of the last century, he is horrified by the destructive powers of the monarchy and impressed by his own arguments in favor of economic laissez-faire, but he too falls back upon the necessity of guaranteeing a pluralistic structure to the social body. The subordinate powers, he argues, should all, by their concurrence, form only one power with the sovereign.[46] No sovereign can either destroy or form these powers; he can only oppress one or another of them relative to the others and thereby jeopardize his own authority, since their function is to contain each other. If the monarchy abuses its power it will only expose itself to a "prompt revolution." "Let them beware, never has an arbitrary monarchical government which forgot the rights . . . of the nation existed except to destroy itself."[47]

Investigation of the history and theory of the monarchy has taught Quesnay and Mirabeau that the state under which they

44. "Traité," sec. 4, 58.
45. *Ibid.*, 63, 65.
46. *Ibid.*, 52.
47. *Ibid.*, 59.

live has violated the principles of its own essence, and in pursuing its erroneous course has risked its own destruction. And the destruction of the monarchy would, they agree, entail the radical transformation of the society over which it presides and from which it draws its very justification. Mirabeau and Quesnay cannot, finally, separate state and society. The mutual reinforcement of the two constitutes the framework of human experience and provides the only legitimate setting for the expression and realization of individual interests. Their discussion of the monarchy has led them to attempt to formulate a coherent philosophy of society in general, but the further they pursue their investigation, the more they encounter the intractable contradictions of their own society.

While Mirabeau clings to the traditional illusion of organic unity, Quesnay has moved toward an ever harsher critique of specific institutions. Quicker to accept new realities and more committed to the independent economic process, Quesnay recognizes wealth as the true source of social power. At the same time, he has no more use than Mirabeau for the specific manifestations of unbridled merchant and finance capital. His insistence upon the unique productivity of agriculture reflects both his recognition of its potential for dynamic economic growth and his desire to promote that growth within a natural order. In this combination he and Mirabeau finally bring their ideas into a common focus.

This agreement, however, did not resolve all of their outstanding differences, notably their attitudes toward private property. Quesnay, in justifying the rights of society against the sovereign, lumped the sacerdotal and military orders with the possessors of wealth and the popular multitude as the component members of the total social body. In so doing, he juxtaposed a social system of estates upon one of classes in a confusion which precisely reflects the reality of mid-eighteenth-century France. Slowly, he and Mirabeau were brought to recognize that their defense of property—the *sine qua non* of their economic program—would force them to distinguish between a traditional idea of property as a diffuse bundle of rights guaranteed from above, and a modern idea of absolute property as an indivisible entity, birthright of every individual by virtue of his participation in the fundamental, material order of nature itself. For the moment they did not yet know that the combination of their respective economics and sociology implicitly proposed a new view of human relations, the implementation of which demanded an increasingly radical program for change. Their investigation of the monarchy had not only revealed the failures of the state, but had also called into question the legitimizing principles of society itself. In their future work they would scrupulously avoid any direct attack on the existing government, but however much they might disclaim it, their purportedly scientific economic program demanded nothing less than a social revolution for the realization of its "neutral" goals.

Toward a Political Economy

In immediate terms, the "Traité de la monarchie" led Quesnay and Mirabeau to a dead end. Unable to cast its conclusions in a form acceptable to the royal censors, they abandoned the project. In long-range terms, however, the very failure of the "Traité" as a publishable reformist tract pushed Quesnay and Mirabeau toward the plane of theoretical social science and the formulation of physiocracy. The new additions to *L'ami des hommes* of 1758–1759 embody their first attempt to dilute the distressing conclusions of the "Traité" into a more general discussion. Their new contributions to that work did not yet constitute a coherent statement of physiocracy, but the major parts, the "Introduction au mémoire sur les états provinciaux," the "Mémoire sur l'agriculture," and the "Tableau oeconomique avec ses explications" provided the outlines of a body of social, political, and economic analysis that would emerge in *La philosophie rurale* (1763) as a fully developed ideology. In other words, this new edition of *L'ami des hommes* contained all the elements of a multi-level transformation of two distinct bodies of thought and their combination in a doctrine that transcended both. What the Tableau expressed as a major revolution in economic analysis, the "Introduction" prefigured in its suggestion of a new ideological perspective, and the "Mémoire" on agriculture articulated as a coherent political economy.[1]

1. *L'ami des hommes, ou traité de la population*, 2 vols. (n.p., 1760), II; all references will be to this edition. Mirabeau brought out the results of

The "Introduction" bears the closest relationship to the problems investigated in the "Traité." It establishes beyond doubt the general framework of the physiocratic ideology, but still carries unmistakable traces of current social realities. Mirabeau, and by association Quesnay, had reached a temporary impasse. Having agreed that the right of property constituted the proper basis for society, they could not yet define it, much less reconcile it with the political forms they knew or justify it independently of those forms. In a few years they would brazenly extricate themselves by abstractly defining property as an absolute economic right and then opting for the despotism of the laws as the only satisfactory check against monarchical or popular tyranny. But even legal despotism bypassed the difficult question of existing laws and social structure, and failed to explain how absolute property would be introduced. Certainly in 1758, Quesnay hardly presumed to question openly the prevailing legal structure of the country, and Mirabeau actively supported it. The "Introduction" expressed the general theoretical perspective they had developed in the "Traité" without resolving the contradictions between that perspective and their own society. For the discussion of potentially problematical specifics, they returned to their economics which they hoped would provide a safer terrain.[2]

---

his work with Quesnay as additions, or new parts, to *L'ami des hommes.* Part 4, first published in 1758, included: "Dialogue entre le surintendant d'O et L. D. H."; "Mémoire sur les états provinciaux," of which the first 51 pages constitute the "Introduction"; "Réponse aux objections contre le mémoire sur les états provinciaux"; and the "Questions intéressantes sur la population, l'agriculture, et le commerce proposées aux académies et autres sociétés sçavantes des provinces." Part 5, first published early in 1759, included: "Mémoire sur l'agriculture envoyé à la très-louable société d'agriculture de Berne," and "L'extrait des six premiers livres du corps complet d'oeconomie rustique de feu M. Thomas Hale." The sixth and final part which appeared later in 1759 included: "Réponse à l'essai sur les ponts et chaussées, la voierie et les corvées," and "Le Tableau oeconomique avec ses explications." In some editions, the various parts correspond to volumes. In the more elegant and commonly used quarto editions of 1758 and 1760, both of which appeared in two volumes, they do not.

2. The "Introduction" first appeared in vol. II of the 1758 edition, and

The "Mémoire sur l'agriculture," which Mirabeau wrote to compete for the prize offered in 1759 by the newly founded agricultural society of Berne, addressed itself to the concrete questions of political economy. Although the proposed subject called for an analysis of Swiss economic conditions and proposals to improve them, Mirabeau used it to develop his and Quesnay's views about France.[3] And even as Mirabeau, with Quesnay's quasi-dictatorial editorial assistance, was elaborating the "Mémoire," Quesnay himself was formulating the first editions of his celebrated and perplexing Tableau.[4] The evolution of the Tableau from the first edition of December 1758 through its first official publication complete with Mirabeau's explanations in the "Explications" of 1759, must be examined as a separate problem of economic analysis, if for no other reason than that economists over the years have treated it as such. But it can only be understood within the larger context of Quesnay's and Mirabeau's thought.

Whatever its intrinsic delights and frustrations, the Tableau

---

the pagination of that edition is identical to that of the 1760 edition. The "Introduction" has received almost no attention from scholars. Weulersse, *Mouvement*, I, 58–59, and Louis de Loménie, *Les Mirabeau: Nouvelles études sur la société française au XVIIIe siècle* (Paris, 1879–1891), II, 201, both mention it briefly and state that Quesnay's influence over Mirabeau is already apparent but not yet total. Both interpretations suggest that Quesnay himself was already in possession of a fully developed liberal ideology. Cf. also Henri Ripert, *Le marquis de Mirabeau: Ses théories politiques et économiques* (Paris, 1910). The more recent accounts of the origins of the school do not mention the "Introduction" at all. Cf. Jules Conan, "Les débuts de l'école physiocratique, un faux départ: L'échec de la réforme fiscale," *RHES*, XXXVI (1958), 45–63; Jacqueline Hecht, "La vie de François Quesnay," *INED*, I, 211–93; and Joseph J. Spengler, "Quesnay: Philosophe, empiriciste, économiste," *INED*, I, 55–74.

3. See *Recueil de mémoires concernants l'oeconomie rurale, par une société établie à Berne en Suisse* (Zurich, 1760), which contains not only Mirabeau's essay but those of the first two prize winners; see also Auguste Onken, *Der Ältere Mirabeau und die Oekonomische Gestellschaft in Bern* (Bern, 1886).

4. See *Quesnay's Tableau* for the first two editions; see also Meek, *Economics*, 28–29.

was designed to serve a purpose. The presence of the various sets of "Maximes" which accompanied every edition bear ample testimony to that larger intent. Specifically, in its early forms the Tableau constitutes a graphic representation of the responsibilities incumbent upon proprietors who would insure the wealth and economic stability of the realm. The pivotal role of proprietors here mirrors their emerging importance in the wider economic physiocratic doctrine. The Tableau provides another approach to Quesnay's and Mirabeau's continuing search for a necessity sufficient to command the obedience of sovereigns. Its economic complexities must, however, be considered in the ideological context established for it by the "Introduction" to part 4 of *L'ami des hommes*.

Mirabeau's opening remarks in the "Introduction" repudiate with one fell swoop much of his own past work and point the direction for all future physiocratic speculation. He is, he maintains, reproducing his "Mémoire sur les états provinciaux" as originally published, but having benefitted from criticism in the interim, he now proposes to investigate its consequences in greater depth by establishing "the general principles of all administration, by which everything holds together." He believes "that to develop clearly . . . the political area it is good to cast a glance over the entire organization," and accordingly he intends "to return to the very formation of societies."[5]

Even if his stated purpose does not appear to differ dramatically from that of the "Traité," the differences are crucial. Instead of limiting himself to his usual preoccupation with the genius of Frenchmen in its specific political manifestations, Mirabeau intends to establish the general principles of all administration and to lay bare those necessary connections between nature and government which, from the origins of society, have determined the proper form of the political machine. Having set out to find

5. "Introduction," 19.

principles within the history of the French monarchy that would provide it with legitimacy, Quesnay and Mirabeau had produced a chronicle of abuses but no commanding principles to oblige reform. History had taught them how the evils arose, but not how to correct them without a direct attack. Confronted with this prospect, they retreated from history altogether and turned to an abstract analysis of the problems grounded in nature. Having failed to find a way to persuade the French government to set its house in order, they turned to the formulation of rules valid for all men in all times and places. Not until 1767, in fact, did Mirabeau finally publish what might be considered the revised version of the "Traité," the *Lettres sur la législation*, divided into three parts entitled "L'ordre légal dépravé," "L'ordre légal rétabli," and "L'ordre légal perpétué."[6] The shift from the origins, progress, perfection, and abuses of the monarchy tells the whole story.

In the "Introduction," Mirabeau, after stating his intention to present the necessary structure of political mechanics, investigates the origins of society. All social organization rests upon the desire to harvest the fruits of one's labor. That desire, illuminated by reason, affords the basis for the recognition that union offers the best means of implementing individual desires. The union itself is what we call society. These mere instincts of desire and greed, however, would constitute a poor basis for the continuance of such a union were they not tempered by intellect and transformed into what we might call a physical law of union. Intellect, in other words, enables us to channel our unbridled passions into the socially acceptable paths of enlightened self-interest. "Interest is thus the first bond of society, from which it follows that society is more or less firm to the extent that those who compose it find in it their greater interest; and it is all the more assured as particular interest is the more protected in it."[7]

6. All references to *Lettres* will be to the 1775 edition in 3 vols. It was first published in *Les éphémérides du citoyen* in 1767, 1768, and 1769.
7. "Introduction," 19–20.

Even now Mirabeau retains some residual traditional doubts about the reliability of self-interest as the basis of social organization. After all, individual interests inevitably tend toward the same objects, the realization of the same desires, and can hardly be relied upon to produce a harmonious community if they are not all "contained the one by the other, and compressed by surrounding weights." He compares the desired interrelationship to that of the stones forming an arch: all contribute to the solidity and height of the construction "by virtue of the gravitational force which should, to the contrary, detach them," but which actually constitutes its essential stability by "the means of the pressure and the totality of the different parts." But an assembly of men, he continues, cannot be regarded as a society unless those who compose it "or the large number who impose it on the others," are interested in the maintenance of the society. Society is emphatically not a fair or a market, a mere passing assembly in which men gather only so long as their business, curiosity, or interest hold them there. Society requires a permanent interest, and Mirabeau cannot imagine an interest more permanent than that of property.[8] His juxtaposition of commercial gain and property suggests how little he thinks of property in purely economic terms, and how little he has yet accepted a thoroughly market view of society.

Mirabeau's discussion of property in the "Introduction" does not proceed with the logical rigor promised by his opening statements. Like subsequent physiocratic theorists, he begins with the traditional concept of the individual's property in himself as the cornerstone of all proprietary rights. But instead of arguing along Lockean lines, as would Quesnay in 1765, or following his own insights in the "Traité" about the individual's obligation to preserve himself, he offers the instinctive horror provoked by the words "rape" or "slavery" as proof of "this truth, that our person belongs to us and that all attempt against this property is infinitely expandable and must, in consequence, be checked if

8. *Ibid.*, 20–21.

we are to have an orderly society; it is also infinitely malleable." Government, he urges, in a theoretical abstraction from the feudal model of "rights in," should steer the primitive proprietary urge into socially constructive forms by giving its subjects reason to think of the country or the province as *my* country or *my* province. Such an identification of interests can only strengthen the public weal. But what, he asks, are we to make of a government the every maxim of which "would seem to disinterest the citizen not only from the public thing, but further from his own, by each day altering and disconcerting property in deed?"[9] Mirabeau's specific property theory at this juncture may not have much to recommend it, but it represents a major step toward formulation of the connection between property and government.

Property, he repeats, "is . . . the strongest bond of a society." Nature endows us with our taste for property together with our natural desire to conserve and extend it. Disputes between competing properties can only be settled by force or arbitration. Force obviously provokes the dissolution of society. Equal men, in disagreement but desirous of preserving society, must place their case before a third party equal to them both but in this instance superior by virtue of a capacity for dispassionate appraisal of their dispute. "This man is by common agreement recognized as judge: *beginning of authority*." In addition, his verdict "bears on principles which he makes the two parties listen to, and these principles become rules for other similar cases: *roots of laws*." Finally, since all societies prosper from avoiding such disputes in the first place, men collect the earliest judgments rendered and promulgate them as "rules of law, by virtue of the consent that man cannot refuse the axioms of equity: *beginning of the laws*." The laws, once established, require a guarantee, for men cannot always be trusted to hear the voice of reason. Government, through equity and force, provides that guarantee. It alone con-

9. *Ibid.*, 21–22.

stitutes the point of the arch; it both rests upon and holds in place the remaining stones.[10]

Government, however, can neither maintain its force nor guarantee equity when it fails to support the laws. Mirabeau here provides a theoretical framework for Quesnay's judgment, expressed as early as his *Encyclopédie* articles, that one person or a small group of people cannot dominate an infinitely larger number of their fellows. Such dominion is, he states, "against nature . . . unless it is by their formal or implicit consent." Furthermore, "this consent always supposes that they who have given it sought their advantage in giving it," and the advantage "cannot be found except in the laws which are the *arrêts* [official resolutions, usually having the force of law] of equity so long as they tend to maintain property, [the] first bond of society."[11] Mirabeau has, indeed, succeeded in extrapolating from the historical specificity of the "Traité" a general theory of social organization. As theories go, it leaves a good deal to be desired, but it faithfully conveys not only his own prejudices, but also his and Quesnay's major preoccupations.

In the "Introduction," Mirabeau cast the debate in the general terms of the nature of social order and the justification for government. Thus methodologically he frees the discussion from the specific investigation of the monarchy and raises it to a new level of abstraction. Nonetheless, he tries to sum up the nature of the relationship between property and the state. The love of property, he argues, can and should be molded into the love of the public good, so that the property, which binds society, is both guaranteed and limited by government.

Mirabeau cannot believe that society could function without subordination and obedience. Yet he is determined to establish property as a presocial right and to endow the laws protecting it with greater authority than that enjoyed by the government

10. *Ibid.*, 22–23. See Rousseau to Mirabeau, in *Précis de l'ordre légal*, (Amsterdam and Paris, 1768), 194–96.
11. "Introduction," 24.

itself. His attempt to establish society on fixed and immutable foundations prefigures that of the physiocrats even as his loving enumeration of traditional structures displays the strength of the ties binding him to his own past. His vision of social structure, in particular, remains unchanged. Society is divided into four orders: the Ecclesiastical, the Noble or Military, the Civil, and the Municipal. Each man, however, depends directly on the sovereign authority, which intersects each of them. Two kinds of laws govern these relations: fundamental laws or laws of title, and laws of regulation or of government. Mirabeau acknowledges the portentous character of the designation of fundamental laws but dares to claim that they do not depend on the government. He recounts the story of a wise man who, when asked where the fundamental laws of the kingdom were located, replied, *"in the Custom of Normandy."*[12]

Mirabeau had every reason to tread lightly as he approached the sanctum of the fundamental law. During the 1750s the Parlements' claims that tended to identify fundamental law with the establishment of an independent political role for themselves had understandably aroused royal suspicions. In identifying the fundamental law with the customary law of Normandy, Mirabeau hoped to remove the concept from this dangerous terrain. The apparent similarity between Mirabeau's fundamental law and that of the Parlements cloaks a crucial distinction. Parlementary claims included the right to participation in the direction of the realm: the Parlements frequently warred with intendants about administrative questions, which Mirabeau would have subsumed under laws of regulation, and then they evoked the fundamental law to legitimize their own intervention. Mirabeau never supported such pretensions. To him the fundamental law merely delimited boundaries that the government could not cross. And those limits were the boundaries of property.

12. *Ibid.*, 36. Cf. Mirabeau's later position, *Lettres sur la législation*, I, 137; and François Dumont, "Royauté française et monarchie absolue au XVIIe siècle," *XVIIe siècle*, nos. 58–59 (1963), 3–29.

Mirabeau's insistence upon the sanctity of property thus laid the foundation for the physiocratic development of natural law. It is impossible, he asserts, "that the Government has anywhere preceded property, because property is necessary to hold men together and to form society. . . . Government, therefore, derives from property," and the laws of title cannot depend on its authority.[13] But if the government does not constitute the source of all social rights, what becomes of Mirabeau's own earlier attachment to the theory of divine right? During the drafting of the "Traité," Quesnay had pointed out to Mirabeau that given the existence of religious pluralism, those who wished to establish a unitary theory of social and political organization must seek its principles elsewhere. Mirabeau showed no alacrity in abandoning religion as a fundamental guarantee of order; but here, in the "Introduction," he tries to come to terms with the problematic claims of religion by arguing that "divine right only embraces everything because God preceded everything, created everything."[14] Quesnay would not have disagreed.

Mirabeau has established two postulates: first, God precedes and creates everything; second, property precedes government. And government has no right to tamper with that fundamental law according to which society rests on property, for it has no right to order society to dissolve itself. His ambiguous reference to divine right explains nothing, particularly since he does not specify whose right is divine. His carefully chosen words suggest, however, that he means not the divine right of kings but of society.

Among the various kinds of property enjoyed by individuals in society, Mirabeau includes physical property in ourselves, such natural (not social) rights and actions as those of fathers in relation to sons, movable and immovable goods, and finally, public property that includes both the real objects held in common (common lands, streets, churches, etc.) and the sense of pro-

13. "Introduction," 37.
14. *Ibid.*

prietorship reflected in the public administration. This list hardly constitutes a coherent property theory, but its very incoherence reveals the tremendous difficulties of constructing such a theory. Mirabeau blends psychological and material, social and natural justifications of property with confusing abandon.[15]

Psychological considerations, rather than any material necessity such as the obligation to stay alive or the right to the fruits of one's labor, still bear the weight of Mirabeau's property theory. They also account for his raising what he calls "our rights and actions" to the plane of a fundamental constituent of property. Society requires that most of its members display a proper sense of subordination, which must be sanctified by nature herself. The family provides the model for necessary social roles, which Mirabeau endows with the force of a natural right inseparable from the fundamental law of property.[16] In a sense this natural subordination forms a transitional link between his earlier defense of legal privilege as a proprietary right and the physiocrats' subsequent reliance upon the market to guarantee social differentiation. Mirabeau's use of the family as the prototype for social subordination thus reflects his position halfway between a divine and a material sanction for natural law. It also suggests that the authority of the father, rather than that of the master or seigneur, constitutes the irreducible minimum of paternalist sensibility. This doctrine renders paternalism assimilable to bourgeois values, as its subsequent endorsement in the Napoleonic Code shows.

Mirabeau's insistence upon the possession of movable and immovable goods as the third facet of property inclines the balance toward the material side, but fails even to mention labor as the justification for such property. Indeed, he does not analyze the origins of property at all. He does, however, argue that even the most paltry material possessions constitute an eminently respect-

15. *Ibid.*, 37–38.
16. *Ibid.*, 39. Mirabeau, however, has abandoned his political paternalism. Cf. *Théorie de l'impôt* ([Paris?], 1760), 19–21, where he violently criticizes paternalist notions of provisioning.

able form of property, which must be treated as more worthy of respect than great wealth because "the greatest evil one can do to society is to disinterest the citizen"; and it is all the easier to "disinterest the poor man than the rich, and much more dangerous, given that the poor are the most numerous and the most useful."[17]

Mirabeau's eloquent, if utilitarian, defense of absolute equality in the right of property constitutes one of his greatest contributions and prefigures one of the more generous features of physiocratic thought. Most of Mirabeau's specific theories about property barely survived formulation, but his recognition of the importance of the psychological aspect of property endured. For Mirabeau property began with the individual's desire for possession. Underlying all the various theoretical rationales, he perceived a primary human drive. Society must respect presocial human rights even as it channels them into respectable social forms. Although Mirabeau's commitment to traditional hierarchy had rested largely on his perception of the necessity to tame the antisocial human beast, he had never condemned man as all bad and had always argued that the principles of order could also be found within man himself. The problem lay in encouraging, by whatever necessary means, the good or sociable at the expense of the bad or antisocial. Through his and Quesnay's investigation of the nature of the monarchy he had come to appreciate the dangers of a traditional order that subsumed all human rights under the aegis of society, and particularly under that of the state. But divesting religious and political institutions of their omnipotence left a dangerous void. By his fourth category of property—public property—Mirabeau tries to fill that void.

All individuals should be encouraged to see their own interest in the public welfare by finding their own sense of property reflected in the sense of public property. Mirabeau's concept of public property as a constituent element of private property derives in part from his continuing preoccupation with the need

17. "Introduction," 40.

for a powerful social cement. In this pursuit he abandons his original doctrine of property as an appendage of social function and substitutes one of presocial property rights.[18] But unlike the early English theorists he could not look to his historical milieu for a satisfactory model.

The distance that separates the "Introduction" from the original *Mémoire concernant l'utilité des états provinciaux,* or even from the "Traité," reveals how far Mirabeau's thought has progressed. By trying to formulate a political theory abstracted from historical experience, he accomplished a personal methodological revolution that led him to abandon historical precedent and ensconce property as the presocial cornerstone of society. In the process, however, he established a dualism at the heart of his political thought. The price he paid to accept the fundamental law that preceded the authority of government was to abandon the laws of regulation, which dictate the practical life of society, to the undisputed control of the government.

Mirabeau thus made no provision for the mediation between private freedom and public authority. Theoretically, the monarch had been divested of his omnipotence and subjected to the rule of laws, but no practical way existed to impose the will of the laws on the monarch. A decade later, in his *Lettres sur la législation,* he would write: "Since men have become inspired to mix in all possible fashion their social institutions and to take precautions against the abuses of power, they have only imagined fragile institutions, have only built edifices founded on the sand, this is to say on the instability and discord of misunderstood interests. They have not yet been able to devise any form of mixed government, or rather of mixed authority, capable of resisting particular exclusive interests."[19] All the physiocrats and many philosophes,

18. *Ibid.,* 41.
19. II, 656. See also Quesnay's letter to Le Blanc on Hume, in Hecht, "Vie de Quesnay," 252; EMHL, Winterthur Mss, group 2, series A, du Pont to Count Scheffer (1773), 20–21.

including even that most independent of fellow travelers, Turgot, agreed with him.[20]

Historically, taxation has furnished the principal grounds for the justification of the limitation of royal authority. If property is both sacred and presocial, by what right does the state appropriate a farthing of the individual's own? In the "Introduction," Mirabeau barely joins this question. The prince, he maintains, enjoys the undisputed right to demand subsidies from his subjects who, on their side, have no right to refuse. If the prince requires financial assistance for the upkeep of the public domain, his purposes serve the interest of all and brook no demur. If he uses his subjects' money for his own "dissipations, liberalities and fantasies, I say only that he violates the law of title, . . . that, in a word, he abuses his power, which is called tyranny" and which corrodes society.[21] But Mirabeau does not suggest any control for such excesses. In principle, taxation is nothing other "than the tribute offered by particular properties to the general property, for . . . their own maintenance." Mirabeau's formulation encompasses the essence of subsequent physiocratic taxation theory, which never resolved the problem of abuse.[22]

Mirabeau's method and arguments clearly foreshadow future physiocratic doctrine on many points. However much traditionalism Mirabeau has maintained, he has shed even more. Physiocracy deliberately incorporated the traditional spirit of ordered community—the claims of society against those of unbridled individuals or even institutions of the ancien régime. But the "Introduction" lacks the essential ingredient of physiocracy, namely, the ultimate sanction of sheer physical necessity which would be

20. For example, Turgot, *Mémoire sur les municipalités,* in Gustave Schelle, ed., *Oeuvres de Turgot,* 5 vols. (Paris, 1913–1923), IV, 576.
21. "Introduction," 42–43. Cf. Mirabeau, *Théorie de l'Impôt,* 406.
22. "Introduction," 54. Cf. Luigi Einaudi, "The Physiocratic Theory of Taxation," in *Economic Essays in Honor of Gustav Cassel* (London, 1933), 129–42; EMHL, Winterthur MSS, group 2, series E, W2-4741, du Pont, "Observations et Recherches."

provided by Quesnay's economics. Mirabeau's reluctant but thorough repudiation of divinely ordained social organization created a void at the center of the system exactly at the point at which Quesnay had proposed to establish a prime physical necessity to govern social action. For Quesnay that prime mover would be his own materialist economics.

In the "Introduction" Mirabeau makes use of what he had learned from Quesnay about the destructive nature of certain taxes and the crippling effects of restrictions on free trade.[23] He similarly insists that agriculture is "the prime source of production, . . . the alimentation of society."[24] He does not, however, succeed in establishing economics as the necessary basis of his political and social theory. But he does abstract the crucial social and political questions from the immediate political situation and thereby create the theoretical vacuum that will be filled by the economics. The "Introduction," in a sense, thus implicitly invalidates the very "Mémoire" it presents, but provides no clear indication of what will replace divine necessity as the center of social gravity.

While Mirabeau concentrated upon preparing his own work for publication, Quesnay returned to his technical agronomic pursuits, presumably with the intent of attacking the problem of the monarchy at its roots. He designed his "Questions intéressantes," which appeared in part 4 of *L'ami des hommes,* for the consideration of the academies and other provincial societies.[25] The questions ask for information that Quesnay deemed necessary to a sound agricultural policy for France. But the seeming naïveté of his honest quest for knowledge frequently masks—as it was undoubtedly intended to—the extent to which he believed himself already in possession of the larger answers. Having elaborated the theory of agricultural development to his own satisfaction,

23. "Introduction," 55–60.
24. *Ibid.,* 48–49.
25. All references will be to the INED, II, edition.

he only needed empirical documentation to answer his opponents.

Quesnay's questions touch upon almost every aspect of French economic life, and in so doing inadvertently highlight the gap between that life and Quesnay's model. Physiocracy never rid itself of the contradictions implicit in the "Questions." If the physiocrats would never publicly entertain the notion that the answer to some of their master's rhetorical questions might be "no," they did increasingly emphasize the necessity for government action and universal education to insure that the answers would become "yes." However much Quesnay might emphasize the technical aspects of his program, its roots were embedded in a social and political problem. In "Questions" he barely touches upon this problem directly; and when he does, as in his discussion of the need for good administration to establish a fitting economic government, he invariably dodges it. In this respect, "Questions" complements but does not advance beyond Mirabeau's "Introduction."[26] It too serves as a transitional document that simultaneously summarizes previous work and points the way to the future. No more than the "Introduction" does it isolate and describe that central force or necessity which would impose social compliance on reigning monarchs. Yet like the "Introduction" it narrows the field in which this essential factor could be sought.

Before formulating the Tableau, Quesnay had to face the problem of adapting his blueprint of economic growth to France. Nor could either of his favorite authorities on economic matters, Cantillon or Hume, be of much help. Cantillon, an Irish banker living abroad, displayed great theoretical sophistication but remained primarily interested in accounting for the mechanics of monetary circulation; and Hume restricted himself to applying Cantillon's analysis to the realities of the English economy.[27] More

26. Cf. "Questions," 657n, where he accepts the existence of *corps* and *compagnies*.

27. Cf. Herlitz, "Development," Adolphe Landry, "Les idées de Quesnay sur la population," INED, I, 49; Eugene Rotwein, "Editor's Introduction"

than either Cantillon or Hume, Quesnay brought to his scientific work a strong normative bias; he wished not merely to understand but to alter the path of development. To recommend that the king suppress major vested interests necessitated the formulation of an absolute law. Quesnay's Tableau was meant to provide such a law, but a proper understanding of the strictly economic problems inherent in its formulation requires consideration first of the "Mémoire" for the agricultural society of Berne. The Tableau challenges the most sophisticated modern commentators, but no amount of puzzle-solving can explain its mechanism without a prior understanding of what it was designed to reveal. Mirabeau's "Mémoire" for Berne, composed during the course of 1759 while Quesnay himself was at work on the Tableau, establishes the context for the Tableau—as Quesnay himself suggested when he proposed that it would furnish an adequate, although partial, introduction to the first publication of the Tableau.[28] The "Mémoire" reveals the political and social problems that motivated Quesnay's economic breakthrough and shows the Tableau for what it was—the analytic instrument rather than the theoretical structure of a new political economy.

"It will seem altogether strange some day," Mirabeau mused in the opening of the "Mémoire," "that there was a time when it constituted a novelty to announce that agriculture was the basis of the prosperity of States, the principle of their force and the only inexhaustible treasure that they could possess."[29] As usual, Mirabeau leaned toward the rhetorical flourish. Identifying agriculture as the source of national prosperity constituted no novelty: it had been commonplace among the ancients, not to

to *David Hume: Writings on Economics* [1955] (Madison, Wisc., 1970) ix–cxi; Engels, *Anti-Dühring*, 260–66.

28. AN, M 784, no. 70. This letter was reproduced by Stephan Bauer, "Quesnay's Tableau Economique," *The Economic Journal*, V (1895), 20, and translated by Meek, *Economics*, 108.

29. "Mémoire," 9.

mention their medieval and early modern successors. He himself, in the first edition of *L'ami des hommes*, had insisted on its primacy in the most traditional terms. The novelty lay in demonstrating, according to the best scientific standards of the day, that agriculture constituted not only the cornerstone of society, but the source of increased revenues for the state. As Quesnay had put it when annotating the manuscript of Mirabeau's "Réponse aux objections," his predecessors had erred in pitying the peasant instead of the state.[30] Only a modernized agriculture could possibly provide the state an adequate financial base to compete successfully in the modern world. In "Questions," Quesnay had elaborated his conviction that agriculture deserved greater support than commerce and manufacture because, unlike those luxury trades, "it belongs to the kingdom in property."[31] A merchant or financier can always go elsewhere.

The notion that possession of land gave a man a particular stake in the good management of society cannot be generically identified as either conservative or liberal. Bodin, Harrington, and Locke all relied upon it, but differed in their conceptions of the nature of property.[32] Political representation of landed property governed English political life and would shortly be introduced as the foundation of the new American Republic. In France, as in England and the American colonies, land constituted the principal base of economic productivity. Quesnay, in dismissing the validity of representation in government, glossed over the difference between feudal and modern property and, in following his own instinctive mistrust of commerce and manufacture as well as Mirabeau's arguments, he tended to exaggerate landed property's qualities as a source of both social stability and economic growth. This combination was not fortuitous.

Quesnay wanted France to enjoy the benefits of wealth with-

30. AN, M 778, no. 3. Cf. Weulersse, *Manuscrits*, 32.
31. "Questions," 637.
32. See J. G. A. Pocock, *Politics, Language, and Time* [1960] (New York, 1973), 104–47, esp. 110–13.

out sacrificing the harmony of traditional social unity. By designating agriculture as the property of the kingdom, he sought to erect a barrier against the dissolvent effects of trade and commerce. The designation of agriculture as social property would insure the continuity and stability of the realm, and best of all insure the nation's control of its own fortunes. But property as Quesnay defined it implied the freedom of the individual to dispose of his own. Just as the nation required absolute control of its produce in order to participate fully in the international market (and maximize the value of its production), might not individuals at home require the same freedom to realize the value of their produce? Had not Quesnay from the start insisted upon the necessity of a free national market in grain? Thus the very private property that he had designed as the fundamental cement of society would be transformed into its most controversial and socially disruptive element. In response to this "nationalization" of agriculture, the seigneurial class would protest the loss of its dues; and the marginal peasantry would protest not only the loss of its traditional rights in the land but its consequent forced entry into the labor market.

Quesnay welcomed the commercialization of agriculture, but never fully faced the social price of economic transformation. In spite of Mirabeau's continued reminders of the damage monied fortunes had already wreaked upon the French community, Quesnay clung to the belief that a market economy could be established without destroying the country's social coherence. Undoubtedly this illusion accounts for much of his insistence upon the doctrine of the exclusive productivity of agriculture, which he had already derived in large measure from the economic analysis of his own milieu. By correctly identifying agriculture as the dominant sector of the French economy, however, he drew attention to that very disequilibrium in the social relations of the nation which he had intended to deny. By exaggerating the role of agriculture he deprived his model of the safety valve of state sponsorship for manufactures or trade, a valve which might have alleviated such tensions.

The Berne "Mémoire" as a whole represents Quesnay's and Mirabeau's attempt to translate the former's economic analysis into a coherent political economy. By formulating an optimal Swiss program for a Swiss audience, they had a unique opportunity to air their views without compromising their position. Throughout Mirabeau's manuscript Quesnay appended extensive comments, mostly pertaining to economic analysis, which Mirabeau incorporated directly, making the finished text a work of collaboration.[33]

The agricultural society, following French fashion, offered a prize for the best essay to explain: (1) the reasons Switzerland should cultivate grain; (2) the general and particular obstacles to such cultivation; (3) the general and particular means the country could offer such cultivators.[34] While disclaiming any desire to compete for the prize itself—his entry took third place— Mirabeau jumped at the chance to consider such interesting subjects in relation to the politically neutral case of Switzerland rather than the highly charged case of France. When publishing at home, he and Quesnay had scrupulously avoided any direct discussion of the "general and particular obstacles" that the large-scale cultivation of grain, which they advocated, would encounter in France. He did not, however, allow the protective Swiss coloration to obscure his primary concern with French conditions. In fact, the transparency of his attempt largely accounts for his failure to carry off the prize.

Mirabeau begins, as he and Quesnay often do, with a brief historical sketch of the questions under discussion. But instead of focusing upon the development of the French state, Mirabeau

33. Cf. AN, M 783, no. 5; Cf. Weulersse, *Manuscrits*, 35–39, which reproduces three of Quesnay's annotations that Mirabeau did not incorporate into his final draft. Meek, *Economics*, 68, also includes a fragment from Quesnay's annotations.
34. "Mémoire," 17.

concentrates upon the progress of the arts, a general category that includes human industry in general and agriculture in particular. From this perspective he treats the period following the barbarian invasions more harshly than he had in the past. The barbarians, he now argues, had "stifled all germ of human industry" and oppressed everything by arms.[35]

Mirabeau credits them with the gentlemanly quality of exempting agriculture from the general destruction, but only because he thought they understood that their existence depended upon it. Thus, while he never relinquished his conviction that feudalism at least preserved the basis for civilization in these dark years— and modern scholarship would hardly dispute him on this point— he no longer offers it as the model for all human organization.[36] Instead, he looks to the recovery of scientific knowledge from Asia, where the barbarians had chased it, to inaugurate the revolution that would revive human progress. In that combination of circumstances "always necessary to great revolutions," the religious quarrels contributed to the general awakening by prodding "the most sensitive part of the human spirit. Everyone studied." The invention of printing hastened the process by disseminating knowledge of the sciences, while princes contributed by supporting artists of all varieties: "It was enough to create a new World; and, nevertheless, Providence fixed at the same epoch the discovery of the one we call by that name."[37]

Unfortunately, all great advances can fall prey to abuse. The new intellectual techniques, foremost among which ranked scientific analysis, equipped society to perfect its own institutions for all time. But society abused them. Entranced by the chimera of mercantile gain, sovereigns pursued erroneous policies to advance useless manufactures and to amass gold within their kingdoms. In the midst of this "universal Idolatry," agriculture almost succumbed entirely. The eternal and circular laws of

35. *Ibid.*, 10.
36. Cf. *Lettres sur la législation*, I, 48–49.
37. "Mémoire," 10; *Lettres sur la législation*, I, 56–57, 221–22.

nature, however, dictate that "reproduction is born in the breast of putrefaction," and even agriculture eventually experienced a renaissance.[38]

The happy rescue of the first art fell to the English. Although blind to agriculture's larger interests and apparently foolish enough to think it could grab the entire wealth of the universe, England proved as enlightened as could be expected of those nations deluded as to the "art of profits." The English thus came to recognize that commerce depends "upon those who sell at first hand," but that it also requires "a strong and continuous production [of] the fruits . . . which assure a useful cargo." Agriculture, Mirabeau insists, is "the only manufacture in which the work of a solitary laborer furnishes the subsistence of a great number of others who can attend to other employments." England's splendor, therefore, dates from its return to these first principles.[39]

Quesnay's and Mirabeau's blueprint of the periodization of European history has not changed, but their understanding of it has immeasurably deepened. They do not doubt that first the Crusades and then the Renaissance, the Reformation, printing, the discoveries, and the scientific revolution have changed the face of Europe. The accelerating increase in knowledge and wealth has enabled society to break out of the prison of subsistence agriculture and local feudal government. The expansion of intellectual and economic horizons has sufficed to create a market with possibilities for capital accumulation and the division of labor. The human mind, freed from the tyranny and slavery of its recent barbarism, now enjoys the power to define and to follow its own best interest. But men have instead fallen under the dominion of an interest that is both vile and "rational in its delirium"—the pursuit of gold for its own sake. Their misapprehension has led them to neglect the only sound basis for wealth.[40]

38. "Mémoire," 11–13.
39. *Ibid.*, 13.
40. *Ibid.*, 12–14.

Quesnay and Mirabeau do not really explain how the English came to understand the importance of agriculture. Nor do they relate the nature of governmental institutions or social organization to the success of the English state. They continue to hold the state responsible for the pursuit of correct economic policies, as Mirabeau said, to give form to the raw material of society. At the same time they allow a much larger role to general historical development than they did previously. In Mirabeau's analysis the raw material of society itself has changed between between the fourteenth and eighteenth centuries. Quesnay and Mirabeau have not filled in the gaps in their thought with speculations and interpretive schemes. They have moved toward a more materialist interpretation than either of them advanced in their early works, but they still accord a decisive role to the state in shaping the material conditions of the national community. They have traced the rise of "economic individualism," even while castigating the deviations it has pursued.

The appearance of agricultural societies, first that of Brittany, now the one of Berne, offers a glimmer of hope that men may indeed be turning toward the correct path. Mirabeau will, accordingly, take this opportunity, not to fight for a prize—"fight is a word proscribed by my conscience"—but to contribute to the spreading of "general views." He modestly acknowledges that actual agricultural practice differs from place to place in accordance with local conditions and must be left to the discretion of the individual. But, he insists, certain general principles cannot be neglected, for they furnish "the certitudes applicable to each Canton." Through an understanding of these general principles the government will be able to determine the kind of support it owes to agriculture—"this plant whose roots constitute its independence and its security, whose trunk establishes its strength, whose branches encompass its extent, whose fruits register its power."[41]

41. "Mémoire," 17.

The society's first question asks whether Switzerland should devote itself to the cultivation of grain. The question, Mirabeau explains, may be read two ways: should Switzerland concentrate on grain production in preference to other crops, or should Switzerland, relative to other nations, be regarded as particularly apt to cultivate grain? The second alternative he wisely brackets. (The second prize winner argued cogently that the Swiss terrain did not even remotely favor grain production.) Even the first alternative he leaves to the discretion of the society. Instead, he proposes to trace briefly "the general reasons that determine the choice of the cultivation of land and its use." His next ten pages, all transcribed directly from Quesnay's manuscript annotations, lay out the central tenets of physiocratic political economy.[42]

Following Quesnay, he begins by dismissing the fictitious hypothesis that the use of agricultural produce should determine the selection of crops or means of cultivation with a view to insuring maximum production of those crops which fulfill primary needs. Today, "neither seas, nor mountains, nor deserts" can cut a country off from commerce—unless "false governmental measures replace, in this respect, the barriers which human industry and constancy have succeeded in crossing." Commerce and communication have shattered the foundations of autarchy so that in any well-administered state, namely in one where the market exists, "*the best use of land is that which procures the greatest profit evaluated in money.*" He explains that a proper evaluation of the produce of land requires consideration of the total product and the net product a given farm can yield. He then demonstrates the method of calculating the net product, as Quesnay had done in the *Encyclopédie* articles, but without ex-

---

42. *Ibid.*, 19, and AN, M 783, no. 5. Cf. *Recueil de mémoires . . . Berne.* The first prize went to Albert Stapfer, deacon at Diesbach, who argues that grain is necessary but that land should only be sown with grain when one cannot make better use of it, and that the obstacles to its cultivation are great (54, 68, 53–100). The second prize went to Jean Bertrand, pastor at Orbe, who argues that grain is necessary but that Switzerland is better suited to livestock (101–47).

trapolating directly from the micro-economic model of a single farm to the macro-economic model of the state.[43]

Inadvertently, Mirabeau had opened Quesnay's eyes to the relationship of social to economic structure and started him thinking about the difficulties of defining property within his general economic model. These new concerns lead him now to discuss the net product not exclusively in relation to the monolithic state, but rather in relation to different social groups, specifically the large proprietors, the small proprietors who cultivate their own land, and the farmers. The proprietors present no problems. Their revenue always depends ("is always established") on the net product, and they enjoy the indisputable right to "exact the price of the rent by virtue of the largest net product which the land can yield." Quesnay adds, as if to underscore the intrusion of market criteria into the heart of Mirabeau's cherished, traditional landlord-tenant relationship, "there are few reasons of State that can legitimately impinge upon this right of property."[44] For the first time Quesnay is unequivocally addressing himself to the nature of property. Here he presents it, unencumbered by historical precedent or feudal obligation, as the economic right of the landowner to demand the highest possible return on his investment.

When he considers the net product in relation to small proprietors, he apparently manifests the same respect for the rights of the individual. The interest of such owner-cultivators would necessarily lead them to prefer the largest total product to the largest net product, and to procure the largest total product by an increase in labor "which pays the wage of the labor attributed to them as a profit because what is consumed in costs furnishes the subsistence of their family." Then turning to the farmers, Quesnay points out that they, like the proprietors, fall into two distinct

43. "Mémoire," 19–21.
44. *Ibid.*, 22.

groups, those who prefer the greatest net product and those who prefer the greatest total product.[45]

His observations upon the behavior of those farmers whose interest leads them to prefer a greater total product lead Quesnay further. He speculates that they can, "in passing, warn us of the damage which can arise from the too great abusive liberty, which exists in allowing the *colon* to so implant himself on the soil of which he is only the cultivator, that, by a popular convention, he lays down the law to the proprietor, who would not find anyone to rent his land if he changed farmers or tried to augment the lease."[46] Only experience, Quesnay shudders, could lead us to conceive of such an abuse, but there actually exists a French province, Picardy, where the entire populace unites to promote it. "The owner has the property of the land and the *colon* that of the exploitation." And the usurped property receives public sanction in contracts and divisions. An occasional proprietor has tried to shake off the yoke, but to no avail. "This abuse," Quesnay concludes, "is not only an injustice against the proprietor, but it is in addition harmful to the land and to the State whose interest is the largest possible net product."[47]

Quesnay has decisively broken his discrete silence about existing property relations and openly repudiated Mirabeau's earlier view, expressed in the "Bref état," that "the best and surest way to draw an income from a land that one cannot exploit oneself is to distribute it to tenants who hold it in property in return for a rent or a share (*quantième*) of its harvest."[48] Mirabeau, of course, was not advancing an economic theory, but describing common practice. And Quesnay himself, for all the communal action of Picardy, must have known that the general phenomenon

45. *Ibid.*
46. *Ibid.*, 23.
47. *Ibid.*
48. "Bref état des moyens pour la restauration de l'autorité du roi et de ses finances," ed. Georges Weulersse, *RHES*, VI (1913), 206.

of dual ownership existed throughout France. But even if Quesnay's explicit recognition of the counter-productivity of French property relations was the inescapable conclusion of his economic analysis, it opened a Pandora's box of opposition to his supposedly neutral economic program and revealed his political economy for the inherently divisive doctrine it was.

According to accepted liberal doctrine, individual interest fired the market and kept it working to insure social harmony and national prosperity. Quesnay shows clearly, however, that the interest of small proprietors and backward tenants—a majority of the French population—favored the greatest total product. Against their interest, accordingly, he had to muster enlightened proprietors, modern farmers, and above all the state, all of whose interests lay in the greatest possible net product. Quesnay is no longer dealing merely with a financial community that the state misguidedly created and might disown. He has raised the spectre of irreconcilable interests within the agricultural sector itself, and in so doing has exposed the depth of the popular commitment to the traditional moral economy. Should he fail to convince the landlords of the true nature of their interests, or worse yet, should he provoke them into an uneconomic defense of their traditional seigneurial rights, he would incite the most powerful members of landed society to assume political leadership of what might have remained mere popular discontent.

Quesnay's insistence upon the absolute nature of the landlord's property, with which not even the state should interfere, challenges the precarious equilibrium of traditional property theory. His argument implies that social function carries no weight as against absolute possession, or at best that social function derives from absolute possession. He has established property as an economic right. To implement his views would, however, require challenging what many regarded as perfectly legitimate forms of property. Quesnay would have to make his own theoretical peace with the nature of property, but in the absence of overwhelming market forces to make the advantages of modern agriculture irresistible, he also needed the state to decide for economic as against traditional property rights.[49]

In turning to a discussion of the net product in relation to population, Quesnay recapitulates the arguments, forged in the *Encyclopédie* article "Hommes," which initially converted Mirabeau. He rejects the old prejudice that a large number of people directly engaged in agriculture favors population and wealth. Mirabeau, whose words at this point Quesnay does not alter, rushes to a qualified defense of his own treatise on population. The author who defended these views, he insists, "considered things more particularly with respect to views of humanity than to economic views." A proper understanding of the question, he now recognizes, requires the combination of the humane and the economic perspectives. He then effortlessly develops Quesnay's argument. An agricultural state comprises several classes of men. "The more cultivation occupies men whose labor produces only their own subsistence, the less the harvests, destined first for the nourishment of the cultivators, yields a surplus to form revenues." Yet this surplus alone can support the rest of the classes in the state. "Thus, at equal product, the more the industry and wealth of the agricultural entrepreneurs saves the labor of men, the more cultivation furnishes the subsistence of other men." Quesnay here resumes the discussion to insist upon the implications of the net product for the social division of labor: those men not directly engaged in agriculture are all the more capable of entering other professions, "as their bread is cooked and prepared, and as they are not attached to the land for the annual reproduction of wealth."[50]

As experience was to prove in both England and France, the great traumatic shift for the working population came with the

---

49. Cf. Roland Mousnier, "L'évolution des institutions monarchiques en France et ses relations avec l'état social," *XVIIe siècle*, nos. 58–59 (1963), 57–72, esp. 67; J. C. Timbal, "L'esprit du droit privé au XVIIe siècle," *ibid.*, 30–39.

50. "Mémoire," 25–26.

ultimate divorce from the land and the necessity to purchase the totality of their daily sustenance in the marketplace. With all residual rights in the soil, with the meager but marginally decisive support of a garden plot or an acre of grain cut out from under them, men became totally dependent on the market, which henceforth governed not only the price of their food but also the price of their labor and hence their power to survive. Given the special place of bread in the eighteenth-century French diet and popular psychology, Quesnay's seemingly innocuous phrase describing it as "cooked and prepared" opens a gulf of social dislocation barely conceivable today. The grain trade debate during the 1760s and 1770s, not to mention during the Revolution, revealed the depth of popular opposition to the buying and selling—to the market governance—of men's lives.

Mirabeau tries to soften Quesnay's dictum by suggesting that if the total product increases through labor-intensive agriculture without prejudicing the growth of the net product, the larger total product will favor population growth. That is all very well, Quesnay sternly reminds him, "but there would be more men and not incomes." Mirabeau will not completely surrender. "It would nonetheless be a great reason of humanity and natural law to augment, as much as is possible, the means of population." As the physiocrats were repeatedly to insist, however, humanitarianism has nothing to do with natural law. Here Quesnay merely points out that the net product rather than humanitarian considerations govern the behavior of farmers and proprietors, who will hardly incline to invest in costs that do not promise to yield a profit. He will concede to Mirabeau only that the humanitarian aspect of population "depends . . . solely upon the morals and customs of a country, or the humanity and domesticity that are in fashion." The seemingly small concession, which yields no ground on the theoretical questions, testifies to Quesnay's persistent respect for the role of human decision in determining the allocation and development of resources. He knows full well that such customs could easily line up against the rational pursuit of the maximum net product.[51] He only hopes that the state will objectively assess the best interests of society as a whole, and its own revenues in particular, and use its powers of persuasion and coercion to transform the economic consciousness of its subjects.

To drive his point home Quesnay turns to the explicit consideration of the net product in relation to the state. We have, he claims, proved that the net product "is all that composes revenues" and affords the state "disposable subjects." A large number of men, fed by a large gross product, remains attached to the land "with no other use than that of drawing from its own subsistence." Such men, "tied, as it were, to the soil, cannot be separated from it without destroying the product that causes them to subsist." From the state's point of view they are worthless, for the state "can draw from them no service or contribution whatsoever without depriving them of necessities. Quesnay reluctantly admits that this portion of the inhabitants "has a right to life like the others, but . . . by the incommunicable weight of its subsistence and employment, can neither contribute to nor participate in that which we call, politically speaking, the prosperity of the *patrie*." Ignorance of the true source of wealth and a lack of analytic sophistication has led to the erroneous idea that the less each individual consumed, the more would be available for the support of others. Even in cities "everything is consumed at a profit," by virtue of rapid circulation. The state, Quesnay concludes, must look to the net product. This general point of view, he concedes, "may be more or less applicable in practice according to the principles and constitutions of the government of Nations, but is always necessary to lay down as the basis of economic science."[52]

Quesnay, in his discussion of the net product, has finally welded his analytic principles into a coherent economic theory, or science as he prefers to call it. Its foundations can be discerned

51. *Ibid.*, 26.
52. *Ibid.*, 26–27.

in the economic articles, but not even in "Impôts" had he stated them cogently. In the Berne "Mémoire" he lays down the central principle that the net product constitutes the basis of national prosperity, and must, in consequence, constitute the primary object of government attention. Having isolated agriculture as the productive sector of the economy, he shows that the introduction of large-scale enterprises in that sector will promote that division of labor which affords the military strength, material well-being, and aesthetic richness of any society. He further argues that increased consumption, when grounded in a healthy productive sector, promotes an increase in wealth which incites the productive sector to further growth. He does not directly tackle the difficult question of the specific nature of the economic contribution of nonagricultural labor: he suggests not only that the simple consumption of such labor endows the product of agricultural labor with a market price and thus transforms it from a commodity of worthless *use* value to one of economically significant *venal* value, but also that it directly contributes to the marketability of agricultural produce.

After following Quesnay's elucidation of the general principles that govern the relationship of state and society to the net product irrespective of particular political arrangements, Mirabeau resumes the narrative and undertakes the application of economic science to the Swiss case. His first words immediately attack the relationship between "the two different styles of economic life and morals," which he asserts "is always a speculation of the greatest importance." We can, he says, truthfully argue that pastoral life in its simplicity most closely reflects "the simple order of nature," while settled agricultural life more closely approximates "the order of political society, which reunites masters and servants, superiority, subordination, commandment, obedience, and different interests."[53] Again, the absence of Quesnay's corrections suggests his concurrence. Mirabeau's words express the

53. *Ibid.*, 28, 29.

two men's concern with the reconciliation of diverging interests. Theoretically, the market to which Quesnay ascribes economic centrality, and which he holds responsible for inaugurating and sustaining economic growth, should assure reconciliation. Practically, it apparently could not. The same reservations that lead Mirabeau to insist upon the order of political society as distinct from a purely economic order also account for Quesnay's ambiguity about the productivity of nonagricultural labor. Both trusted properly scientific observation to foster nothing less than a veritable economic transformation, but neither trusted it to guarantee social stability. Ultimately, their fear of social disorder proved so strong that it affected their formulation of their economic system.

Mirabeau proceeds to articulate vigorously the social hazards of industrial concentration. First, he warns the Swiss not to be deceived by their country's apparent assets for raising livestock as against the cultivation of grain. A pastoral economy requires the support of cultivation, even as successful cultivation requires livestock. Furthermore, he interjects in an apparent non sequitur, many countries have ruined themselves through their failure to understand that costs must be subtracted before the profits of any economic enterprise can be calculated—an error that leads them to regard industry as more profitable than agriculture. Take the great wealth that Lyon purportedly draws from its vast textile industry, he argues. Foreign raw silk, and the gold and silver for embossing, must be subtracted as costs, as must the wages of the workers, who must be considered, in the language of calculation, as machines requiring daily and costly maintenance. These men "are so little at the disposition of the State that if the industry stops for one instant they must flee and go elsewhere to seek work or they perish of misery." Mirabeau cannot help wondering what remains as true wealth once these costs have been subtracted; he answers, "nothing but that which constitutes the fortune of the entrepreneurs." The state gains nothing.[54]

54. *Ibid.*, 30–32.

Mirabeau concedes that the maintenance of these machines we call workers "is subsistence; that this subsistence is consumption; that consumption excites production in giving its fruits a value; and that by this chain of relations, industry enlivens agriculture." But the disadvantages of industry, he hastens to add, affect more than economic performance. The encouragement of industry "changes the principles, alters the morals and entangles the policy of great States." Even in lesser states which adopt liberty as their guiding principle, industry threatens the social fabric. A merchant or great manufacturer has at his disposition all the machines that he supports. Some of them thus command ten thousand machines called workers. "What would become of public liberty on an election day, etc., if these machines made a popular disturbance?" The republic in question would "immediately and necessarily become an oligarchy or something worse."[55]

Mirabeau has heard of the practice of landlord control over tenant votes in England, but he dismisses this rumor with the cheerful reflection that if such were indeed the case, the English Parliament would soon feel its repercussions. As a general rule, he insists, large proprietors either reside on their lands, in which case they share the values of their tenants so that the influence they exercise simply realizes the tenants' own aspirations; or they reside in cities, in which case they are no longer proprietors except by virtue of a "convention which stipulates the dues which their farmers bring them; and those who live on their lands barely know them, far from being disposed to risk anything for them."[56]

Mirabeau's arguments in favor of the necessarily constructive social role of landed proprietors prove nothing. Quesnay's economic scheme makes clear that the landlords, or their farmers, employ wage labor exactly as do industrial entrepreneurs. Mirabeau's arguments do, however, reveal the way in which he and Quesnay hoped to circumvent the political and social dislocation of a large labor force. Rather than admit that any divorce

55. *Ibid.*, 33, 34.
56. *Ibid.*, 34.

of labor from the land entails the mass insecurities and resistance inherent in any labor market, they maintain that the natural agricultural order insures social harmony even as it moves from traditional to market structures.

The threat of dislocation comes from all areas of the nonagricultural sector—wage labor and employers of labor alike. This identification of capitalists and workers within an economic sector dominates the physiocrats' entire system of social classification. Class is determined by function, not income level. At the same time, the physiocrats actively support a market differentiation between owners of capital and owners of labor. In this respect, physiocracy represents a transition from the organic medieval view to the modern economic view, and it attempts to fuse features of both. Mirabeau voices the essence of their sentiments in his discussion of agricultural laborers. Agriculture infuses the hard realities of the economic model with a spirit of humanity that reflects the divinity itself. From this point of view, "Men are no longer machines: they are our fathers, our brothers, and our children."[57]

In the light of Quesnay's demonstration of the economic superiority of agriculture and his own demonstration of its political and moral superiority, Mirabeau feels that he can definitely advise the Swiss to pursue the cultivation of grain. He warns them, however, that such an undertaking invariably encounters general and particular impediments. He does not regard the particular impediments to the cultivation of grain resulting from the Swiss climate and soil as insurmountable and suggests that the advantages of a complementary livestock economy might counterbalance them altogether. He apologizes that his discussion of general hindrances may raise issues apparently unrelated to Swiss conditions. But, he warns, "Political evils are all contagious: maybe the epidemic is in its neighborhood. Haphazardly, I speak to the universe. May those who have elicited my voice pardon

57. *Ibid.,* 38.

me the extension of my facilities."[58] And with this fair warning, he treats his audience to a course in the evils besetting France.

Above all else, restrictions upon free trade in grain hinder the development of the agricultural sector and the realization of a maximum net product. Historically, governments have displayed an unfortunate inclination to try to control the grain market in the interests of social justice. Their actions may have been justified before the revival of commerce, but the improvement of roads now "open from one world to the other" and the flourishing of competition and greed have made them untenable today. "Grain is like water; it will always seek its level."[59] The price mechanism suffices to insure the proper distribution of the world supply.

So there will be no possible misunderstanding, Quesnay takes over to describe the wondrous workings of the market. Patiently, he explains that governmental attempts to ascertain price levels and to stimulate national production of particularly lucrative commodities can only result in the misery of authoritarianism, special interests, and monopoly. Fixing prices causes even greater harm: those who would judge price levels in a country in which price legislation prevails confuse "the moral error with reality." No, the only way to judge the benefits of the grain trade is to consider those countries where uniform prices prevail. "There human life and subsistence will have been the least in danger and compromised."[60]

Quesnay, as he had done in "Grains," outlines his argument that a high price of grain does not jeopardize popular well-being. On the contrary, so long as prices remain stable, a higher price merely serves to indicate a generally higher standard of living that includes higher wages for the national work force. Traditionally, he insists, the ordinary wage for a day's labor has settled around a twentieth of the price of a *septier* of grain, evaluated

58. *Ibid.*, 38–39.
59. *Ibid.*, 39, 41.
60. *Ibid.*, 43–44.

at the common year (the average or mythical "normal" harvest). Should this common price rise, the wages of labor will rise with it. Nor will rising wages increase costs and therefore cut into the profits of entrepreneurs. Needless to say, with a constant net product, such would be the inevitable result. But the whole point is that the net product does not remain constant.[61]

By means of arithmetical calculation, Quesnay demonstrates that since the price of grain does not affect most production and distribution costs, which are determined not by wheat-consuming men but by animals, machines, and ships, most of the increased returns afforded by a higher price accrue to the proprietor of land. The great advantages of a higher price may not be immediately apparent in countries where men perform most of the agricultural labor, but except for human labor the increase in revenues "is to the profit of all kinds of proprietors and the State." In the economy as a whole, an increase of one-third in the wages of labor only occasions a rise of one-fifth in the costs of production. While manufactured goods will have increased in price by one-fifth, the income of the proprietors will have doubled.[62]

In any state, Quesnay points out, "if you except the *rentier* and merchants engaged in foreign trade, each man is either a proprietor or a wage earner." According to Quesnay's calculations, both proprietors and wage laborers benefit from an increase in the price of grain. Furthermore, merchants may always be trusted to use their ingenuity to secure their own profits. The *rentier* may indeed lose, but as Quesnay sternly warns, his selfish interest cannot be permitted to influence state policy. That general good must be identified with the specific good of the proprietors and wage laborers both of whom ostensibly benefit from a high price of grain.

Thus for Quesnay, capital and labor share identical interests. But he knows very well that others are not likely to see it his

61. *Ibid.*, 47–48.
62. *Ibid.*, 50.

way.[63] In fact, rents rose steeply during the eighteenth century while wages lagged far behind. The landed proprietors did not effect an agricultural revolution; they continued to draw their dues and rents in kind and to reap the rewards of the rising prices. Even as Quesnay argues in favor of the consolidation of small plots into large farms yielding maximum net product, he admits that a rising price of grain would increase proprietary revenues "in the increase of *dîmes* [tithes], of *champarts* [rents], etc., an object which must still be regarded as a revenue of the proprietor." Aside from this explicit reference, Quesnay does not dwell upon the actual structure of French property. His silence undermines his argument that equality of prices will "alone greatly augment the revenues of land, without the inhabitants paying more dearly for their bread." No such results could be expected in the absence of profound structural transformation.

During the liberalization of the grain trade in the 1760s the proprietors drew larger revenues, but the populace did not receive commensurably higher wages. Under the residual seigneurial mode of exploitation, the proprietors' rents consisted of dues in kind, which bore no necessary relationship to the net product. These dues might represent the totality of the peasants' wheat crop, for example, and its appropriation by the lord would leave the producer with enough rye and lesser grain to feed the family and provide for the seed for the next year's sowing, but hardly anything to generate the capital requisite for major investment in the most modern means of production. Nor did the bonanza of rising prices tempt the seigneur to undertake direct exploitation himself. Finally, in the absence of a strong national market, prices continued to vary dramatically from region to region, so that purchasers of bread, urban and rural, faced the periodic hardship of exorbitant prices against a backdrop of the cumulative misery induced by wages that did not keep pace with the cost of living.[64]

63. *Ibid.*, 50–51.
64. See Labrousse *et al.*, 473–97; and Robert Forster, *The House of*

Had the price rise been accompanied by the transformation of agriculture into a rationalized capital sector, the standard of living of the working population might have improved in conformity with the general trend, although undoubtedly not as much as Quesnay predicted. The English experience shows, however, that such relative social harmony and economic well-being themselves succumbed to the strains of wholesale transfer of a large segment of the labor force into an industrial milieu.[65] In France the experiment was doomed from the start because the landowners could satisfy their desire for economic gain through their possession of seigneurial rights and eminent domain, which assured them the agricultural surplus with its increasing market value. Quesnay's program, whatever his intentions, indisputably benefited the large proprietors at the expense of the laboring population and introduced divisiveness where he had expected

---

Saulx-Tavannes (Baltimore, 1971). René Girard, *L'abbé Terray et la liberté du commerce des grains, 1769–1774* (Paris, 1924), deals with the different responses of various provinces. Ernest Labrousse, *Esquisse du mouvement des prix et des revenus en France au XVIIIe siècle* (Paris, 1933) emphasizes throughout the variations between years and areas. Louise Tilly, "The Food Riot as a Form of Political Conflict in France," *Journal of Interdisciplinary History*, II (1971), 23–58, esp. 35–45, on the other hand, emphasizes the emergence of a national market in France during the eighteenth century. A thorough critique of this argument must await another occasion. But her evidence, based upon three urban price series, is hardly conclusive, particularly since she does not touch upon problems of price formation. All the available monographic literature suggests that even when prices in different regions happened to coincide, their convergence could have reflected accident as much as the existence of an altogether problematical national market. Cf. Georges Frêche, "Etudes statistiques sur le commerce céréalier de la France méridionale au XVIIe siècle," *RHES*, XLIX (1971), 541, 181–224; Jean Letaconnoux, *Les subsistances et le commerce des grains en Bretagne au XVIIIe siècle* (Rennes, 1906); and Ruggiero Romano, *Commerce et prix du blé à Marseille au XVIIIe siècle* (Paris, 1956), for good regional studies.

65. See Edward Thompson, *The Making of the English Working Class* (London, 1963), and "The Moral Economy of the English Crowd in the Eighteenth Century," *Past and Present*, no. 50 (1971), 76–136; and A. H. John, "Aspects of English Economic Growth in the First Half of the Eighteenth Century," in E. M. Carus-Wilson ed., *Essays in Economic History* [1962] (London, 1966), II.

to insure harmony. The free trade in grain, which he wished to see founded on a beneficial "irrevocable law" of nature, became the symbol for the destruction of all community and social conscience.[66]

Quesnay and Mirabeau both understood that French property relations did not readily lend themselves to a rational capitalist system of production. Mirabeau, quite in conformity with Quesnay's views, reiterates his opposition to *rentes* and *rentiers*, which he now presents in more precise economic language. Loans guaranteed by land "were a usury in Morality before they were one in Religion." And aside from such considerations they wreak real abuse on agriculture by tending to fragment fortunes and properties. "For me to be the proprietor in fact of the land of my neighbor, it is not always necessary for him to have transferred the property to me; it suffices that this contract (*rente*) attribute its fruits to me and mine in perpetuity." Furthermore, although in theory the debtor can always buy back the land, events conspire to favor the interests of the lender whose independence from the costs of upkeep and from "the calamities which destroy the fruits of the earth" leave him in secure posession of an increasing surplus. The surplus enables the creditor to invest in further *rentes* while the debtor whose lot remains henceforth "to work and risk for others" sees his own fortunes each day encumbered by new debts. Such a financial system undermines all agricultural innovation. Had the creditor truly purchased the land, it would have "passed into the hands of a possessor in a position to exploit it." As it is, the income is siphoned off with no commensurate reinvestment.[67]

Despite the destructiveness of its private manifestations, Mirabeau sees the most serious effects of the constitution of *rentes*

---

66. "Mémoire," 53. Cf. AN, F^{11} 223, F^{11} 265, and F^{12} 715. For a regional study of the problems of maintaining order in provisioning, see Camille Bloch, *Le commerce des grains dans la généralité d'Orléans* (1768); *d'après la correspondance inédite de l'intendant Cypierre* (Orleans, 1898).

67. "Mémoire," 60–61.

residing in its public aspect. The state itself, by borrowing from individuals, fosters a prohibitive interest rate and attracts the capital that should go into the productive sector of the economy. For this reason, Quesnay, who himself takes up the pen to drive the point home, argues that the high interest rate constitutes neither more nor less than a tax upon the productive life of the nation—upon those who do not borrow as much as upon those who do. Any tribute levied upon the venal value of merchandise results in a decrease in the financial returns to the agricultural sector and jeopardizes the process of reproduction. For, just as everything that comes from the earth and passes into direct consumption must return to the earth "either in fertilizer, or work, or the influence resulting from the presence of the master, all the portion which is transformed into merchandise and which seeks its retribution afar must return to it in money." Mirabeau adds, "All commerce other than that of property can only enrich you with the spoils of another similar to yourself."[68]

Quesnay's and Mirabeau's discussion of the interest rate once again reveals the contradictions inherent in their political economy. Throughout his economic work Quesnay consistently argues that money is only one commodity among many. He thus rejects the notion that a large stock of money specifically benefits a nation. Theoretically, money should, in consequence, obey the normal market laws of supply and demand, and investment should no more require regulation than the grain trade. In fact, were he to accept this hypothesis entirely and to argue from the historical case, he would have to conclude that *rentes* represented a better investment than agriculture and that the flow of funds obeyed the natural laws of the market. Such a conclusion, however, ran directly counter to his understanding of the productive process. Drawing upon the method of his metaphysics, he instead argues that the high return on *rentes* represents an artificial rather than a natural phenomenon. To correct that distortion of the natural order requires a conscious policy

68. "Mémoire," 62, 64, 68.

upon the part of the state. Quesnay's attitude toward interest did not, as has so frequently been argued, reveal a residue of medieval attitudes so much as it revealed his appreciation of the distortions that the growth of the state had introduced into the workings of a natural economic process.[69]

Quesnay and Mirabeau also believed that as political arrangements, *rentes* distorted the institution of property by separating possession of its income from possession of the means of production. The arrangement they castigate did not characterize the *rentier* relationship alone. It also dominated the relationship between *seigneurie* and exploitation. Although they do not attack existing seigneurial property relations frontally the way they do the structure of *rentes*, they do permit themselves a description of the proper nature of property. Property should be an economic unit. The income from production should accrue to those responsible for production so that their immediate and visible interest lies in constructive reinvestment. Commerce should be the direct exchange between properties so that its profits return directly to production. Only such direct property can guarantee the working of the market, for only such direct property brings individual interest into conformity with the maximization of the net product. The doctrine is generous in its conviction that labor or production affords the natural title to ownership of the means of production. But it also displays a classical liberal ruthlessness in refusing to consider the relations of production within the agricultural sector. In other words, Quesnay and Mirabeau understand property to mean the legal title to the net product or surplus of the social production of wealth. They insist that the state guarantee property rights to those immediately engaged

69. Cf. Quesnay, "Observations sur l'intérêt de l'argent: Par M. Nisaque," *Journal de l'agriculture, du commerce et des finances*, IV (1766), 151–71; and Raymond de Roover, "The Concept of Just Price: Theory and Economic Policy," *Journal of Economic History*, XVIII (1958), 418–34, and "Scholastic Economics: Survival and Lasting Influences from the Sixteenth Century to Adam Smith," *Quarterly Journal of Economics*, LXIX (1955), 161–90.

in this productive process. They do not, however, question the social structure that assures no more than a subsistence—although possibly a comfortable one—to those engaged in the labor that produces the surplus.

The less generous side of their property doctrine emerges forcefully when they turn to the consideration of enclosures. Mirabeau assumes responsibility for most of the discussion and whatever traditional sensibilities he may still harbor fail to encumber his economic rationality. He dismisses customary rights, communal practices, and all such nonsense with a stroke of the pen. Only the most unenlightened sentimentality can fail to recognize that they interfere with the natural law of the net product, which private property alone can guarantee. The industrious proprietor owes his prosperity to God and the sweat of his own brow; he is entitled to enjoy the fruits of his toil and to dispose of them as he alone sees fit.[70] "In a word, it is to my sense a barbarous law to impede the proprietor from enclosing his field, his pasture land, his woods. It is to violate the laws of property, basis of the laws: and this prohibition, under whatever pretext it may introduce itself, is unworthy of any legitimate Government and, for all the more reason, of a Government founded on equity and liberty."[71]

Mirabeau makes his point with considerable force, but Quesnay, wishing to leave no possible ambiguity, adds a final warning. Everything, he reminds us, grandly encompassing all political and social organization, can be reduced essentially "to the cultivation of wheat, to the causes and means necessary and favorable to the success of this cultivation." The Government's most important duty is to encourage this cultivation and to prohibit all impediments. "The cogs of the machine cannot satisfy their use without the aid of those who set it in motion and who regulate its movements. But if they themselves have a poor knowledge of the construction of the machine and its effects, their help and

70. "Mémoire," 70–77.
71. *Ibid.*, 77.

their attention will only bring obstacles and disarray." What does it matter, he later repeats, what we draw from the earth "if we draw from it the best net product evaluated in money?"[72]

The "Introduction," the "Questions intéressantes," and the "Mémoire" for Berne constitute a logical intellectual progression independent of their fortuitous publication under the common rubric of *L'ami des hommes*.[73] In the "Introduction," Mirabeau, extrapolating from the all-too-actual specificity of the "Traité," elaborates the general outlines of a political theory. In a fundamental change in method, he attempts to build a general model of social and political organization. His model expresses his own earlier traditionalism by emphasizing the claims of community over those of the individual, but breaks with it by presenting society—as opposed to a divine-right monarch—as the source of political principles and obligations. His instinctive mistrust of the free play of individual self-interest distinguishes his liberalism from that of his English predecessors and accounts for his retention of an absolute sovereign as the guarantee of social order and undisputed custodian of the laws of regulation. At the same time, his commitment to the claims of individuals as against political authority leads him to insist upon the individual's pre-social property rights as the foundation and legitimization of all society. He repudiates his earlier attempt to legitimize political authority as a form of political property independent of society and shows how laws arose from and are justified by the social arrangements among individuals. Finally, he insists that these original fundamental laws constitute the *noli me tangere* of all society and command the respectful allegiance of the sovereign himself.

Mirabeau's theory embodies what were to become the central

72. *Ibid.*, 78, 80.
73. Mirabeau's "Réponse à l'essai sur la voierie," which appeared in pt. 6 in 1759, is much more an occasional piece and does not fit directly into the development of his and Quesnay's joint work. See AN, M 783, no. 13.

tenets of physiocracy but still lacks the necessity for which Quesnay had called during the formulation of the "Traité." Quesnay's simultaneous work on the "Questions," in which, despite the rhetorically interrogative form, he tries to codify his economic knowledge in relation to the actual state of France, attacks the problem from the economic side. His work confirms Mirabeau's position in the "Introduction" by emphasizing both a natural order of economic production and the necessity for a regulatory authority to insure the implementation of that order. But it does not solve the problems of the "Introduction"; it fails to establish the general rules that can simultaneously provide the authority for government and justify constraining the properly economic behavior of individuals.

The "Mémoire" for Berne fills the empty space of the "Introduction" and the "Questions." The net product, it announces, constitutes the undeniable rule (in both meanings of law and yardstick) for social and economic behavior. The governing principle of the net product allows Quesnay and Mirabeau to show the economic nature of property and to repudiate traditional, noneconomic property forms without jeopardizing the sanctity of the principle of true property. Similarly, they distinguish between true and false self-interest. The implications of their thought, which include the eradication of all traditional safeguards for marginal population and the repudiation of traditional seigneurial incomes, evoke all the hardships and social dislocations of economic transformation. They hope that their insistence upon the primacy of the agricultural sector will, contrary evidence notwithstanding, ensure the preservation of community. Whether it would or not, they insist that the net product constitutes that necessary law of social and political behavior which brooks no contradiction. By promising a new necessity to enforce their political theory even as it threatens existing political and social institutions, their political economy bore within itself the ideology that would set them against the most entrenched interests of their society.

The Tableau

When Mirabeau announced in *Philosophie rurale* that the stability of society rested upon three major inventions—writing, money, and the Tableau économique—he indulged in one of the more grandiose and sectarian of those expressions which regularly exposed the physiocrats to the ridicule of their contemporaries. The Tableau baffled those unable to decipher its arithmetical calculations, offended the more sophisticated who were skeptical of its pretensions, and evoked disagreement from many excellent economists. Subsequent commentators, less encumbered by the ideological passions aroused by the contemporary debate over the optimal social allocation of economic resources in France, also have disagreed about its meaning and significance. But since Marx's "rediscovery" of the physiocrats, many economists of various persuasions have recognized the Tableau as a milestone in the development of economic thought. Schumpeter regarded it as the first portrayal of the "circular flow of economic life," and more recent students of economic equilibrium and the stationary state have seen it as a major precursor of their own efforts.[1] If history neither realized the program of the physiocrats

1. *La philosophie rurale* (Amsterdam, 1763), 4; see François Véron de Forbonnais, *Principes et observations oeconomiques*, 2 vols. (Amsterdam, 1767), esp. vol. II; Jean-Joseph-Louis Graslin, *Correspondance entre M. Graslin . . . et M. L'abbé Baudeau . . . sur un des principes fondamentaux de la doctrine des soi-disants philosophes économistes* (London and Paris, 1777). See also Joseph A. Schumpeter, *Economic Doctrine and Method* (London, 1954), 52, and Michel Lutfalla, *L'état stationnaire* (Paris, 1964).

TABLEAU ÉCONOMIQUE.

Objets a considerer, 1.° Trois sortes de dépenses; 2.° leur source; 3.° leurs avances; 4.° leur distribution; 5.° leurs effets; 6.° leur reproduction; 7.° leurs rapports entr'elles; 8.° leurs rapports avec la population; 9.° avec l'Agriculture; 10.° avec l'industrie; 11.° avec le commerce; 12.° avec la masse des richesses d'une Nation.

DÉPENSES PRODUCTIVES relatives à l'Agriculture, &c	DÉPENSES DU REVENU, l'Impôt prélevé, se partage aux Dépenses productives et aux Dépenses stériles.	DÉPENSES STÉRILES relatives à l'industrie, &c
Avances annuelles pour produire un revenu de 600.ᵗᵗ sont 600.ᵗᵗ	*Revenu annuel de*	*Avances annuelles* pour les Ouvrages des Dépenses stériles, sont 300.ᵗᵗ
600. produisent net............	600.ᵗᵗ	300.ᵗᵗ

Productions .... moitié passe ici *Ouvrages, &c.*

300.ᵗᵗ reproduisent net.......	300.ᵗᵗ	300.ᵗᵗ
150. reproduisent net.......	150.	150.
75. reproduisent net.......	75.	75.
37.10. reproduisent net.......	37.10.	37.10
18.15. reproduisent net.......	18.15.	18.15.
9...7...6. reproduisent net.....	9...7...6.	9...7...6.
4..13...0. reproduisent net.....	4..13...9.	4..13...9
2...6..10. reproduisent net.....	2...6..10.	2...6..10
1...3...5. reproduisent net.....	1...3...5.	1...3...5
0..11...8. reproduisent net.....	0..11...8.	0..11...8
0...5..10. reproduisent net.....	0...5..10.	0...5..10
0...2..11. reproduisent net.....	0...2..11.	0...2..11
0...1...5. reproduisent net.....	0...1...5.	0...1...5

&c.

REPRODUIT TOTAL.............. 600.ᵗᵗ de revenu; de plus, les frais annuels de 600.ᵗᵗ et les intérêts des avances primitives du Laboureur, de 300.ᵗᵗ que la terre restitue. Ainsi la reproduction est de 1500.ᵗᵗ compris le revenu de 600.ᵗᵗ qui est la base du calcul, abstraction faite de l'impôt prélevé, et des avances qu'exige sa reproduction annuelle, &c. Voyez l'Explication à la page suivante.

nor validated the full extent of their claims for economic science, it has at least granted them respect and renewed interest.

Ironically, much of the present popularity of Quesnay's Tableau rests on a misunderstanding and a disregard of its intentions. Many of the giants of political economy have displayed intellectual charity and imagination by divesting the Tableau of its outmoded pretensions and assimilating its revolutionary economic technique to their own frame of reference. But in the process they have distorted Quesnay's intentions. Schumpeter cannot be faulted for his generous recognition of Quesnay's analytic genius when he writes that "no economic proposition of Quesnay's rests upon any theological premises or would be affected by discarding what we know about his religious beliefs. This proves ipso facto the purely analytic or scientific nature of his economic work and leaves no room for extra-empirical influences." Nor can Marx be faulted for his refusal to reproach the physiocrats: "Like all their successors they thought of these material forms of existences—such as tools, raw materials, etc.—as capital, in isolation from the social conditions in which they appear in capitalist production; in a word, in the form in which they are elements of the labour-process in general, independently of its social form —and thereby made of the capitalist form of production an eternal, natural form of production." Both these adulatory appraisals repudiate some part of the physiocrats' own perception of the nature of economics and its integral relationship to their political and ideological preoccupations. And anachronistic evaluation only worsens in the work of scholars lacking the broad historical knowledge and cultural sensitivity of a Schumpeter or a Marx.[2]

Whereas economists have erred in abstracting physiocratic eco-

2. Joseph A. Schumpeter, *History of Economic Analysis* (New York, 1955), 233; Karl Marx, *Theories of Surplus Value* (Moscow, 1969), I, 44. Cf. Robert V. Eagley, "A Physiocratic Model of Dynamic Equilibrium," *Journal of Political Economy*, LXXVII (1969), 66–84, and *Structure of Classical Economic Theory* (Oxford, 1974); and Izumi Hishiyama, "The *Tableau Economique* of Quesnay—Its Analysis, Reconstruction, and Application," *Kyoto University Economic Review*, XXX (1960), 1–45.

nomic analysis from its larger setting, historians have erred in increasingly viewing the Tableau as a perfect model of pre-Revolutionary society. The very normative commitments the economists would dismiss, along with their historical context, color the physiocrats' own intrepretation of their historical milieu. Had the physiocrats been content merely to describe what incontrovertibly existed they would never have become enmeshed in those polemical struggles which characterized their careers; nor would they have found it necessary to extrapolate so radically from the political realities of their time when formulating a political theory to support their political economy.[3]

Quesnay's economic analysis arose within a context provided by Mirabeau's original ideological commitments. Both the economics and the ideology became transformed in the course of the Quesnay-Mirabeau collaboration. The new formulations emerged as a coherent political economy with its own new ideological implications in the "Mémoire" for the agricultural society of Berne. Chronologically, the Tableau belongs to the same period, but intellectually, for those not particularly interested in early models of static or dynamic equilibrium analysis, it seems to add little to the understanding of physiocratic political economy and ideology. Many of the scholars who have most admired the physiocrats as being early, rigorous liberals, have omitted it altogether from their discussions of physiocracy.[4]

According to Mirabeau, writing endows humanity with "the power to transmit, without alteration, its laws, its pacts, its annals, its discoveries." Money "binds all the relations between

3. Herbert Lüthy, *La banque protestante en France* (Paris, 1959), II, 24–25, and *François Quesnay und die Idee der Volkswirtschaft* (Zurich 1959); Jean Molinier, "Le système de comptabilité nationale chez François Quesnay," INED, I, 100; and Pierre Goubert, *L'ancien régime* (Paris, 1969). See also Lars Herlitz, "The *Tableau Economique* and the Doctrine of Sterility," *Scandinavian Economic History Review*, XI (1961).

4. Cf. Eugene Daire, "La doctrine des physiocrates," *Journal des Economistes*, XXVII (1847), 349–75, XXVIII (1848), 113–40; and Charles Gide and Charles Rist, *Histoire des doctrines économiques*, 7th ed. (Paris, 1947).

well administered (*policées*) societies."[5] In Mirabeau's presentation of key discoveries, neither fire nor the wheel nor other inventions rank with writing and money—only the Tableau. Writing and money share the property of organically binding human beings into society and of facilitating their social commerce. Notwithstanding their dependence upon human will, Mirabeau implicitly presents them as strictly material phenomena in contrast to the arbitrarily man-made laws of government. Writing and money constitute indispensable links in human social development, the signs, as it were, of the progressing interconnectedness or mutual dependence called society.

However fantastic Mirabeau's comparison of writing, money, and the Tableau, his insistence on considering the Tableau as a successive stage in social integration cannot be avoided. The Tableau, he explains, "is a derivative of the two others and completes them equally in perfecting their object: It is the discovery of the Tableau économique which, becoming henceforth the universal standard, embraces and aligns (*accorde*) all the correlative portions or quotas which must enter into the general calculation of the economic order." Would, he moans, that he had sufficient genius to deduce or even designate and arrange "all the political truths, derived from this study." He promises, however, that the remainder of his work will divulge some of them. The more one deepens one's own understanding of the Tableau, he explains, the more one will be surprised "to find certitudes where one had feared paradoxes, and to see the highest politics become simple, infallible, in conformity with the rules of the Gospel, of Morality and to touch without effort its true goal which is the happiness of humanity."[6] The Tableau demonstrates the necessary order of political relations—that is, of the formal relations of men in society, which must reflect their economic relations.

Mirabeau's extravagant claims for the eternal significance of the

5. *Philosophie rurale*, 19.
6. *Ibid.*

Tableau have sadly obscured his own insight and closed off serious discussion. The writing and money to which he compares the Tableau enjoy the double property of being both things and signs: the written word and hard currency both exist but also represent thoughts and values. Mirabeau particularly saw in them the tangible signs of increasing socialization. Similarly, he saw the Tableau as both a thing and a sign: it had real existence and it represented a social reality. The Tableau, however, unlike the word and the coin, did not circulate. It did not constitute a medium of communication, but rather a theory or a model of communication. As such, it represented the unique intellectual creation of a single individual who proposed to reveal the rules of social communication between all individuals. It held the essence of such communication to be economic in nature—the transmittal of material goods and services. By confusing the properties of a written word or a coin with those of a theoretical construct, Mirabeau discourages pursuit of the useful element in his flamboyant comparison.

Mirabeau is trying to express his and Quesnay's conviction that his age has witnessed the emergence of a qualitatively new level of social exchange and integration. His preposterous comparison with writing and money tries to convey the meaning he cannot quite articulate. The Tableau, he says, derived from both writing and money and complements them both. It realizes, as it were, the fullness of their discrete potentials by completing the process of social unification. Or rather, since the Tableau does nothing on the level of social action, it represents the completion of a historical process; specifically, of the irreversible creation of a market society in which all men are indissolubly linked by necessary market relations. The Tableau expresses what he elsewhere calls "the economic circle," which constitutes the central human reality determining political relations in an ordered society.[7] The Tableau is thus the sign of the completion of the market just as printing (that is, the extension of writing to the middle classes)

7. *Ibid.*, 61.

and money had been the signs of its emergence. It is also the sign of the transposition from the economic to the political and moral planes, and expounds the rules of their interdependence. Finally, it explains according to scientific principles how the interdependence reflects an immutable moral order. So it is at once the sign of a historical reality and the scientific tool for explaining that reality.

To grasp this vision fully requires an appreciation of Quesnay's metaphysics and of his conviction, echoed by Mirabeau in the opening pages of *Philosophie rurale*, that a natural order exists, and that it reflects divine intent and constitutes "the principles and basis of moral order on earth, the principles and basis of natural right and natural law." Against this immutable purpose, human governments can do nothing: "The order is immutable, Sovereigns and Subjects can only stray from it to their disadvantage. Disorder, it is true, is the work of ignorant or perverse men, but order is the work of the supreme wisdom and the true government of societies. Perfect government is not of human institution; there is nothing men can either add to or remove from this Theocracy; their happiness consists in a conforming to it."[8] The Tableau embodies the dualism inherent in Quesnay's original metaphysics. Like the natural order it purports to illustrate, the Tableau was presented by the physiocrats as both a description of the economic basis of society and as a guide to human action; it thus embodies their attempt to fuse idealism and materialism into a single all-encompassing truth about reality and human perception.

The Tableau économique represents a revolutionary breakthrough in economic analysis and reflects the historical reality of its conception; but it also embodies the specific perceptions of the man who conceived it. Quesnay, while committed to advancing pure economic analysis and to restoring the financial resources of the French monarchy, remained deeply concerned with those relations of men in society to which he had been drawn by Mira-

8. *Ibid.*, xviii.

beau. The physiocrats' political and ideological preoccupations led them at once to attempt to reform the political structure of their own society and to develop a science of society capable of prescribing necessary rules of human conduct and political organization.

The physiocrats wrote before the emergence of the social sciences as discrete disciplines; they lived in a society groping for a bridge between traditional and market views of itself and still lacking a modern framework for political action. Quesnay's admirers, like Le Trosne, Baudeau, and the more independent Condorcet, were economists, political theorists, sociologists—even sometime anthropologists. They, as well as others such as du Pont, Le Mercier de la Rivière, and Roubaud, were also eighteenth-century administrators, propagandists, and aspirant politicians. All, including the least sectarian, notably Condorcet, Morellet, and Turgot, believed that their intellectual and ideological concerns constituted inseparable facets of a single project of understanding. The more sectarian also believed that they could interpret the will of God with the precision of physics and that their correct interpretation would dictate action. The instinctive fear of the social conflict implicit in the realization of their supposedly nonpartisan model led them to insist all the more upon the divine inevitability of their prescriptions, with which they forged the theory of a free market economy through the dialectical resolution of the conflicting claims of materialist individualism and the traditional notions of order and community. Quesnay tried to cram the whole of these aspirations and contradictions into a single Tableau, which would function as merely the household accounts of an agricultural kingdom while providing the rules of what Mirabeau called "economic science, immortal base of our subsistence, of our morals, and of all in a word that can be truly called the fundamental science of the government of States."[9] No wonder the model strained a little at the seams and

9. "Tableau oeconomique avec ses explications," in *L'ami des hommes,* pt. 6 [1759] (Amsterdam, 1760), II, 120, henceforth, "Explications." Two

continues to baffle the finest minds. The Tableau lends itself to no single solution except at the expense of its own rich complexity. As an analytic tool it can do no more than suggest the contradictions of the political economy and ideology it serves.

The designation "Tableau économique" refers in a general way to the graphic representation devised by Quesnay to portray the circulation of the net revenue among the classes of an agricultural kingdom. Throughout a decade of controversial attention the Tableau assumed a number of different forms. In some instances the changes amount to little more than a uniform increase in the magnitude of the quantitative values ascribed to the revenue, advances, and respective shares of the productive and sterile sectors. In others, the changes entail a significant revision of the form of representation. The differences between the different tableaux make it impossible to refer to the Tableau économique as a single entity, as one might refer to *The Social Contract* to mean Rousseau's treatise on government irrespective of edition. No single edition may be taken as definitive. A generic Tableau exists only in the sense that each of the tableaux represents a stage in a changing process of analysis. And this analysis can only be evaluated in relation to the larger questions which themselves shaped its development.

The Tableau made its first public appearance in December 1758 when Quesnay sent Mirabeau a hand-drawn diagram entitled "Tableau oeconomique," which has subsequently become known as the first edition. Early in 1759, Quesnay sent Mirabeau a second and very similiar edition. The third edition was printed in very few copies at Versailles late in 1759. This version, which departed in certain crucial particulars from the first two, con-

---

successive manuscript versions of the "Explications" are at the Bibliothèque de l'Arsenal, in the Fonds de la Bastille, no. 1201. Both drafts bear Quesnay's editorial annotations. Aside from a few very general and not directly pertinent reflections, Quesnay's corrections deal with technical economic points and are far fewer in number than those he affixed to the "Traité,"

stituted the immediate prototype for the fourth edition published
and analyzed by Mirabeau as "Le Tableau oeconomique avec
ses explications," in part VI of *L'ami des hommes* in 1759. The
succeeding versions, published as the diagrams, or tableaux, of
Philosophie rurale (1763) follow the same format. *Philosophie
rurale*, however, also introduced a new version of the Tableau,
the *précis*. The *précis* marks no analytic departure from the
earlier models; it simply eliminates the many stages of the circulation of the revenue in order to present an abbreviated diagram of
the entire process of circulation. Quesnay's final version of the
Tableau, the "Formule du Tableau économique," which he used
in his "Analyse de la formule arithmétique du Tableau économique" (1766), does, however, introduce an important analytic
departure as well as a profound, if unavowed, ideological development. It also ominously, if inadvertently, pointed the way to a
split between the economic analysis and the full economic science.
Significantly, du Pont, in his edition of Quesnay's writings,
Physiocratie (1767), included only the textual material related
to the Tableau, but no diagram.[10]

Quesnay himself had originally promulgated the view that his
economic science could not be reduced to numbers or graphical
representations by the explications and maxims with which
he equipped all versions of the diagram. Like the succession of
tableaux, that of the written commentaries affords an indispensable guide to the development of both science and doctrine. The

10. *Quesnay's Tableau* contains the first three editions of the Tableau.
That of the "Explications" is in Mirabeau, *L'ami des hommes*, pt. 6 (all
references will be to vol. II of the 1760 edition). Until recently, most
discussions of the Tableau dealt with the "Analyse de la formule
arithmétique du Tableau économique de la distribution des dépenses
annuelles d'une nation agricole," which first appeared in the *Journal de
l'agriculture* (1766), and which was also included in du Pont's *Physiocratie*
(Leyden, 1768). It is reprinted in INED, II; all references will be to that
edition and will be cited as "Formule." Lars Herlitz, "The Tableau
Economique and the Doctrine of Sterility," *Scandinavian Economic History Review*, IX (1961), points out the significant differences between the
zigzag and the "Formule."

explications elucidate the significance of the numbers, and the maxims establish the contours of the world they purport to reduce to certainty. If Quesnay succeeded as Mirabeau claimed, in doing for "the economic world what physicists have vainly attempted to do for the physical world," he did so as much by his words as by his numbers.[11] An understanding of physiocracy requires strict attention to the changing relationship between words and numbers in their chronological sequences.

For the two centuries following the formulation of the first Tableau, an aura of mystery shrouded the true sequence of development. No one could definitely identify the earliest versions of the zigzag, nor even state with certainty how many versions had preceded the public introduction of the Tableau in 1759 in part VI of *L'ami des hommes*. The story of the search for and proper identification of the early editions of the Tableau has been amply recounted elsewhere. The efforts and mistakes of generations of perplexed Tableau *afficionados*, apparently including the physiocrats who followed Quesnay and Mirabeau, culminated in 1956 with Marguerite Kuczynski's discovery of the third edition. Her joint publication with Ronald Meek of the facsimile of that edition, complete with English translations and accompanied by reproductions of the first and second editions, as well as by exhaustive notes comparing the variations between the third edition and *L'ami des hommes*, *Philosophie rurale*, and *Physiocratie*, solves all technical problems of identification and provides the indispensable source for all subsequent discussions of the Tableau.[12]

11. *Philosophie rurale*, 42–43.

12. Meek, *Economics*, 265–72, and "The 1758–9 'Editions' of the *Tableau Economique*," in *Quesnay's Tableau*, vii–xx; and Marguerite Kuczynski, "The Search for the 'Third Edition' of the *Tableau Economique*," in *ibid.*, xxv–xxxiv. See also her *Tableau économique von François Quesnay* (Berlin, 1965). Kuczynski does not inform her readers that the "Third Edition" which she located at EMHL can be found in a copy of *Philosophie rurale* in which either Quesnay or du Pont undoubtedly had it bound. All references will be to the Kuczynski and Meek edition, *Quesnay's Tableau*.

When Quesnay first sent his zigzag (as he termed the early tableaux) to Mirabeau in December of 1758, he included a covering letter explaining his intent: "I have tried to construct a fundamental Tableau of the economic order for the purpose of displaying expenditure and products in a way that is easy to grasp, and for the purpose of forming a clear opinion about the organization and disorganization which the governments can bring about. You will see whether I have achieved my aim."[13] The diagram that accompanied the letter depicted the circulation of a revenue of 400 livres between productive and sterile expenditures and was followed by twenty-two "Remarques sur les variations de la distribution des revenus annuels d'une nation," which bear a distinct formal resemblance to the fourteen "Maximes de gouvernement économique" that had accompanied "Grains."[14]

Two or three months later Quesnay again wrote to Mirabeau, this time expressing concern at having heard that Mirabeau was still "bogged down in the zig-zag." "It is true," Quesnay apologized, "that it relates to so many things that it is difficult to grasp their concurrence, or rather to perceive it as self-evident. One can see in this zig-zag what occurs, without understanding its common denominator, but that is not enough for you."[15] And then Quesnay reviews the mechanism of circulation, much as he had reviewed that of production on the margin of the manuscript of the Berne "Mémoire." One of the main problems of the Tableau, he insists, lies in the relationship between men and wealth. Specifically, in the zigzag "wealth is regarded in relation to men, and men relative to wealth." The second major

13. AN, M 784, no. 70. The letter was reproduced by Stephan Bauer, "Quesnay's *Tableau économique*," *Economic Journal*, V (1895), 20, and translated by Meek, *Economics*, 108. I have not followed Meek's translation completely.

14. AN, M 784, no. 71; *Quesnay's Tableau*, xviii; Meek, *Economics*, 109–14. See INED for "Grains" and Meek, *Economics*, 72–81, for translations.

15. AN, M 784, no. 70. Meek, *Economics*, 115, offers a slightly different translation.

problem concerns the process of the distribution of revenue, "which ensures that the revenue is returned together with men's subsistence." Finally, he explains, when properly understood the zigzag will show at a glance "how much wealth and how many men there are and how they are employed, their interrelationships and their influence on one another, and the whole essence of the economic government of agricultural states."[16]

Having bravely laid out what one small Tableau, a mere zigzag, could show, Quesnay admits that its ideas would themselves "be very elusive if they were not fixed securely in the imagination by the Tableau." But the zigzag, "if properly understood, cuts out a whole number of details and brings before your eyes certain closely interwoven details which the intellect alone would have a great deal of difficulty in grasping, unravelling and reconciling by the use of the method of discourse." The Tableau therefore constitutes by Quesnay's own admission an abstraction from his larger political economy. He underscores the relationship between the new tool and his and Mirabeau's previous common endeavors by proposing that the second edition (enlarged and amended), which he is sending under separate cover, might find its proper place at the end of Mirabeau's "Mémoire" for Berne, "together with an introduction written by yourself if you thought it worthy of it."[17]

The second edition—"this Little Book of Household Accounts" —follows exactly the same format as the first, except that the revenue now totals 600 livres, with all other figures increased accordingly, and it is followed by twenty-three annotated maxims under the title, "Extrait des économies royales de M. de Sully."[18] Somewhat later in 1759 Quesnay followed his second edition

16. Meek, *Economics*, 116–17.
17. *Ibid.*, 117.
18. *Quesnay's Tableau*, xviii–xix; Meek, *Economics*, 120–25. Quesnay said he was going to have three copies printed and two have since turned up, one at the Archives nationales, the other at the Bibliothèque nationale. Cf. British Economic Association, *Tableau Oeconomique by François Quesnay* (London, 1894).

with the famous third, "the very fine edition in quarto" to which du Pont had referred and which Forbonnais had described.[19] This privately printed and circulated Tableau duplicated its immediate predecessor in showing the circulation of a revenue of 600 livres, but differed from it slightly in presentation. The format designed by Quesnay for this occasion eliminated the columns of explanatory remarks to the right and left of the diagram which had encumbered the first two editions. It added a few lines of print at the top of the page under the rubric, "objects to be considered," and slightly altered some of the wording of the identifications on the face of the Tableau itself. This edition included, besides the actual diagram, an "Explication" and a set of twenty-four maxims with extensive notes, again entitled "Extrait des économies royales de M. de Sully." The diagram of the third edition is the mature zigzag. The version of the Tableau which Mirabeau used throughout his "Tableau économique avec ses explications" in *L'ami des hommes* replicates it exactly except for a few additions to the summary section called "total reproduction." The version used in *Philosophie rurale* raises the revenue to 2000 livres and also incorporates an extended account of the total reproduction, but with the exception of a highly suggestive minor change in labeling, follows the format of the third.[20] Both Mirabeau's "Explications" and *Philosophie rurale* incorporate the twenty-four maxims. They differ from the third addition, however, in dropping the notes to the maxims and its entire "Explication."[21]

19. P. S. du Pont, "Notice abrégée," in Onken, *Oeuvres*, 155–56; EMHL, Winterthur MSS, group 2, series B, P. S. du Pont, *L'enfance et la jeunesse*, ch. 13, 6; Forbonnais, *Principes et observations oeconomiques*, I, 161–62.

20. The headings for the columns of expenditures are changed from "dépenses productives" and "dépenses stériles" to "classe des dépenses. . . ."

21. "Explications," 183–90. The chapter heading reads: "Tableau économique considered relative to the conditions necessary to the free play of the machine of prosperity" (*Philosophie rurale*, 341–55). There are some stylistic changes between the two, but the object of each maxim remains the same.

When compared to Mirabeau's "Explications" or *Philosophie rurale*, the third edition appears a very spare, scientific text. Quesnay personally testifies that he had designed the original Tableau not only to clarify his own thoughts about political economy, but also to establish a mathematically necessary rule for the behavior of sovereigns—specifically for the fiscal policies appropriate to the French crown.[22] The formulation of the first edition undoubtedly accounts for the clarity and authoritativeness of Quesnay's discussion of the net product in the "Mémoire." But Quesnay continued to perfect his analytic model and, confusingly, to endow each successive edition with an increased burden of words.

The first edition established the pattern for the organization of these words. The "Remarques" following the diagram begin as follows: "From the preceding Tableau, it can be seen that in the order of the regular circulation of 400 millions of annual revenue, these 400 millions are obtained by means of 600 millions of advances, and are distributed annually to four million heads of families." Then after dividing the population into proprietors and workers, he adds, "But in this distribution it is assumed . . ."[23] The twenty-two assumptions establish the conditions for the proper functioning of the Tableau. The remarks include, in prescriptive form, the essence of physiocratic political economy, but since their substance recurs essentially unaltered in each subsequent Tableau, the interesting question concerns precisely the successive forms of that recurrence.

The introductory paragraph of the "Extrait des économies royales de M. de Sully" in the second edition repeats the formula of the "Remarques" but raises the revenue to a base of 600 livres. The maxims that follow recapitulate the content of the "Remarques" and increase their number by one. It demands for each person the freedom to cultivate his fields according to "his in-

22. AN, M 784, no. 70, first and second letters from Quesnay to Mirabeau. Cf. Meek, *Economics*, 108, 115–17.
23. *Quesnay's Tableau*, app. A, n.p.

terests, his means and the nature of the land . . . in order that he may extract from them the greatest possible product" in terms of market value. This addition clearly reflects the intervening composition of the "Mémoire" for Berne.[24] The notes, appearing for the first time in this edition, elaborate the economic reasoning behind the positive commands embodied in the maxims themselves.

Where the second edition manages merely to stretch the form established for the first, the third modifies it radically. The explanatory material in the columns of print on the faces of the tableaux of the first two editions reappear, but in considerably expanded form as the "Tableau économique avec ses explications," which follows the diagram and precedes the "Extrait des économies royales de M. de Sully." In addition, the "Explication" attempts a quantitative evaluation of the potential wealth of the territory of France "given advances and markets."[25] The "Explication" renders explicit the presuppositions of the diagram and describes its actual workings.

Quesnay's contemporaries frequently launched their attacks on physiocracy with repudiations of his virtuoso sallies into conjectural statistics, claiming that any reasonable adult knew that France produced nothing like the product his figures suggested. But none of the forms of the Tableau depends upon the exactitude of Quesnay's mathematical calculations. Simple arithmetical errors, which he frequently commits, do not invalidate the method of calculation. More important, he never claims that his figures measure existing French conditions. Beginning with the third edition, he always explicitly states that he is computing the product France could yield in a perfect state of cultivation. Small-scale cultivation, he explains in terms directly echoing those of the Berne "Mémoire," flourishes only where the lack of wealth reduces men to grubbing for a mere subsistence. "This thankless type of cultivation, which reveals the poverty and ruin

24. *Ibid.*, app. B, 3, 6.
25. *Ibid.*, i–xii.

of those nations in which it predominates, has no connection with the order of the tableau . . . where the annual advances are able, with the aid of the fund of original advances, to produce 100 percent."[26] In other words, Quesnay offers an analytical model for the description of the economic structure, performance, and strength of an imaginary state. He is describing not any given country, but a carefully defined kingdom in which "agriculture produces 100 percent." He admits at the end of the maxims of the second edition and repeats at the end of those of the third, "Without these conditions, an agriculture producing 100 per cent, as we have assumed it to do in the Tableau and as it does in England, would be a fiction." But he adds, "Its principles are no less certain."[27] If the Tableau should be measured against any historical reality, it should be measured against that of England. Quesnay's lengthy note on the respective stocks of money in England and France underlies his preoccupation with England as the model of a modern wealthy nation.[28]

The "Explication" of the third edition thus elaborates what are only short notes in the first and second editions into a short treatise on the distribution of the revenue in, and the potential aggregate wealth of, an agricultural kingdom. Modern economists who seek in Quesnay's work the equivalent of GNP must consult these notes, not the Tableau. But England—or a country whose agriculture reproduces 100 per cent—affords the raw material for his arithmetical calculations and the model for his own most empirical work. Marxists and others who argue that in Quesnay's work the material base always determines the superstructure, must accordingly recognize that the material base of the Tableau was an analytic construct abstracted from Quesnay's knowledge of England. Quesnay, nevertheless, was overwhelmingly preoccupied with French development, the potential of

26. *Ibid.*, v, vi. For examples of Quesnay's arithmetical errors, see Kuczynski's notes, 6.

27. *Ibid.*, 21, app. B, 6.

28. *Ibid.*, ix–x. See *Philosophie rurale*, ch. 7.

which the Tableau revealed. In the third edition as in the first two, the model for France appears in the "Extrait des économies royale de M. de Sully," which contain Quesnay's assumptions about the circulation of revenue.

None of the maxims of the early editions—those of the third were retained verbatim in both Mirabeau's "Explications" and *Philosophie rurale*—directly applied to mid-century France. Fictitious conditions again emerge as the necessary preconditions for the functioning of the Tableau. The maxims, which differ significantly from the explanatory remarks by raising political considerations, in effect call upon France to institute these preconditions. The new addition to their number—in the third, as previously in the second, number 21—"assumes that the land employed in the cultivation of corn is brought together, as far as possible, into large farms worked by rich husbandmen." That is, it implies as does the "Mémoire" a social upheaval of enclosure and a political readjustment of property rights guaranteed by the state itself.[29] Yet Quesnay indisputably intends his Tableau to serve the interests of that state. In this sense, the Tableau bears the direct legacy of his earliest economic work, "Fermiers": A higher net product from the agricultural sector affords increased revenues for the personal uses of the ruling class and the public uses of the state.

None of the tableaux can be understood outside this political context, for fiscal exigencies governed the original formulation, as Quesnay so clearly informed Mirabeau. In his first letter announcing the Tableau, Quesnay describes his zigzag as "a way of meditating on the present and the future," and expresses amazement that "the Parlement proposes no resources for the reparation of the state except economy" despite the need for a reallocation of resources. Even so, he counsels against despair about the apparent ineffectiveness of individual efforts, "for the appalling crises will come and it will be necessary to have recourse to

29. *Ibid.*, 15.

medical knowledge."[30] In the interim, he continues to design tableaux to establish the rules of economic organization necessary for the permanent solvency of the monarchy.

Although scholars have never ignored the political aspect of the Tableau—Conan even argues that the entire early physiocratic program can be reduced to one of fiscal reform—they have tended toward a narrow reading that ignores the complexity of Quesnay's thought. The progression of the first three tableaux demonstrates that from the outset he proceeded on three levels. In the diagram itself he depicted the process of the distribution of the revenue and illustrated the magical effect of an increased velocity of circulation. In the explanatory notes, which ultimately mushroomed into the "Explication" of the third edition, he developed his economic analysis in textual form. Finally, in the "Remarques" or "Maximes," he elaborated the principles of his political economy. No one of his approaches makes sense without the others, but each remains methodologically distinct. Where the diagram depicts the mechanism of circulation, the explication analyzes the productive process, and the maxims establish the conditions requisite to both optimal distribution and maximum productivity. Quesnay uses the Tableau to bind together his micro- and macro-economic understanding of capitalist production with his aim of raising the over-all performance of the economy—in particular, the revenues of the crown.[31] He asks his mechanism to resolve the contradictions that had led him and Mirabeau to abandon the "Traité de la monarchie."

The two strains of thought that Quesnay asks the Tableau to join were fundamentally different. While capitalist production requires, as he repeatedly insists, a free market, including security

30. AN, M 784, no. 70; Meek, *Economics*, 108. I have not used Meek's translation.

31. See Bert Hoselitz, "Agrarian Capitalism, The Natural Order of Things: François Quesnay," *Kyklos*, XXI (1968), 637-64, on Quesnay's capitalist theory of production; see also Jean Bénard, "Marx et Quesnay," INED, I, 105-30.

of property and autonomy of the individual, the commitment to the existing French state presupposes an acceptance of a social system with feudal property relations and paternalist notions about the social allocation of resources through a tightly regulated market. Quesnay at first assumed that the state could introduce, through administrative fiat, the necessary conditions for the free market his economics required. The new maxims introduced in the second and third editions, which call for freedom to plant and the introduction of large farming units respectively, raise the spectre of political individualism within the monolith of the state itself. In addition, the extensive new notes to the maxims of the third edition dwell insistently upon the contrast between France as is and the necessary order of the Tableau.[32]

Quesnay's first three editions of the tableau resolutely avoid any mention of the social and political community to which Mirabeau had introduced him, but this silence haunts the Tableau like the ghost at the feast. The ideology implicit in the economic analysis and that implicit in the political economy do not mesh. The contradiction might not seem to matter in this specifically economic context were it not that it reflects back upon the mechanism of the Tableau and upon all attempts at its interpretation.

The third edition marked the end of one sequence even as it inaugurated another. In Mirabeau's "Explications," and even more in *Philosophie rurale*, the focus of attention shifts. While the diagram remains essentially identical to its prototype, the explanation disappears, and the maxims, freed from the apparatus of their notes, appear as a few self-contained pages.[33] These two works, of 160 and 412 quarto pages respectively, address themselves exclusively to an extended explanation of the Tableau. There constructions, however, represent successive and significant

32. I regret that I have not been able to read Kiyoaki Hirata, *F. Quesnay: La création des sciences économiques* (Tokyo, 1965), available only in Japanese, which may bear on some of these questions.
33. "Explications," 183–90; *Philosophie rurale*, 341–55.

shifts in focus. The "Explications" consider the Tableau relative to its own operation and to a series of questions about the larger concerns of political economy. *Philosophie rurale* rigorously follows the formula, announced on the face of the third edition diagram and retained in the "Explications" diagram, of "objects to consider"; it traces in succeeding chapters: (1) three kinds of expenditure; (2) their source; (3) their advances; (4) their distribution; (5) their effects; (6) their reproduction; (7) their relations between themselves; (8) their relationship to population; (9) to agriculture; (10) to industry; (11) to commerce; (12) to the mass of the wealth of a nation.

Both works retain the Tableau at the center of their investigations. Mirabeau's "Explications," as indicated by its title, claims to do no more than to elucidate the diagram's workings. It studies the relationship of the Tableau to all aspects of economic life, not to mention morals, customs, and taxation, and devotes its introduction to the nature and scope of economic science. By doing so it simultaneously reduces the importance of the diagram in relation to the textual attempt to expound a coherent and inclusive political economy, and vastly exaggerates its importance as the symbol not only of a political economy but of a world view. *Philosophie rurale* openly announces the extremes to which it pushes this tendency by the claims of its subtitle: *Economie générale et politique de l'agriculture, réduite à l'ordre immuable des loix physiques et morales, qui assurent la prospérité des empires*. Mirabeau, in his preface, announces the eternal significance of economic science from the perspective of Quesnay's dualistic metaphysics. Throughout the text he intersperses mathematical calculations and economic analysis with reflections upon the Tableau as the infallible guide to the dictates of natural law, and therefore the necessary arbiter of the relations of men in society.[34]

Philosophie rurale marks the full evolution of the zigzag. Indeed, its introduction of the abbreviated form, the *précis*, heralds

34. On the extent of Quesnay's authorship, cf. Meek, *Economics*, 37n.

the 1766 appearance of the "Formule" even as its text prefigures
Quesnay's "Observations sur le droit naturel des hommes réunis
en société" (1765) and Le Mercier de la Rivière's *L'ordre naturel
et essential des sociétés politiques* (1767). But *Philosophie rurale*
marks no decisive break with earlier physiocratic writings. It
grows directly from them; its more universal claims and more
general terminology merely indicate the rising level of abstraction dictated by the contradictions at the heart of Quesnay's
thought.[35] And those temperamental materialists—Marxists and
non-Marxists alike—also err when they seek the true Quesnay
only in the specifically economic analysis while ascribing to his
disciples the responsibility for the ideological aspects of the
doctrine. The concept "tutelary authority" for which the disciples
are regularly reproached, makes its appearance in *Philosophie
rurale*.[36] The need for such an absolute authority derived directly
from Quesnay's and Mirabeau's analysis of French society.

Thus the progression of changes in the zigzag and the slow,
irregular introduction of new elements into the different sections
of the text of the Tableau graphically illustrate the interconnectedness of Quesnay's thought and the piecemeal emergence
of the mature physiocratic doctrine. The economic analysis
cannot be understood apart from Quesnay's and Mirabeau's
early work.

The vast literature devoted by modern economists to physiocracy demonstrates conclusively that the Tableau does not work.[37]

35. An interesting indication of these contradictions can be found in
Quesnay's attitude toward Hobbes. He openly repudiates Hobbes's vision
of society as founded on struggle in *Droit naturel;* yet the whole point of
his own political theory is to guard against just such a struggle of individual interests. Cf. Heinz Holldack, "Der Physiokratismus und die
absolute Monarchie," *Historische Zeitschrift,* CXLV (1932), 533.

36. *Philosophie rurale,* 296–98.

37. Cf. Henri Woog, *The Tableau Economique of François Quesnay: An
Essay in the Explanation of Its Mechanism and a Critical Review of the
Interpretations of Marx, Bilmovic, and Onken* (Bern, 1950); Friedrich
Engels, *Anti-Dühring* (New York, 1970 [1939]), 266–77 (the key section

In 1766, three years after his adherence to the *Secte*, du Pont still encountered difficulties in explaining it to his own satisfaction.[38] Although since his time, numerous economists have succeeded in explaining it to their own satisfaction, none of their reconstructions has convinced a majority of their peers.[39] One of the roots of this general frustration lies in the Tableau itself. As a formally symmetrical mathematical model, the Tableau promises the delights of balanced, simultaneous equations and holds out the lure of a mathematically precise solution. The physiocrats, in their intensive propaganda about its virtues, intentionally furthered the illusion that it contained scientifically verifiable answers to the problems besetting France—the secrets, as it were, of perpetual, equilibrated motion.[40] Everyone who devotes much time to the study of the Tableau succumbs in some measure to the disease—the answer, one knows, can be unearthed by just a little more work. Yet no physiocrat other than Quesnay himself appears to have understood the mechanism. And Quesnay

on the Tableau was written by Marx); A. Bilmovic, "Das allgemeine Schema des wirtschaftlichen Kreislaufes," *Zeitschrift für National Ökonomie*, X (1944), 199ff.; Ronald Meek, "Problems of the *Tableau Economique*," [*Economica* (1960)] repr. in Meek, *Economics*, 265–96; Almarin Phillips, "The *Tableau Economique* as a Simple Leontief Model," *Quarterly Journal of Economics*, LXIX (1955), 137–44; Akiteru Kubota, "Essai sur les perturbations du système d'équilibre dans le *Tableau Economique* de François Quesnay," Science Council of Japan: Division of Economics, Commerce, and Business Administration, Economic Series, no. 24.

38. EMHL, Winterthur MSS, group 2, series B, W2–4577, "Préliminaires de l'explication du *Tableau oeconomique*" [1766?]. There is no published work corresponding to this manuscript, which seems to be trying to explain the "Formule" version of the Tableau. Du Pont gets as far as outlining twelve articles which should be treated and starting an introduction and then breaks off.

39. Cf. Mark Blaug, *Economic Theory in Retrospect*, rev. ed. (New York, 1968), 27.

40. Cf. Nicolas Baudeau, *Explication du Tableau économique à Madame de****, extracts from *Les éphémérides du citoyen* of 1767 and 1768 [1776] (Paris, 1967), 168.

ended his life studying geometry, convinced that he had squared the circle.[41]

The puzzle of the Tableau invites caution. The model's inconsistencies cannot be resolved by the introduction of extraneous variables, or by rearrangement of the chronological sequence of the diagrams, or by attempts to make it fit modern equilibrium theories. Had economic analysis advanced to its present level of sophistication in Quesnay's time, Quesnay would undoubtedly have delighted in expressing his insights in the equations of the Harrod-Domar model of dynamic equilibrium. But the contradictions in his work would nonetheless have remained.[42] An input-output presentation may well help modern economists unfamiliar with physiocracy understand the mechanism of the Tableau, but it cannot explain how Quesnay developed the model in the first place.[43] Quesnay wanted to use economic analysis as a scientific rule for political and social policy. His Tableau can only be understood in reference to the analytical tools available to him and the specific historical problems he wished to solve.

In one respect, the econometric fallacy in Tableau exegesis resembles the historical fallacy. Modern economists usually treat the givens of the Tableau as if they represented a historical reality instead of the projections of a highly abstract model. In fact, the Tableau constitutes, in the econometricians' language, a counter-factual argument, and suffers as do all such arguments from the confusion between its reliance upon concrete historical facts and its development of hypothetical situations logically derived from the initial, real data. Moreover, the Tableau itself presents not historical data but a counter-factual theoretical

41. François Quesnay, *Recherches philosophiques sur l'évidence des vérités géométriques avec un projet de nouveaux élémens de géométrie* (Amsterdam, 1773).

42. Eagley, "Physiocratic Model."

43. Phillips, "*Tableau Economique* as a Leontief Model"; Blaug, *Economic Theory in Retrospect*, 28–29.

model. Solving the Tableau entails solving a rudimentary mathematical model that purports to describe not an actual historical condition but a possible and desirable one. Quesnay was interested both in the mathematical structure of his model and in its ability to reflect accurately a desired reality so as to afford an indisputable guide to policy. He always risked having his mathematical formulation acquire a life of its own; he thus exposed himself to the danger of solving the mathematical problem as an independent exercise and then claiming that his solution precisely reflected the human situation, or conversely, of allowing his political commitments to distort their supposedly exact, mathematical expression. Modern economic analysis has proved of incalculable assistance in attempts to construct modern models of old economic structures and has even helped in the construction of economic theories of, for example, feudal societies. But it cannot be expected to reconcile the inconsistencies of a model of a hypothetical economic reality.

Between the explanations and the maxims of the various tableaux, Quesnay states the economic and political conditions requisite to the functioning of his zigzag and describes the process of circulation they embody. Despite this care, his work contains numerous gaps about his own presuppositions and encompasses all the tensions of his general, evolving ideology. Quesnay designed his economics as a tool for restoring the finances of France, but he illustrated its analytic propositions by a country other than France and postulated requisite political conditions that could not occur in France. In the successive versions of the tableaux, Quesnay increasingly tries to incorporate his understanding of capitalist production into a precapitalist economy and political system.

The early evolution of the Tableau shows how Quesnay came to create a model with insoluble problems. An investigation of the evolution of the zigzag will reveal how the analytic contradictions of the Tableau were implicit in the earlier formulations and slowly surfaced as the contradictory demands placed upon the model increased. Herlitz is therefore wrong in arguing that the most serious inconsistencies in the Tableau only come fully to light in its latest incarnation as the "Formule," although they are prefigured in the *précis* of the pivotal *Philosophie rurale*.[44]

Since Adam Smith first insisted upon the fundamental distinction between the mercantile and the agricultural systems, it has been common to emphasize the opposition between the physiocrats and their mercantile predecessors. The physiocrats' battles with the leading French neomercantilists of their day seem to confirm this verdict. A significant break did occur eventually, but the line of continuity from the mercantilists to the physiocrats is no less significant. Quesnay did not immediately jettison the essentially mercantilist point of view that characterized the economics of his immediate predecessors. On the contrary, he retained many of their assumptions; in particular, in his concept of the net product he emphasized aggregate rather than per capita indicators as the barometer of economic performance. He broke with the mercantilists more over methods than goals. His conviction that agriculture (domestic production) rather than foreign trade constituted the best means to raise aggregate output; his insistence that quality of population mattered more than its quantity; and his intransigent belief that direction of the economy through monopoly, privilege, and regulation frustrated exactly those objects it was designed to promote, all set his thought in direct opposition to that of the neomercantilists. His close analysis of capitalist agriculture as it had developed in England convinced him that the road to true wealth and power led to the separation of men from the land—the introduction of a market in labor power. Despite his insistence that agriculture afforded the only disposable surplus, he clearly understood that the introduction of capitalist relations of production into all sectors of the economy afforded the only sound basis for competi-

44. Herlitz, "*Tableau* and Sterility," 14–15.

tion in the modern world. His analysis of production therefore demanded a market basis for all social as well as economic relations, and whether or not he chose to admit it, directly undermined his initial commitment to a unitary conception of the state.

As a corollary of this system of production, all economic operations—the production and consumption of commodities as well as the allocation of labor—must participate in a commercial system that assesses their worth in monetary terms. Quesnay decided, in other words, that the ordinary business of life had no social or political significance if it could not be measured in monetary terms. In this fundamental tenet of his economics he once again betrays his debt to the mercantilists. By the time Smith wrote *The Wealth of Nations*, market relations had so fully developed in Britain that the monetary expression of economic processes could be taken for granted, and analytic discussion once again focused on how to maximize the social production of wealth— although this time with the tacit acceptance of a new political and social system reflected in economic analysis by the new emphasis on per capita rather than aggregate indicators. Quesnay, caught in a transitional period of both historical development and economic analysis, still had to argue that without such monetary expression there would be no social production of wealth.

Quesnay insisted that only the capitalist rationalization of agriculture in particular and the economy in general could make production take the form of commodities to be exchanged for specie. He opposed merchant and finance capital in practice, as well as the value of monetary stocks in theory; he did not oppose commercial transactions in general. On the contrary, he believed that commercial transactions create the economy or are identical with it. Without a market there can be no economy, only subsistence. But he wanted a complete circular flow: the money realized through the sale of commodities must immediately return to the production of commodities in order to maintain the level of economic performance. Exchange occupies a central position in physiocratic economics. If Quesnay repudiated the mercantilist notion that exchange contributes to the increase of wealth, he believed, as all successive economists would, that there would be no wealth at all without it. Supply without a monetary value—without adequate demand—creates only misery and economic stagnation.

Quesnay's emphasis on the primacy of demand in assuring economic performance underlies the central mechanism of the Tableau and reveals the extent of his debt to Cantillon and Hume. But Quesnay's economic analysis entailed more than his insight into the importance of demand. It also inadvertently predicated a revolution in the productive sector and thus carried an unavowed and proto-classical insistence upon the decisive nature of supply. For if the labor market that Quesnay advocated had been instituted, he might have assumed, as his successors did in viewing a different historical situation, that supply would create its own demand.

The role of demand appears decisive to economists studying relatively developed economic systems. When Cantillon looked at France, taking the existing social relations of production for granted, he rightly insisted that the owners of land commanded the decisive margin of purchasing power and that their consumption decisions would dictate the level and nature of output of the economy as a whole. He also understood—in his major contribution to economic analysis—that with a given monetary stock, an increase in the velocity of circulation will have the same effect as an increase in the monetary stock itself. Quesnay took over Cantillon's formal analysis in its entirety. But he also tried to extend it to include the production of commodities. His attempt constitutes his central contribution to economic analysis —the vision of economic life as a complete circular flow. But his integration of his separate understandings of production and exchange was never complete. His analysis of capitalist production pointed to quite different conclusions than the social and political premises underlying his and Cantillon's picture of the social process of exchange. For if, instead of predicating a revolutionized productive sector, Quesnay had concentrated on the difficult problems of that economic transformation itself, he might have understood that the creation of a market in labor power would have distributed the aggregate purchasing power of the landowners among a vast number of individual workers and agricultural entrepreneurs. In all justice, as Mirabeau's paean to the market for boots and nails in *Philosophie rurale* testifies, he did understand it in an abstract way.[45] He did not, however, inject his understanding into the formal model of the Tableau. Instead of integrating his two analytic positions, or jettisoning one of them, Quesnay superimposed one upon the other. Their superimposition accounts for many of the inconsistencies of the Tableau.

The five basic zigzag diagrams share a number of common characteristics.[46] By abstracting from the explanatory notes on the face of the first two, the diagrams can be reduced to a simple graphic representation of the distribution of a base revenue equal to two monetary units. The monetary unit, M, itself represents the amount Quesnay allotted for the support of one working family—in either agriculture or manufacture—of three persons above the age of infancy.[47] Its value equals that of half the annual advances of productive expenditure, or the amount received by each class of expenditure. The circulatory process described by the Tableau shows the expenditure of the initial net product, 2M, from the beginning of the economic period (one year) when its monetary value is realized, through its sale by the farmers and transferal, in payment of the rent, to the proprietors of the land. The period ends when the net product has been spent "to the

45. *Philosophie rurale*, 57: "There will be more purchases and sales of shoes than of laces and rich fabrics of great labor."
46. See *Quesnay's Tableau* for reproductions of the first three. The third edition, reproduced in this book, was the model for "Explications" and *Philosophie rurale*.
47. *Quesnay's Tableau*, app. A, n.p.

last farthing."[48] In the initial act of expenditure, the proprietors divide their income equally in transferals to the two other classes of expenditure that now each command one unit, M, of money. Each class then exchanges M/2 for the products and labor of the opposite class and expends M/2 on the products and labor of its own. The process continues through a succession of twelve such mutual expenditures until the entire revenue has been expended and the process starts anew with the sale of the re-generated net product by the farmers.[49]

Quesnay specifies in the explanatory notes to the first edition how the expenditure of wealth relates to population—a relation-ship the clarification of which was one of the key aims of the Tableau. "The proprietor, who spends the revenue of 400 livres draws his subsistence from it. The 200 livres distributed to each class of expenditures can support one man in each; thus 400 livres of revenue can enable three heads of families to subsist."[50] And one of them enjoys a standard of living twice as high as the others. Here lies the first miracle of the Tableau. By its illustra-tion of the multiplier effect inherent in an increased velocity of circulation, it shows how the funds necessary for the support of a single family can be stretched to support two additional families. In the explanations accompanying the second and third editions, Quesnay calls attention to the same phenomenon, although in the third, the relationship between wealth and density of popula-tion has taken third place in the order of important lessons. Even Mirabeau, with his special interest in population, relegates his discussion of the Tableau's contribution to population theory to the third chapter of his "Explications."[51]

But the miracles depicted by the zigzag do not rest solely on the multiplier effect of expended revenue. From the earliest

48. Cf. Herlitz, "*Tableau* and Sterility," 17–18, who rightly argues that the zigzag exhausts all possibility of expenditure.
49. *Quesnay's Tableau*, app. A, diagram.
50. *Ibid.*, app. A.
51. *Ibid.*, app. B and iv; "Explications," 146.

version Quesnay includes on the face of the diagram a central column of figures, connected by a horizontal dotted line to the succeeding productive expenditures, and equal in value to those expenditures. The dotted line carries the words "reproduce net." Herlitz has argued that the figures of the central column do not represent real quantities of M and should not, therefore, be included in any calculation of the total units of M circulating in the Tableau. Those figures serve merely to remind the observer of the 100 percent reproductive powers of productive expenditures. They do not directly affect the mutual expenditure phenomenon of the zigzag itself, for they are not intersectoral expenditures. Rather, they logically represent the effects of intrasectoral expenditures within the productive sector, where by definition any expenditure generates a physical output equivalent to its own monetary value—or as the physiocrats would say, reproduces 100 percent. They indicate that the unit M (half of the total amount of 2M passing through the farmers' hands and spent within their own sector) regenerates an identical unit M. Those two units provide for the reconstitution of the revenue.[52]

Furthermore, according to Quesnay the reconstitution of the annual advances presupposes agricultural costs, "which are also regenerated each year," amounting to 2M (which reproduce—a 100 percent reproduction—to form the annual advances). Roughly half of these costs consist in wages paid to agricultural labor and afford an additional M, which can support another family. Thus the total of 3M "which are generated annually from landed property" could enable the appropriate multiple of twelve persons to subsist "in conformity with this order of circulation and distribution of the annual revenue."[53] The second edition reproduces the same analysis practically verbatim except for the increase in the base revenue, which requires a value of 300 for M, and the addition of a definition of circulation by which "is here meant the purchases paid for by the revenue, and the distri-

52. Herlitz, "*Tableau* and Sterility," 14.
53. *Quesnay's Tableau*, app. A, n.p.

bution which shares out the revenue among men by means of the payment for the purchases at first hand, abstracting from trade which increases sales and purchases without increasing things and which represents nothing but an addition to sterile expenditure."[54] The third edition incorporates the argument of the second, as does Mirabeau's "Explications."[55]

Total reproduction in all of the basic zigzag models, as stated at the bottom of their diagrams, thus amounts to 4M: 2M revenue plus 2M annual advances. The third edition includes, in addition, the interest on the primitive advances "which the land restores," while the "Explications" includes the interest on both primitive and annual advances and gives the values of taxation and the tithe as well as their advances and interest on the advances from which it nonetheless abstracts.[56] Their inclusion would change the quantitative level of expenditure, but not its qualitative distribution, since the premises of the Tableau dictate that taxation and the tithe fall directly upon the already-regenerated net product. This position, which obtains consistently from the third edition on, represents a clarification and strengthening of Quesnay's sense of the necessary inviolability of property as against his attitude in the first and second editions where he had toyed with the notion that "taxation is detrimental to the revenue."[57] From the third on, he solves the problem inherent in having the proprietors and the state live off the same net product by arguing that any increase in the demands upon the revenue presupposes additional production to supply the requisite surplus. That assumption, which reappears each time the physiocrats build a model and abstract from public revenues, reflects his growing understanding of the importance of private property to a functioning market, and it vitiates the arguments of recent scholars who hold that the revenue accruing to the proprietors has no

54. *Ibid., app.* B, 2.
55. *Ibid.,* v; "Explications," 147–48.
56. "Explications," 146.
57. *Quesnay's Tableau,* app. A, app. B, 4.

necessarily private character and could just as well devolve upon the state.[58] Even the first and second editions specify, in their seventh maxim (which the third edition and the "Explications" retain), "that taxes are not destructive or disproportionate to the mass of the nation's revenue; that their increase follows the increase of the revenue."[59] *Philosophie rurale* and later the "Formule" both insist explicitly upon the necessity of the absolute character of property in land as a guarantee of the proper functioning of the economy.

The progression in Quesnay's treatment of the rights of property suggests the extent of his prolonged effort to move evermore of the positive assumptions of his political economy initially contained in the maxims into the functioning or technical explanations of the zigzag itself. Whether or not landlord property enjoys security does not of course directly affect the abstract mechanism of distribution, but as Quesnay came to understand, it would affect the structure and functioning of the free market economy, which the successive tableaux claimed to portray. Quesnay's treatment of the sanctity of landed property reflects the fundamental contradiction of his model and goes far toward explaining the differences between the physiocratic and the Ricardian attitudes toward rent.

Quesnay and Ricardo were observing the same socioeconomic transformation from very different vantage points in time and space. From the viewpoint of the ancien régime, Quesnay analyzed the emergence of a market economy in England and recognized that the maximum efficiency of capitalist production rested upon complete security and autonomy in the individual disposition of the means of production and their product. But he applied this understanding to his own historical milieu in which he, quite reasonably, believed land to constitute the only surplus-yielding means of production, and in which property in

58. Warren J. Samuels, "The Physiocratic Theory of Property and the State," *Quarterly Journal of Economics*, LXXV (1961), 96–111.

59. *Quesnay's Tableau*, app. A, app. B, 4–5; "Explications," 185.

land was defined by residual seigneurial standards. Ricardo, on the other hand, with his understanding of nascent industrial capitalism, saw property in land as the title to a scarce resource the total value of which turned not upon its uniform and absolute productivity, but rather upon the marginal demand for the product of its least efficient unit. While Quesnay tried to infuse outmoded property relations with the force of emerging market possession, Ricardo recognized that new forms of property rendered the economic claims of an obsolete political title increasingly contrary to the larger social interest.[60]

Quesnay's determination to respect existing political forms as the external structure and principal beneficiaries of his new economic model colors the entire sequence of tableaux. The early zigzag did not, for example, portray the functioning of the entire economy. The nature of the discrepancy appears in the representation of total reproduction. Abstracting from (discounting) all taxation, tithes, and interest payments, the first four models show a total reproduction of 4M. The process of revenue distribution supports reproduction by permitting maximum consumption at market prices, while the process of mutual sales between the classes of expenditures converts commodities into money. Quesnay believed even agricultural products to be worthless without the quality of venal or market value. So the distribution of the revenue brings the entire economic process into the purview of market operations. Everyone, in the world of the Tableau, lives off the revenue: Quesnay explicitly stipulates that all production assumes a capitalist form and leaves no doubt that he views labor as a commodity.[61] But the Tableau does not depict the productive process; it assumes it.

In the first edition, Quesnay restricts his remarks about reproduction to the observation that the expenditure of the revenue 2M gives M to each class of expenditures "in addition to the

60. Cf. David Ricardo, *The Principles of Political Economy and Taxation*, Everyman Edition [1911] (London, 1948), 33–45.

61. *Quesnay's Tableau*, 15.

advances which are maintained intact."[62] He adds, while discussing the possible extent of population, that the costs of the class of productive expenditures are also regenerated each year. The second edition repeats the same formula. Neither of the first two editions attempts to describe the reproductive process nor to tie it to the distribution of the revenue.

In "Fermiers," "Grains," and the "Mémoire" for Berne, Quesnay had already developed his ideas about capitalist reproduction in the agricultural sector and had established his theory of exclusive productivity. In "Fermiers" and "Grains," he extended his micro-economic analysis of the capitalist structure of a single farm to the kingdom as a whole. The disposable surplus that had first figured on the basis of a single firm afforded the qualitative prototype for the disposable surplus of the kingdom as a whole. His macro-economic analysis accordingly consisted in multiplying the product of the single firm by the number of existing (or imaginary) firms. The procedure involved a complete abstraction from (discounting of) marketing and transactions costs, which he arbitrarily reduced to zero. At the same time Quesnay ascribed to market operations the faculty of creating value, for he understood social as well as economic development as the progressive incorporation of all economic activity, including the employment of labor, into the purview of the market. He simply stipulated that the ideal market, as the reflection and embodiment of the natural order, should introduce no artificial costs. Within its confines value must exchange for equal value.[63]

Quesnay also believed that all social value must be realized in the market value. The mere increase of population contributed nothing to the progress of civilization. The original configuration of the zigzag represents his attempt to fuse his own understanding of the surplus-producing capacity of capitalist agriculture and notions of circulation gleaned from Cantillon with his growing ideological commitment to the market as the symbol and agency

62. *Ibid.*, app. A.
63. Cf. *Philosophie rurale*, 4.

of social progress. Market values for agricultural produce, as well as for manufactured commodities and labor, constitute the necessary precondition of the zigzag: without market value, there is no revenue. But no more than it registers the reproductive process does the zigzag offer any account of price formation. The zigzag in its original forms bears only a tangential relationship to the central process of economic production. With the passage of time this basic discrepancy emerges more clearly as the physiocrats attempt to close the economic circle and to show the relationship between cash and commodity flows. In fact, the attempt to correlate these two flows became the major preoccupation of subsequent economists who sought to elucidate the Tableau.

The first two editions make only a passing reference to the commodity flow. Both state that the "two classes spend in part on their own products and in part mutually on the products of one another."[64] The third edition attempts a more explicit treatment of the money-commodity exchange. The class of productive expenditures ostensibly receives its original unit, M, of cash "by means of the sale of the products which the proprietor buys from it." The accompanying explanation stipulates that the products of this class amount to 1200 livres (4M), disposed of among a unit equivalent in value to M bought by the proprietors, another bought by the class of sterile expenditures, another consumed within the class of productive expenditures itself, and a final unit used for the feeding and maintenance of livestock." The explanation continues, "Thus of the 1200 livres worth of product, 600 are consumed by this class [productive expenditures], and its advances of 600 livres are returned to it in the form of money through the sales which it makes to the proprietors and to the sterile expenditure class."[65] In his "Explications" Mirabeau reaffirms that the product of the class of productive expenditures amounts to 1200 livres. He then explains how the proprietor

---

64. *Quesnay's Tableau*, app. A, app. B, 2.
65. *Ibid.*, ii–iv.

spends half his revenue on agricultural produce, "which comes to the same as if he had received half his revenue in productions."

Mirabeau in many respects offers us our best guide to the Tableau. Not having invented it, he had to work at understanding it—"I was not able to know his Tableau in all its extent except by working through it for my own use and making my own explanation of it"[66]—but he also had to verify his understanding in discussion with Quesnay. Not for him the tampering in which du Pont and Baudeau may have indulged: Quesnay's immediate presence and collaboration commanded orthodoxy. Mirabeau's perplexities therefore must be taken seriously. How, for example, could he have proposed that the proprietors might just as well have received half their revenue in agricultural commodities? Unless the proprietor pays money for his produce, the Tableau will not even begin to function. Without market value, no society can exist. Mirabeau's slip should not have been allowed past the eyes of the master. That it escaped Quesnay's censorship suggests that Mirabeau's confusion reflected a real problem. First, it betrays the weakness of physiocratic value theory—the identity of goods and value under the assumption of an exogenously determined price. Second, it betrays the existence of a market external to the Tableau. Agricultural products had to command a monetary equivalent from the start in order for the farmers to pay the proprietors a revenue in cash. The Tableau was designed not to incorporate the circulation of the total annual reproduction, but merely the total annual surplus.

Listen to Mirabeau as he attempts to describe the total process: "Each year the advances of the productive classes cause the regeneration of the advances and the revenue; similarly each year the revenue and these advances are consumed and reproduced; each year also the advances are consumed by the Farmer; they themselves constitute the costs or the expenditures that he assumes for their reproduction and for the reproduction of the revenue, which is the net product which cultivation yields above and beyond costs."[67] Restated, the above passage might read: capital investment in agriculture yields high enough returns to cover the replacement of working capital (interest on fixed capital subsequently included) and to produce a surplus, here rent. For the economy to function at full capacity—to reproduce 100 percent —the entire net social product must be consumed and the working capital replaced. As a problem in accounting, the process could be described thus: each year the farmer consumes the working capital; the working capital covers the costs for its own replacement and the regeneration of the surplus.

The zigzag did not originally depict the consumption of the entire social product. On the contrary, it specifically depicted only the consumption of those goods purchased by the monetary equivalent of the net product. In the first two editions Quesnay simply stipulated that the working capital be maintained intact. In the manufacturing sector the necessary replacement could be easily effected simply by holding back the extra money afforded by the accelerated rate of exchange in the process of circulation. Given the net reproductive character of expenditure within the productive sector, the same process could account for the regeneration of the working capital of agriculture, but not for the additional yield of the revenue without the intervention of an additional stage of production.

The initial expenditure of the revenue, 2M, sends M to each of the other two classes. The subsequent twelve exchanges record a total additional transfer of M to each class. Of its total receipts, 2M, each class spends M within its own sector. This process leaves the class of sterile expenditures in possession of the M in resources necessary to reconstitute its advances. Granted that everything the class of productive expenditures spends upon itself reproduces

67. "Explications," 142. In this instance Mirabeau so little understood the economics that he simply transcribed Quesnay's marginal comment directly into his text. Bibliothèque de L'Arsenal, Fonds de la Bastille, no. 1201, "Le Tableau économique," manuscript no. 2, 9.

100 percent, the circulatory process leaves it in possession of the 2M necessary to reconstitute its advances—but with no 2M for the revenue. One therefore has to assume the existence of additional costs equal to M, as Quesnay did, that reproduce the additional 2M. The only alternative to this procedure lies in concentrating upon the total of expenditure instead of its direction, so that anything the farmers spend, whether for seed or their household, ranks as productive expenditure and therefore can be assumed to reproduce 100 percent. Following this line, the total receipts, 2M, of the class of productive expenditure can be assumed to double, and the regeneration of both advances and revenue can be explained. But this method of understanding also raises the dour spectre of the nature of the contribution of the nonagricultural sector to reproduction. Can the process of circulation alone link the two sectors of the economy, as Quesnay so clearly wished to believe?[68]

Since the class of sterile expenditures does not use its share of the revenue in agricultural production, the proposed solution for the regeneration of the total product does not affect it, but it does present problems of its own because it receives, in all, 2M, when it only requires M to reconstitute its advances. In the first two editions, Quesnay describes the remaining M as left for "expenditures" and "wages" respectively.[69] In the third he implicitly recognizes the problem he has created for himself. On the one hand, when speaking of M as a receipt from the point of view of the sterile class, he describes it as the payment of the wage bill. On the other hand, when speaking of it as a unit of agricultural products transferred from the class of productive expenditures, he describes it as composed of two subunits with M/2 being consumed for subsistence within the class and M/2

68. Cf. Eagley, "Physiocratic Model," 83; Herlitz, "*Tableau* and Sterility," 49. Quesnay's reliance upon the process of expenditure to link the two classes reveals his deeper confusion between the relative roles of supply and demand.

69. *Quesnay's Tableau,* app. A, app. B, 2.

being taken for external trade. If one follows the basic assumption of the early zigzags, that M supports one household in either the class of productive expenditures or in that of sterile expenditures, disposal of the receipts of the class of sterile expenditures presents no problem. The members of the class turn their advances into one unit of product, which they sell to the proprietors in return for their share of the revenue. With half that share they buy raw materials from the farmers. During the year they receive an additional M from the farmers, half of which also goes for raw materials. These raw materials are turned into commodities, which pass to the farmers in return for the farmers' expenditures, while the remaining M (M/2 twice retained for expenditure within the class) reconstitutes their advances.[70]

This solution could be taken simply to represent Quesnay's basic premise about the nonproductive nature of nonagricultural labor, if he himself did not introduce the question of wages. It would be possible to accept his postulate, frequently expressed elsewhere, that any given unit of commodities embodies one-half unit of raw material and one-half unit of subsistence for the worker.[71] At the end of the production period both have been consumed and labor itself receives no special payment. Were it not for the rigid structure of the Tableau, a situation could be imagined in which farmers with agricultural produce above the nation's subsistence needs—total subsistence demand—paid laborers to transform the excess of agricultural supply into commodities to satisfy other social demands. This procedure would increase the market value of the farmers' product, at least by the value of the labor-power it would now embody. Given Quesnay's larger political economy in which farmers are clearly identified as capitalist entrepreneurs whose net reproductive activities pay the wage bill of national labor—agricultural and sterile alike—this reading would seem to make sense. Furthermore, Quesnay's own admission that the farmers' payment to the artisans consists in wages

70. *Ibid.*, iii.
71. Cf. "Dialogue sur les travaux des artisans," INED, II, 885–912.

would seem to support it, as would his early statements about the nature and benefits of the division of labor. This solution, however, fails to take account of Quesnay's particular vision of the division of labor as promoting the natural realization, under advanced social conditions, of the necessary value of agricultural produce rather than promoting an increase in value of agricultural produce.

The earliest versions of the zigzag attempt to depict precisely Quesnay's concept of the realization of value through the social division of labor. Suppose that each unit M which passes through the hands of the class of sterile expenditures represents equal amounts of subsistence goods and raw materials, under the assumption of zero transactions costs and zero profit on the production and sale of nonagricultural commodities. Suppose further, as Quesnay claims, that the advances in hand at the beginning of the economic period consist in subsistence goods and raw materials. Then, during the period the manufacturing sector would transform two units of subsistence goods and raw materials worth 2M (advances in kind and one unit purchase from the agricultural sector) into two units of commodities also worth M each, which it would sell to the proprietors and farmers respectively. The manufacturing sector would acquire in addition an extra unit of M from the farmers, which would reconstitute its advances. This solution leaves only the problem of the transformation of the last unit of money into the produce and raw materials necessary for the production of the commodities required to make up the advances. Since Quesnay initially designed the zigzag only to demonstrate the support provided for surplus population by an increased velocity of circulation and to suggest a proper pattern of expenditure to the crown and landowners, he ignores the problem. In fact, in the later model of the "Formule," Quesnay closed the economic circle by having each economic period begin with the artisans purchasing from the farmers a unit of produce.[72]

72. Herlitz, "*Tableau* and Sterility," 16–18.

Economists, however, have been much more concerned with the inconsistency in the mathematical formulation. Accepting Quesnay's statement that the class of sterile expenditures contains half as many members as that of productive expenditures, they have trouble balancing the relationship between input and output and that between commodities and money.[73] On the basis of their understanding of the population/money ratio, Meek and Eagley, for example, postulate a 2:1 ratio of manufactured output to raw material input—a ratio they regard as central "to determining the Sterile Class's productive function." Eagley points out that the manufacturing sector produces two units of manufactured goods for sale to the proprietors and farmers, and then during the exchange process purchases a second unit of agricultural goods (the first unit was the advances). Then, following Quesnay's statement in the third edition, he identifies the major problem: "One half unit of this purchase is consumed as the Sterile Class's wage bill. What about the remaining one half unit?"[74]

Eagley, on the questionable assumption that all manufactured goods purchased by the classes of sterile and productive expenditures from the class of sterile expenditures are capital goods, argues that the "static-equilibrium conditions described by the Tableau imply that the depreciation allowances to replace fixed capital are the sole source of the Productive or Sterile Class's demand for manufactured capital goods." He then adds that Quesnay "is inconsistent, if not outright misleading, in his definition of agricultural and manufactured output," because while he gives the gross output of the Productive Class, he gives only the net output of the Sterile Class.[75] Eagley proceeds on the basis of Quesnay's numerical variables to reconstruct a static equilibrium model of the Tableau. It reveals that the static equilibrium output is "three units instead of two as indicated in Quesnay's Tableau.

73. Cf. Woog, *Tableau Economique,* and Herlitz, "*Tableau* and Sterility," 20–23.
74. Eagley, "Physiocratic Model," 68; Meek, *Economics,* 277.
75. Eagley, 69–70.

By netting out depreciation costs, and giving the Sterile Class's output in net terms, Quesnay could present a Tableau in which the annual advances of the Sterile Class would appear to reproduce only themselves, but nothing more. This was a useful gambit to support the sterility doctrine. But it was less than candid on Quesnay's part."[76] The sterility of nonagricultural labor has usually aroused justifiable criticism from subsequent economists, but there is no justification for attacks on Quesnay's integrity or for the characterization of his economic analysis as a "gambit." Indeed, an uncharitable critic might argue that Eagley, by postulating a capitalist structure for the sterile sector, against all historical evidence and all evidence of Quesnay's grasp of the economy of his own society, lays himself open to the charge of pursuing a flagrant gambit. Happily, Eagley's sound general conclusions do not depend upon acceptance of his premises. In fact, the confusion about the input-output ratio of the sterile sector results more from Quesnay's error in calculation than from his ideological bias.

For Quesnay, the first function of his initial tableaux was to demonstrate that the revenue could support two households on the basis of M consumption per household in addition to the proprietor, whose establishment consumes 2M. The basic model therefore depicts three households, with each nonproprietary household subsisting on the basis of M. Onto this basic model Quesnay grafted another household in the agricultural sector, which also subsisted on the basis of M in wages generated by the costs of the annual advances. The significance lies in the grafting. Quesnay's procedure in relation to taxation and tithes demonstrates his willingness to add units to the productive sector on the assumption that the net reproductive character of such activities would generate the additional net product necessary to increase social revenues. He seems to have followed exactly the same procedure in his addition of another household to the productive sector. Subsequently, he simply stated that the pro-

76. *Ibid.*, 70.

ductive sector contained twice as many households as the sterile sector. But half as many households in the sterile sector never meant that these households subsisted on M/2. By definition they subsist on M. Twice as many households in the productive sector means that they subsist on M per unit, or a total of 2M. Which brings back the problem of Quesnay's difficulty in reconciling his understanding of capitalist production with his understanding of the circulation and the role of money as the foremost social bond in what remained more a traditional than a possessive market society.[77]

The assumption that Quesnay's zigzag and subsequent tableaux represent an attempt to fuse two discrete circular flows, premised on different economic and social systems, does not itself "solve" the problems of the Tableau économique. If Quesnay did add an extra household to the productive sector, he should logically have added enough additional labor to the sterile sector to use up or to transform the surplus production of the additional agricultural labor so that it would command a market value. Meek argues that Quesnay tried to solve this problem by premising an export of agricultural raw materials, through the agency of the class of sterile expenditures, equal to M/4. And Quesnay did state that such an export would take place. But as Eagley points out, this solution creates other problems;[78] and Quesnay certainly did not postulate any additions to the nonagricultural labor force. He apparently believed that the increment of agricultural production which furnished the advances would realize its value in an agricultural commodity market off to the side of the Tableau. Later, in *Philosophie rurale*, Mirabeau introduced a phrase which perfectly captures the shadow structure I am postulating. The column of figures under the designation productive class, he writes, "represents the amounts . . . of the pulsation of the economic

77. Cf. *Philosophie rurale*, 5.
78. Meek, *Economics*, 282–86; Eagley, "Physiocratic Model," 69.

pendulum against the walls of reproduction."[79] The relationship between the circular flow of economic reproduction and the distribution of the revenue afforded by the net economic product is tangential.

In subsequent diagrams and writings Quesnay tried to resolve some of the problems arising from the initial contradiction, but he only complicated them further. He never did abandon the original format. His contradictions provided a graphic manifestation, not so much of eighteenth-century France, as of the dilemma facing nonbourgeois, nonrebellious, pre-Revolutionary advocates of a capitalist market. This understanding of the dual function ascribed to the Tableau as an abstract model—quite apart from its presumed correspondence to historical reality—cannot make mathematical sense of the variables it presents, but can afford a perspective from which to consider the Tableau as the first effort in economic model-building.

If the Tableau originated as a demonstration of Cantillon's premise that velocity of circulation was equivalent to an increase in the money in circulation, and that this increase permitted an increase in the population which could exist on a finite revenue, it soon lost sight of its initial purpose.[80] It retained the corollary insight that demand creates its own supply as the rationale for its configuration. But Quesnay, insisting upon a free market and substantial division of labor as the necessary material base for the maximum benefit from the rapid circulation of revenue, began to grant priority to the role of a balanced distribution of the revenue in guaranteeing fiscal solvency and stable economic growth.

Not until the third edition does Quesnay introduce his pregnant notion that "this expenditure may go more or less to one side or the other," with all its implications for economic regression and economic development.[81] From that point on, however, the role

79. *Quesnay's Tableau*, iv-v; *Philosophie rurale*, 23.

80. Cf. AN, M 784, no. 70, Quesnay to Mirabeau; Blaug, *Economic Theory in Retrospect*, 22-23.

81. *Quesnay's Tableau*, i.

of the Tableau as the yardstick of economic performance encroached more and more upon its original purpose. This aspect of the Tableau has also attracted considerable attention from modern economists interested in static and dynamic equilibrium analysis and the concept of the stationary state. Some excellent work has been devoted to this problem, although much of it is seriously weakened by inattention to or distortion of Quesnay's own economic hypotheses and general world view.[82]

Herlitz, for example, exposes the mathematical limits within which increased expenditure on agricultural products yields increasing returns. He shows that the beneficial progressions depend upon the simple productivity of nonagricultural labor and also shows by econometric methods that the mechanism of the Tableau requires two equal sides in order to substantiate its own claims. "Concerned as they were," he writes of the physiocrats, "with the problem of the maximum effect of expended revenue, they first determined the desired course of expenditure and then derived from this their doctrine of the completely unproductive nature of the sterile 'expenditure class.' "[83] Although Herlitz is correct in insisting that extraneous commitments led Quesnay to repudiate the concept of simple productivity of nonagricultural labor, which should have been the logical corollary of his conception of capitalist production, it does not follow that Quesnay's techniques of mathematical progression determined the doctrine of sterility. On the contrary, his commitment to the doctrine of sterility arose from ideological considerations, strengthened by his exposure to Mirabeau's traditional world view. Furthermore, it was mathematically irrelevant to the first two editions of his zigzag in which the mathematical progression demanded only

82. Lutfalla, *L'état stationnaire*, 127–37; Eagley, "Physiocratic Model"; and Hishiyama, "*Tableau Economique.*" See also Paul Samuelson, "Dynamics, Statics, and the Stationary State," *Review of Economic Statistics*, XXIV (1942), 58–68, which deals with the general concepts but not specifically with Quesnay.
83. Herlitz, "*Tableau* and Sterility," 35.

three columns to show how the division of the revenue between two classes supported an extra unit of population.

Since the labeling of the columns does not carry any particular significance in the early diagrams, scholars have generally ignored its central feature: in the first four zigzags, the three columns are labeled, from left to right, "productive expenditures," "expenditures of the revenue," and "sterile expenditures." In the accompanying explanatory texts Quesnay does refer to them as "classes" of expenditure.[84] But by classes he meant kind or classification. Initially, these classes bore no necessary relationship to living, breathing men. As time passed, and he increasingly tried to integrate his vision of economic production into the framework of the zigzag, the classes came to refer primarily to men, and the operative variable became the nature of the labor performed by the members of the class. But the early tableaux indisputably reflect the point of view of the crown, and all that matters is the way in which those who hold the revenue—those possessed of the legal title to the economic surplus—spend their money. On this level the early zigzags reflect the point of view developed in "Fermiers" and treat the kingdom as an estate to be exploited rationally. The focus upon expenditures rather than human beings marked a fateful depersonalization of the economic process. Quesnay stands as one of the most extreme exponents of that fetishism of commodities to which Marx was to call attention as a major characteristic of early bourgeois economic thought.[85]

The early zigzags carry another message: the proprietors of the revenue must spend it. Quesnay wishes the Tableau to demonstrate to the crown and to the seigneurial proprietors that expenditure "to the last farthing" affords greater economic returns than saving. The physiocrats' general attitudes toward saving and interest gave rise to considerable debates with their contemporaries and to much subsequent review, frequently ending in

84. *Quesnay's Tableau*, app. A, app. B, 2.
85. Marx, *Capital*, 3 vols. (Moscow, 1961), I, 71–83.

the judgment that they had preserved a traditional opposition to usury on moral grounds. One could argue that Quesnay's view of the role of interest more closely approximates Schumpeter's notion of "zero interest rate" than it does scholastic prohibitions of usury, but only by doing some violence to the historical dimension of Quesnay's analysis.

Lüthy has frequently pointed out how closely Quesnay's Tableau mirrors the real condition of France under Louis XV. While his one-sided interpretation willfully slights the capitalist character of Quesnay's analysis of agricultural production and ultimate commitment to a market basis for all social and economic relations, it vividly illuminates certain problems of the early zigzags, as well as their persistent opposition to merchant and finance capital.[86] Lüthy rightfully deprecates "a certain pseudo-Marxist conception of 'capitalism' as a uniquely bourgeois fact, a prepossession to ignore the socio-economic structures of the *ancien régime* as an economy monopolized for the profit of royal society and its constituted orders and to hold as historically negligible the manipulation of the freest revenues of the kingdom —Quesnay's net product." For as he further argues, the agricultural base provided most of the income of the court, either through seigneurial dues or through the extensive mortgages which, he suspects, decisively crippled the economic power of the nobility. The Tableau, however schematic it may be, "contains the quasi-complete analysis of this 'society of proprietors' which is at the center of the *ancien régime*." It has the inestimable merit of exposing the existence "at the very center of the regime and of the economy, of a fairly large and composite and, above all, very powerful society which, appropriating without counterpart the 'net' social product for its own profit is, economically, only consuming and which determines the circulation of the wealth of the 'agricultural kingdom.' "[87]

86. Lüthy, *Banque protestante*, II, 687–89.
87. *Ibid.*, 24.

The ancien régime, according to Lüthy, also supported a society of merchants and financiers who lived off an altogether different form of activity—commerce—which communicated with the agricultural sector only through the high society of "State, Church and Court."[88] But Lüthy notwithstanding, Quesnay emphatically stresses the strength of the bonds uniting the elite of the two societies and particularly emphasizes the contamination with which merchant and finance capitalists had infected the patterns of all ruling class economic behavior. While Quesnay accepts the political form—specifically existing property rights—of the appropriation of the surplus, he also believes that it can only be justified if the titleholders expend the totality of their revenue as the necessary lubricant of the entire economic process. He repudiates interest and saving because they draw part of the surplus out of the economy and thus rob society of part of the social product of its labor and capital.[89] The opposition to finance capital heralds the future as much as it echoes the past, however much Quesnay obscures the point.

Once again the contradiction between the capitalist structure of production and the seigneurial form of landed property plagues Quesnay's model. Had the capitalist entrepreneurs owned the land they exploited—a contingency which the physiocrats periodically consider and usually reject—and particularly had the same people owned both the land and the productive capital, Quesnay would undoubtedly not have seen saving and interest as such inevitable depletions of the total social product. Looking at the France of his day, however, he saw saving in the form of *rentes* and interest in the form of the exorbitant price of royal loans. He judged them simply as potentially productive capital diverted from its proper role as productive expenditure, or healthy demand, which would stimulate the decisive agricultural supply. Within the agricultural sector the accumulation of capital

88. *Ibid.*
89. *Quesnay's Tableau,* 3.

presumably resulted from saving, and investment certainly carried interest, although interest was presented as depreciation costs necessary to guarantee productive reinvestment.[90] But seigneurial property, supported by the state, negated the extension of such agricultural investment. Under those conditions capital accumulation normally transpired outside the agricultural base, even while feeding upon it.[91] Many opponents of the physiocrats, such as Forbonnais, did not so much disagree with this analysis as with the conclusions Quesnay drew from it. Forbonnais ascribed great importance to money as "fictitious real estate" and believed that the returns from such investments constituted the mainspring of economic development.[92]

Recent scholarship substantiates Quesnay's insistence upon agricultural development, the internal market in mundane rather than luxury commodities, and optimal market conditions as reflected in the marked reduction of transactions costs and improvement in transportation facilities. Reed, for example, has argued that with as little as 10 or 20 percent of total costs of cereals ascribed to transactions, a 10 percent decline in the per unit cost of making transactions in the market can result in a substantial rise in real income.[93] And Bairoch has argued, by something of a sleight of hand, that overseas commerce made no appreciable contribution to the early stages of industrial transformation in England.[94] Quesnay's bias against commercial enterprise as well

90. *Ibid.*, v. Interest on the annual advances is calculated at a rate of 10 percent.

91. Lüthy, *Banque protestante*, II, 687–89.

92. Forbonnais, *Principes et observations oeconomiques*, I, 168. Cf. Baudeau's attack on this concept in "Critique raisonée," *Les éphémérides du citoyen*, 1767, vols. V, VI, VII, VIII.

93. Clyde G. Reed, "Transactions Costs and Differential Growth in Seventeenth Century Western Europe," *Journal of Economic History*, XXXIII (1973), 177–90. I am indebted to Professor Stanley Engerman for pointing out that Reed's figures are inaccurate, but concurring, as an economist, that the general argument holds up.

94. Paul Bairoch, "Commerce international et genèse de la révolution industrielle anglaise," *Annales ESC*, XXVIII (1973), 541–71.

as his instinct to reduce transactions costs in his model to zero accorded with a major aspect of historical development.

The most convincing analyses of early economic development have been based, like Quesnay's, on England—the first nation to develop a capitalist agriculture and a modern industry. England, unlike France, had managed to divest itself of seigneurial property and to generate an agricultural revolution. The effects of the English lead on French economic development remains the subject of controversy. Quesnay based his analysis upon the English model while accepting French political institutions, which supported seigneurial property. This international marriage might result in what he considered to be the "natural order," but it never recommended itself to monarchs faced with critical political exigencies. As Forbonnais said, the natural order may never have been altered in its essence, "but its consequences have been modified by circumstances that concern the conservation of societies." Principles must be calculated according to this double optic, just as "the natural right of man is seen to bend under the right of society." It would hardly be more reasonable, he concluded, to administer the economic business of a state bound by external relations according to "the principles of the natural order of things only, than to sacrifice the hierarchies established in the constitution to the purely philosophical idea of the equality of conditions."[95] Quesnay fully shared Forbonnais' scorn for such chimerical philosophical speculations, but he failed to recognize that his solid notions of market production might themselves appear to be mere speculations in the political configuration of France.

Quesnay's insistence upon the pivotal role of consumption has been confirmed by the experience of mature industrial nations, but has yet to be proven for the process of economic development itself. Forbonnais, for example, agreed that money destined for investment was diverted from its "natural function as the

95. Forbonnais, *Principes et observations oeconomiques*, I, 148.

sign of commodities," but advised against wasting arguments over necessities. France, as a powerful and prestigious nation, had to defend its international position, and to that end it had to command public credit.[96] How could the king realistically divest himself of his tax-farmers and his bankers? Forbonnais had a point. France had been extraordinarily successful, whatever the long-range consequences of its course. Nations, like human beings, can progress too far on faulty premises to be able to change voluntarily. Quesnay's course would have entailed political upheaval and a great, if temporary, setback.

Quesnay sought to promote French economic development. His texts and those of his disciples abound with plans to match the English example, to increase French wealth, and to promote increased social division of labor. Nevertheless, scholars have discussed at length whether physiocracy looked backward or forward—whether the Tableau depicts a static or a dynamic equilibrium. Since Quesnay asserted that the Tableau constituted a tool for analyzing the present and the future, it seems strange that his intentions should still occasion so much doubt. The best recent econometric reconstructions of the Tableau all concur in seeing it as a dynamic model.[97] They frequently modernize Quesnay's premises in order to achieve their results, although their arbitrary intrusions do not necessarily do violence to Quesnay's intentions. Quesnay did design the Tableau as a model of economic growth. But in order to show the beneficial results of growth to the crown and the nation, he presupposed the crucial transformation the model was supposed to promote—a capital-intensive agriculture and a market value for the entire social product. When he capped his performance by ensconcing his dynamic agriculture within an inflexible traditional framework,

96. *Ibid.*, 154.
97. Herlitz, "*Tableau* and Sterility"; Eagley, "Physiocratic Model"; Lutfalla, *L'état stationnaire*, 167–77.

he single-handedly created the stationary atmosphere that characterizes his models.

Soon use of the Tableau required a manipulation of figures in order to arrive at the desired results. As Quesnay tried to close the economic circle and to account for the flow of commodities as well as that of money, he forced his model so far beyond its original purpose that it lost all conviction as an accurate reflection of existing conditions. The contradictions between the economic system and the social and political superstructure fostered an impression of a specifically economic deadlock at the heart of a model explicitly created as a blueprint for growth.

Because of the peculiar character of Quesnay's method, the viability of the mathematical reasoning embodied in the Tableau has been identified ipso facto with the viability of his general analysis of growth. But the mathematics do not necessarily reflect the deeper implications of the political economy. Hence the question posed by Rogin and echoed by Meek: how does the Tableau meet objective standards as a prescription for public policy?[98] Forbonnais attacked it on just those grounds. Subsequently, when the physiocrats as a sect devoted their energies to securing and defending the freedom of the grain trade, Linguet, Galiani, and Necker, among many, attacked their program as either materially unrealizable because of insufficient harvest and inadequate transportation, or socially so divisive as to destroy the fabric of society. This grain trade debate raised issues that far transcend the present context, and I intend to treat them in a subsequent study, but the violence of the debate reveals the sensitivity and reality that the physiocratic vision of society could touch.

The physiocratic program provoked powerful opposition which prevented its realization. But according to objective economic standards, would its realization have been efficacious? Economics,

98. Leo Rogin, *The Meaning and Validity of Economic Theory* (New York, 1958), 50; Meek, *Economics*, 367.

for all the mathematical precision of its tools, is no more scientific today than it was in the 1750s. The question remains. Kula, in his superb studies of "feudal" (that is, seigneurial) economies and emerging capitalism, argues forcefully for the necessity of just such agricultural development as the physiocrats prescribed, on the grounds that even relatively advanced industrialization can occur in pockets and feed upon the backward regions of the country, while the backward regions continue their traditional routine, discourage the formation of an internal market, and depress wages even in the more advanced regions. In terms reminiscent of Quesnay's analysis, if not his conclusions, Kula describes how rural exploitation under absentee feudal landlords can continue indefinitely, siphoning off peasant savings through the relatively higher price of small units of land, discouraging direct landlord creation of estates based on economies of scale, forestalling capital accumulation by promoting luxury consumption at the landlord's place of residence, and offering no incentive for the replacement of human labor by machines with a complementary development of nonagricultural employment. He adds, confirming a judgment made by Quesnay and later in much greater depth by Marx, that merchant capital constitutes the principal beneficiary of this socioeconomic configuration since it can profit from the economic dualism and draw profits from both sectors at once.[99] In evaluating the validity of Quesnay's developmental scheme it is less useful to consider its eventual applicability in France than its actual applicability as an analysis of seventeenth- and early eighteenth-century English development. From this point of view Quesnay deserves the recognition as a great economic historian which his contributions should long since have earned him.

In a final ironic twist, Forbonnais, despite his defense of merchant and finance capital in France, describes its potential as

---

99. Witold Kula, "Secteurs et régions arriérés dans l'économie du capitalisme naissant," *Studi storici*, I (1959–1960), 569–85, esp. 572, 576.

an exploiter of less developed regions, and thereby inadvertently confirms Quesnay's analysis:

The influence of money in the commerce between nations has produced yet another remarkable effect. The people richest in monetary capital have established for themselves a revenue upon the territorial and industrial production of people less rich in money. They have advanced them, at great interest, the capital necessary to production; and, having, through the dependence of their debtors, become the arbiters of price, they have forced them to accept a mediocre wage in kind composed of the goods their country lacked. By this policy, the exchanges of all nations have fallen into their hands, and having become, under the name of agents and brokers, the proprietor, they have, by a necessary consequence, reserved for themselves alone all the direct correspondence that nations could support between themselves by virtue of their natural productions and their reciprocal needs. They have even succeeded in stopping production by stopping consumption when their political interests have so dictated. This stroke of authority was only able to succeed for the very moment when it was used. Eyes have been opened to the danger of these liaisons and this passive commerce. The calculation of political independence has been substituted for that of a pretended merchant economy which did not exist.[100]

Forbonnais does not, of course, mean to describe the relationship of merchant and finance capital to agriculture within France. Nor does he, more than Quesnay, expect a political revolution within France. And yet the conclusions of both men's analyses led exactly to the political issue.

One must marvel at Quesnay's performance. It has convinced scores of economists much better technically equipped than he to try to resolve the apparent contradictions of his economic model. But as with the larger political economy, of which the Tableau was both tool and symbol, the origins of those contradictions lay much deeper than a capricious terminology or technical naïveté. The contradictions arise primarily from the social, political, and ideological context of the endeavor.

100. Forbonnais, *Principes et observations oeconomiques*, I, 146–47.

Quesnay's theory of value provides a final illustration of his method and its limits. It as much as any single feature of his economics has challenged the imagination of his interpreters. Implicitly, as early as "Fermiers," and quite explicitly in "Hommes," he rigorously denies the use-value of agricultural goods. His subsequent writings merely reinforce this early stance: value consists in price, or in the market value with which he identifies price. Quesnay's deep, intrusive materialism never prompted him to modify his position on this question, although the development of his more philosophical work reveals that vis-à-vis value, as vis-à-vis all other questions, he harbored a profoundly dualistic attitude.[101]

Quesnay's fundamental economic premise, that nature alone affords an economic surplus, betrays the depth of his materialism. Only those things which satisfy the needs and desires of men have value. How do we reconcile this commitment to the value in essence of material goods with the oft repeated identification of value and price—particularly in the absence of any satisfactory physiocratic discussion of price formation? The answer, its complex implications notwithstanding, is simple: man, however material a being he indisputably may be, is a social animal. The reverence of nature never meant, for Quesnay, a return to simple, primitive conditions. Social relations—advanced society—constitute material human reality. And economic production and exchange, constituting as they do the material foundation and expression of that social reality, reveal the essential structure of that natural order—men reunited in society.[102]

Like Marshall, Quesnay could have said that "Political Economy or Economics is a study of mankind in the ordinary business of life; it examines that part of individual and social action

---

101. See H. Bartoli, "Le problème de la valeur chez les physiocrates," in *Mélanges économiques dédiés à M. le professeur René Gonnard* (Paris, 1946), 25–37; and Hannah R. Sewall, *The Theory of Value before Adam Smith* [1901] (New York, 1968), 80–91.

102. *Philosophie rurale*, 17.

which is most closely connected with the attainment and with the use of the material requisites of well-being."[103] But Quesnay never would have restricted his definition to only one part of individual and social action, for he believed economics to be the science of the totality of human society. And unlike the members of the classical school whose period of sway separated his career from that of Marshall, Quesnay could never accept utility or human preference as the criterion for value. Such subjectivism challenged both his historical experience of the free play of individual interests—in eighteenth-century France they demonstrably did not work to further economic progress—and his commitment to a conception of an order that transcended the possible errors of individuals. Notwithstanding his frequent references to the price set by the international market, he never undertook a serious investigation of the nature of price formation. Value, and in consequence, price—at least the good price—existed independent of selfish human desires. Like the natural order of which it formed a constituent element, value belonged to the normative, not to the positive sphere. God not man created that ideal market in which the natural price was formed.

Speaking of the Tableau in *Philosophie rurale*, Mirabeau describes the physiocratic vision of the market. The two parts of the revenue—productive and sterile—he argues,

apparently so distinct in their destination, have nonetheless, in the economic order, as in the moral order, a single and identical goal which is to bind, to unite, to defend and to serve society. The *Tableau économique* shows us that he who renders nothing to society must expect nothing from it, and that exactly he who believes his existence [to be] the most indifferent and independent, nonetheless influences, with his whole physical weight on the political rotation, by the effect of his expenditure in the economic circle.[104]

No wonder that with so much riding upon expenditure its level should be set by extrahuman necessity. Had not Quesnay in the

103. Alfred Marshall, *Principles of Economics*, 6th ed. (London, 1910), 1.
104. *Philosophie rurale*, 61.

"Traité" explicitly sought just such a necessity? The Tableau, with its attempt to construct an economic model of political relations, provides the shape of that necessity, its general guidelines, as it were. But beyond the direction of expenditure lies the level of expenditure. Social stability and economic development—fraught as they were with irreconcilable contradictions—both rode upon the good price. That Quesnay left the establishment of that price in the hands of God, in order that it command the respect of socially divisive men, differentiates him less from Marshall and Böhm-Bawerk than it does from Ricardo and Smith.

Quesnay's economics does not, however, rest solely with the Tableau and his formal emphasis upon the role of demand. His analysis of capitalist production in agriculture earns him a well-deserved place as the major forerunner of classical economics; the larger implications of his economic thought point directly towards an emphasis upon the primacy of supply. But his political and historical milieu imposed its own requirements upon the development of his analysis. The contradictions at the center of his political economy reveal nothing so much as the strength of the existing obstacles to rational French economic development.

❧ 8

Conclusion

The physiocratic doctrine of Quesnay and Mirabeau heroically, if unsuccessfully, attempted to construct a synthesis of the statist and "feudal" strands of French political thought, buttressed by a rigorous market economics derived from the observation of English development. The doctrine thus proposed a blueprint for French development that would simultaneously ensure economic revolution, individual freedom, and social harmony. These promises proved as mutually irreconcilable as the liberty, equality, and fraternity subsequently promised by the Declaration of the Rights of Man and the Citizen. Nevertheless, in emphasizing the necessity for all three, the physiocrats isolated the essential ingredients of capitalist liberalism. Furthermore, their insistence upon the need for an authoritarian rather than a representative government, and their failure to discuss the political mechanisms for transforming French society, revealed a deep understanding of the problems confronting reformers who would move France from the traditional to the modern world. Their rejection of politics in the modern sense betrays their conviction that the confrontation of different interests would produce deadlock or social warfare rather than smooth progress. It reveals an understanding that the modernization of France turned not upon the confrontation between clearly defined classes, but upon the confrontation between two world views—that implicit in the theory of the Tableau and that of the ancien régime—each of which embodied a discrete social system. The physiocrats, like the philosophes and many subsequent French social scientists, thus passed in silence over the problem of political implementation. In so doing, they unwittingly built into the model itself the very contradictions their model purported to resolve.

The conflicting strands of physiocratic thought found expression in the concept of legal despotism, which wedded a market society based on capitalist relations of production to an authoritarian government. Theoretically, the government did no more than a liberal representative government did, namely ensure the optimal workings of the market; but its unitary power betrayed a deep fear that, on the political level, the workings of the market would not produce the desired results. Furthermore, the configuration of legal despotism strongly resembled that of the absolute monarchy shorn of its directive powers. Mirabeau had convinced Quesnay of the primacy of the social system over the coercive government. Quesnay had convinced Mirabeau that a viable social system must be determined by economic necessity and that national life must have an absolute focus or center of gravity. Physiocratic political theory thus resolved the dialectical tension between society and the state that had plagued previous French political thought by combining a revolutionary economic world view with a commitment to the preservation of a traditional political order. The physiocrats apparently remained unaware that their resolution of the conflicting claims of feudal society and absolute monarchy carried its own contradictions, and that they were if anything less tractable than those it replaced.

The contradictions embedded in physiocracy affected all aspects of the doctrine including its sociology and economics. The physiocrats never openly espoused the class analysis implicit in their economics and subsequently attributed to them by economic determinists. Quesnay moved from the totally depersonalized classes of expenditures to the somewhat more human classes of activities. He never proclaimed, however, that classes turned exclusively upon the relations of individuals to the means of production, or even to the level of their income irrespective of its source. He thus merged a traditional view of estate member-ship (social identity through form of activity) with a modern view of class membership. Agricultural or "productive" classes receive primacy independent of the economic status not merely because they belong to the capitalist sector, but also because they are bound across class lines by a sense of fraternity. Similar dif-ficulties plague the Tableau itself. Traditional order and the market economy are arbitrarily wedded in the diagram, but are never merged.

The cornerstone of physiocratic thought, absolute property, should have forced the resolution of some of these contradictions. Property constituted the basis for individual autonomy and freedom. It bore the full weight of physiocratic economic in-dividualism and constituted both the means by which the in-dividual participated in society and the rationale for government. As such it could forge the link between society, economy, and political life. Yet the physiocrats persistently denied property political representation. Propertied interests, they repeatedly affirmed, do not conflict. The physiocrats knew full well, how-ever, that social interests and political interests do conflict. In repudiating that social and political conflict, they simultaneously repudiated the notion of class struggle within a modern capitalist economy and the notion of struggle between feudal and capitalist forms of property. They thus unwittingly perpetuated the long-standing cleavage between state and society enunciated by Bodin.

Physiocracy is rarely presented as an organic part of En-lightenment thought. Some recent studies of the Enlightenment have included the physiocrats, but usually in a partial and unin-tegrated fashion. Yet physiocracy has little historical meaning apart from the Enlightenment, which itself cannot be fully under-stood apart from physiocracy. The physiocrats participated directly in the attempt to forge a theoretical basis for individual-ism. They contributed substantially to the articulation of the social sciences. They shared the philosophe commitment to science as the proper tool to redefine the laws of society and to education as the proper tool to transform human consciousness. At every turn physiocratic thought echoes the larger eighteenth-century intellectual consensus. Specifically, the physiocrats, like the other philosophes, drew upon a combination of French and English intellectual traditions and attempted to weld them into an ideology appropriate to the reformation of French society.

Drawing upon work in the natural sciences and upon the natural law tradition as well as Lockean psychology and Newtonian physics, they gradually mounted an assault on the divinely sanctioned traditional order. The old order did not, however, come under a single unified attack. Most of the philosophes reintroduced one or another aspect of traditional thought into their blueprint for change. Carl Becker, acutely sensitive to the psychological tensions underlying bold intellectual advances, maintains that the traditional legacy ultimately weighed heavier in their world view than the commitment to innovation. He exaggerates, but he has a point. Furthermore, the social and economic contexts in which the philosophes developed their positions imposed specific resistances to the unfettered development of a natural and individualistic society.

The Enlightenment established the contours of modern thought, carried as it was by a rising tide of political, social, and economic transformation. The philosophes of various countries, however, never effected the changes they propounded without political assistance. Their discrete contributions to that new world view which came into its own in the nineteenth century cannot be divorced from the philosophes' specific national and chronological contexts. Heirs to a common intellectual tradition, they were also members of different cultures and products of different socioeconomic systems and political traditions. The individual contributions to the Enlightenment all reflect the tensions experienced by individuals attempting to reconcile cosmopolitan intellectual convictions with the full range of personal and local experience. Thus the debates over the forward-looking or backward-looking, optimistic or pessimistic character of the Enlightenment as a whole neglect the specific working out of the contradictory impulses wracking individual philosophes.

Deeply conflicting commitments also shaped the formulation of physiocratic doctrine. Despite the idiosyncracy of the physiocratic attempt to adapt natural law doctrine to French conditions, the physiocrats worked within the same limitations and for the same general goals as the other philosophes. A close analysis of physiocratic texts would reveal few theoretical propositions that could properly be termed original except Quesnay's specific economic analysis. Like so many philosophes, the physiocrats followed the path hewn by Montesquieu and attempted to study the entire social phenomenon. Political theory, social theory, and economic theory remained for them, as for other philosophes, relatively undifferentiated but nonetheless susceptible to rational analysis. The general interest in society owed much to the renewed appreciation of man's primarily social identity that had been promoted by Lockean psychology. Nevertheless, eighteenth-century French social science anticipated Durkheim in implicitly regarding society as a phenomenon *sui generis*—one that had a life independent of that of its members. The philosophes, accordingly, sought to analyze the social mechanism.

Significantly, while the English theorists concentrated on describing the social activity that surrounded them, the French philosophes devoted most of their efforts to the theoretical study of government and its proper relationship to the social body. Their most characteristic speculations led to a preference for "enlightened" despotism or for democracy. The specific preferences of Voltaire or Rousseau for enlightened despotism or democracy had more in common with physiocracy than superficial divergences would suggest. And all differed profoundly from the Anglo-Saxon tradition. Whatever the internal quarrels, the mainstream of eighteenth-century French political thought tacitly accepted certain specifically French historical lessons, in particular that government cannot be a simple emanation of society. State and society operate on separate planes and obey different rules. Society should, ideally, determine the appropriate government, but experience shows that it rarely does. Natural law cannot be assumed to realize its own dictates. Even a country's culture, many argued, depends on its government. Enlightened despots or a general will were called upon to force social behavior on antisocial human beings. Like physiocratic political proposals, these too had an authoritarian cast. The physiocrats' legal despot did, however, differ in one crucial respect from the alternative authorities: the interest he embodied was defined in strictly rational economic terms. And that interest, the net product, dictated all social function including the action of government.

The other philosophes, many of whom had originally admired aspects of physiocratic thought, later ridiculed and ultimately rejected the physiocratic doctrine as a whole. Quesnay and Mirabeau themselves invited this fate by insisting upon the necessary unity of their new science. They intended to explain and to direct the totality of life in society, not some fragment thereof. Well might they claim that they intended to liberate human beings from the chains of ignorance and to ensure the optimal social development, their contemporaries insisted that their science merely reimposed old constraints. Furthermore, few enlightened Frenchmen could accept the physiocratic position on the grain trade, which they understood merely as a willingness to let the poor starve. The other philosophes sought to free the human spirit by different means. The enlightened despot and the general will might be authoritarian, but at least they appeared to embody the freedom of creative human intelligence. Men would reshape the world according to their own vision of natural law and social advantage. The forms of government, like the willingness to infringe upon the rights of property in the interests of provisioning, both testified to a measure of faith in human genius.

Like the physiocrats, however, the other philosophes, fighting in the name of human freedom, faced a profound contradiction. They had no evidence that unbridled individualism would necessarily contribute to the general social good. Furthermore, they deeply believed that society shaped the individual. To reshape him, therefore, required stringent means—beginning with the reshaping of society itself. Such a transformation could only be effected by human genius—always the property of rare individuals, not of humanity at large. The philosophes, accordingly, proposed the conquest of government by genius and the subsequent transformation of society by government. Education would mediate between government and society and help to prepare new generations for enlightened social participation. An enlightened elite should exercise authority in the name of the true social interest. The formula rested on the desperate conviction, born of the rejection of political struggle, that the forms of the ancien régime could be put to the service of its own destruction.

The physiocratic position rested upon similar assumptions but pursued a different solution. The physiocrats sought a new social gravity that would command the obedience of the state. A truly economic society, they argued, required no coercion. The net product proclaims rules that brook no human intervention, genial or otherwise. The physiocrats thus implicitly espoused the view that society will shape government, which will do little more than guarantee the natural workings of society. The physiocrats, however, never explained how the desired transformation would occur. They always proclaimed that the implementation of their economic program would naturally produce the desired results. They scrupulously avoided the possibility that the implementation of their program might instead produce revolution. They did, assuredly, know that most Frenchmen preferred immediate advantage to long-range economic self-interest. Their profound authoritarianism betrays their mistrust of self-interest as perceived by their contemporaries. It is easy now to see that they should have recognized the revolutionary implications of their proposals. In all likelihood, however, they did not.

The individualism that the philosophes sought to propagate derived largely from the English and Calvinist traditions. It had received political implementation only in England where it rested upon an unusual harmony between state and society, not to mention a firm economic base. The philosophes understood that their own society rested upon no such unity, much less unity with the state. They could not, however, sacrifice their vision of a new world of human dignity and social progress. Their respective solutions drew upon the same venerable French traditions which endowed the state with the responsibility for creating a national, as opposed to a particularistic, society. Quesnay and Mirabeau merely pushed the argument one step further by rejecting any human intervention and ascribing the optimal form of society to the dictates of nature.

Like the other philosophes, the physiocrats built a fundamental contradiction into the heart of their thought. Their discussions moved confusedly from how society was to how it ought to be. Indeed, they justified their program for radical change by arguing that it would realize the natural law. Their authoritarianism rested upon the certain knowledge that actual, flesh-and-blood men were not enlightened men; their justification for change rested upon the claim that enlightened man was natural man. They, therefore, built their science of society upon a construct or an ideal type, rather than upon an analysis of the actual French human nature.

French social science thus began not only as an analysis of French society, but also as a confused extrapolation from English experience, as transmitted by English theorists who were describing their country's prevalent social relationships. The French theorists understood the difference and did not seek to emulate England. They did, however, wish to profit from certain aspects of English success, in particular individual freedom and national economic power. As they came increasingly to understand that French society would not spontaneously generate these benefits, they came increasingly to rely upon the state to force enlightenment upon society. Their approach, however, stretched thinner and thinner the claim that their state was only realizing society's inner will. Their science acquired a strong ideological component and its implementation rested more upon social engineering than upon natural processes. Science, in a word, had become politics.

The Revolution that swept away a monarchy unwilling or unable to profit from the instruction of the philosophes vindicated the lurking fears common to all eighteenth-century French social thought. From the physiocratic perspective it also introduced a fateful irony: in guaranteeing that absolute property for which the physiocrats had campaigned, the Revolution assured the triumph of the peasantry—those recalcitrant defenders of the total product. Absolute property emerged victorious, but one of its most immediate casualties was economic development. Peasants do not belong to the world of the Tableau. They subsist, and in subsisting reject the brave new world of social interconnectedness based on economic exchange. Were it not for that one flaw, the Napoleonic Empire might readily be portrayed as physiocracy triumphant. As it was, economic individualism triumphant retarded the French economic "take-off" for at least half a century, and those Saint-Simonians who surrounded the second Napoleon turned once again to a strong state to force modernization upon uneconomic individuals.

The French faced a particularly poignant deadlock between state and society. Some societies, notably the English and American, built industrial-capitalist systems from the bottom up with society commanding the compliance of the state; others, notably the German and Japanese, built them from the top down with the state forcing the pace upon society. In both instances the transformation occurred more swiftly than in France, and national social theory bore a corresponding stamp. English and American individualism was more public, more part of the natural order; German and Japanese individualism, more private, more romantic, and in its virulent forms, more extreme. French social theory remained committed to the individual as the basis of society and made him the rationale for all social programs; yet it also remained suspicious of him as inherently antisocial. French social theory continued to insist upon reforging the individual in the name of individualism.

As Quesnay so well understood, in destroying the traditional world view the philosophes were destroying the only objective reference point in human debates. By denying the role of God as absolute authority, they were destroying the possibility for any absolute authority. Man as the source of knowledge became both subject and object, and all judgment accordingly became relative to the point of view of the observer. Quesnay did argue that the rule of arithmetic could provide a new absolute standard, but he was never willing to trust even that rule to human beings. God must guarantee science. Human intelligence, capable of mathematical reasoning, could not be an accidental product of the material universe. Human intelligence is a light from God that informs and makes sense of otherwise irrational material life. Once that divine authority is dismantled, science, like everything else, becomes the product of human whim and subject to the vagaries of human passion: it lacks that necessity which can command unquestioning obedience.

The political, social, and economic theory of the English and Scottish Enlightenment carried the irrefutable authority of success. The social transformation immortalized by Locke, Hume, Adam Smith, and their contemporaries emerged from their descriptions as "classical" liberalism and "classical" economics. As their society increasingly set the pace, and therefore the model, for international development, their analyses of a specific national history acquired the stature of natural law, or organic necessity. No other European nation, however, spontaneously generated an industrial revolution. The late-comers all sought to remodel societies that, in different degrees and for different reasons, lacked the market basis from which the English had secured their individualism and begun their ascent to world economic power. European thinkers and administrators therefore had to reconcile the normative patterns of English success with quite different historical conditions. Loathe to sacrifice the norm itself, yet fully cognizant of the resistance of their own populations to a market society, they increasingly built a political silence into the heart of programs the implementation of which remained essentially a political question.

Social science grew from an ideological commitment. The philosophes marshalled science to justify their assault upon the traditional order. Science would secure individualism against the domination of irrational authority. Science, however, could not transcend the human beings who practiced it. Men made science where once God had made men and the absolute truth to which they were permitted partial access. The liberation of the human mind from the constraints of the traditional world view has permitted a vast expansion of human facilities. Individualism has opened human dignity to beings once relegated to unselfconscious and exploited subsistance. It has not, however, brought a new certainty to human affairs. The anxiety attendant upon uncertainty plagues modern thought. As a result, social scientists continue to present ideological positions as natural laws and vehemently deny their *parti pris*. Scientific accuracy, where it is possible, advances human knowledge. It cannot, however, decide upon the optimal social development. Sooner or later human judgment intervenes and takes its stand in favor or one or another value or social group. The physiocrats and the other philosophes, who set the terms of the debate, knew that self-interest provokes conflict. That they dodged the issue in favor of value-free science and social harmony does not justify their heirs continuing to do so.

Bibliographical Note

Aside from the directly relevant texts and manuscripts cited in the notes, my study rests upon reading and research in four general areas: works on Quesnay in particular and the history of economic thought in general; the work of the physiocratic school, with special reference to the right of property and the debate over the grain trade, including manuscript sources and unpublished administrative correspondence; secondary studies of eighteenth-century social and economic history (particularly the great regional monographs); and the general history of the Enlightenment, including the literature of reform as well as that of "high" thought.

I have consulted the following archival materials:

Archives nationales: series AD (IV, 1); F^{10} (esp. 222, 252–53, 285); F^{11} (esp. 223, 264, 265); F^{12} (esp. 50^1, 105^1, 149, 713, 715); H (esp. 1501–10, 1510^2, 1511, 1512, 1515, 1518); K (esp. 885, 906, 944, 1317); M (778–785).

Archives départementales: Seine et Marne, B (262); Yvelines (Etude Huber).

Bibliothèque nationale: Manuscrits français (6680–87, 7771, 10911, 11347, 14295–96); Fonds Moreau (1092).

Bibliothèque de l'Arsenal: Fonds de la Bastille (1201).

Eleutherian Mills Historical Library: Longwood Manuscripts, group 1, series A; Winterthur Manuscripts, group 2, series A, B, C, E, F.

In 1957, Jacqueline Hecht compiled an exhaustive bibliography of works by and about Quesnay, see INED, I. Marguerite Kuczynski's introduction to François Quesnay, *Oekonomische Schriften*, 2 vols. (Berlin, 1972), adds some additional references, particularly to manuscripts and works in German. It now constitutes the best edition of Quesnay's early work in any language.

The basic bibliography for the physiocratic school remains that provided by Weulersse, *Mouvement*, supplemented by his *La physioc-*

ratie à la fin du règne de Louis XV, 1770–1774 (Paris, 1959), and his *La physiocratie sous les ministères de Turgot et de Necker, 1774–1781* (Paris, 1950). Edgar Faure, *La disgrâce de Turgot* (Paris, 1961), and Henri Grange, *Les idées de Necker* (Paris, 1974) are also useful, as are the recent dissertations by John W. Rogers, Jr., *The Opposition to the Physiocrats* (Ann Arbor: University Microfilms, 1971), and Steven L. Kaplan, *Subsistence, Police, and Political Economy at the End of the Reign of Louis XV* (Ann Arbor: University Microfilms, 1974). Robert Mandrou, *La France au XVIIe et XVIIIe siècles* (Paris, 1968) remains a standard bibliographical introduction. Eberhard Schmitt, *Repräsentation und Revolution: Eine Untersuchung zur Genesis der kontinentalen Theorie und Praxis parlamentarischer Repräsentation aus der Herrschaftspraxis des Ancien régime in Frankreich (1760–1789)* (Munich, 1969), includes a useful bibliography of German works not usually found in the French and English literature. For the Enlightenment as a whole, Peter Gay's masterly bibliographical essays remain indispensable, *The Enlightenment: An Interpretation*, 2 vols. (New York, 1966 and 1969). The Institut national d'études démographiques bibliography, *Economie et population: Les doctrines françaises avant 1800* (Paris, 1956), is also invaluable. See in addition Alexandre Cioranescu, *Bibliographie de la littérature française du dix-huitième siècle*, 3 vols. (Paris, 1969).

I regret that Keith Baker's *Condorcet: From Natural Philosophy to Social Mathematics* (Chicago and London, 1975), and Giorgio Rebuffa's *Origine della ricchezza e diritto di proprietà: Quesnay e Turgot* (Milan, 1974), appeared too late for me to take more than passing account of them in the notes. I believe, however, that their conclusions are compatible with those of my own work. Two new articles on the Tableau appeared as this book was going to press: T. Barna, "Quesnay's *Tableau* in Modern Guise," *Economic Journal*, LXXXV (1975), 485–96; and W. A. Eltis, "François Quesnay: A Reinterpretation," pt. 1, "The *Tableau Economique*," *Oxford Economic Papers*, XXVII (1975), 167–200. Both approach the Tableau from a modern economic perspective, but do not address the problems most relevant to this study.

A more detailed bibliography can be found in my "The Forging of a Bourgeois Ideology: A Study in the Origins of Physiocracy," Widener Library, Harvard University.

Index

Absolutism, 104-5, 117, 164, 167, 179, 181, 190; *see also* Authority, Property, *and* State

Agricultural society of Berne, 38, 204, 218, 221, 224, 249

Agriculture, 11, 12, 23, 58-59, 66, 92-94, 109, 110, 115, 116, 119, 122-23, 126-28, 155, 165, 198, 207, 266, 271-72, 300; capitalist, 100, 122, 272, 280, 283, 293, 296; history, 221-24; importance, 50, 111-15, 125-26, 199, 218-20, 224-25, 235, 245; improvement, 56, 107, 126; revolution in, 93, 238, 300; subsistence farming, 53-54, 121-22, 223; *see also* Farmers, Grains, Land, Production, *and* Quesnay

Agronomes, 76, 93, 110, 126, 161

Alembert, Jean le Rond d', 76; see also *Encyclopédie*

Anarchy, 10, 177, 196

Ancien régime, 10, 12, 16, 21, 27, 28, 29, 55, 61, 72, 117, 168, 176, 190, 191, 192, 215, 278, 293-94, 304, 310; indictment of, 196-97; opposition to, 108

Année littéraire, 76

Aristotle, 9, 70

Arithmetical calculation, 9, 59, 91, 146, 237, 246, 261, 262, 287

Authority, 18, 22, 43, 49, 106, 141, 159, 181, 194, 195, 210, 214-15, 244, 304; absolute, 9-10, 64-65, 267, 313; and dependence, 179-80, 250; ecclesiastical, 197; legitimate, 177; nature of, 168; physiocrats'

support of, 45-46, 62, 174; traditional, 172, 177

Barbeyrac, Jean, 22, 86, 87

Baudeau, Abbé Nicolas, 46, 253, 282

Bayle, Pierre, 83

Becker, Carl, 307

Bertin, Henri-Léonard Jean-Baptiste, 58, 64

Bilan de l'Angleterre, 95

Bodin, Jean, 104, 181, 188, 219

Boerhaave, Hermann, 76, 79, 80, 80n, 81

Boisguilbert, Pierre de, 20, 63, 88, 94, 107

Bossuet, Jacques Bénigne, 105, 182

Bourgeoisie, 28, 29, 44, 45, 61, 143, 212

Buffon, comte de, 76, 81, 84

Burlamaqui, Jacques, 22, 86

Cantillon, Richard, 95, 96, 98, 110, 113, 120, 123, 127n, 134, 145-51, 156, 157, 166, 217, 218; *Essai sur le commerce*, 95, 145, 146, 158n; Mirabeau's debt to, 145-51, 157, 158; Quesnay's debt to, 273-74, 280

Capital, 27, 102, 237, 283, 293, 294, 300; investment, 127, 161, 238, 283, 295

Capitalism, 10, 29, 60-61, 103, 110; free market, 25, 60; industrial, 11, 29, 279; *see also* Agriculture *and* Production

Cartesianism, 77, 78, 80, 81, 83, 84; *see also* Neo-Cartesianism

The Origins of Physiocracy

Designed by R. E. Rosenbaum.
Composed by York Composition Company, Inc.,
in 10 point Linotype Janson, 3 points leaded,
with display lines in Centaur.
Printed letterpress from type by York Composition Co.
on Warren's Number 66 text, 50 pound basis.
Bound by John H. Dekker & Sons, Inc.
in Columbia book cloth
and stamped in All Purpose foil.

Library of Congress Cataloging in Publication Data
(For library cataloging purposes only)

Fox-Genovese, Elizabeth, 1941–
    The origins of physiocracy.

    Includes bibliographical references and index.
    1. Physiocrats. 2. Quesnay, François, 1694–1774. 3. Mirabeau, Victor de
Riqueti, marquis de, 1715–1789. 4. France—History—18th century. I. Title.
HB93.F69   330.15′2   75-36999
ISBN 0-8014-1006-1

GLASSBORO STATE COLLEGE